PRAISE FOR *HOW TO USE CUSTOMER DATA*

T0309283

'Dr. Scheuing is one of the world's greatest experts on the intersection of data protection and marketing, approaching both with a genuine customer-first perspective. In always seeking to balance innovation and privacy in a rapidly changing technological world, Dr. Scheuing's clear thinking and expert knowledge are a must-read for all marketers. This book captures the challenges faced by marketers and makes sure they remember that behind the data are real people searching for relevant products and services to live their best lives.'
Chris Combemale, CEO, UK Data and Marketing Association (DMA)

'This great book is a must read for anyone working at the crossroads of marketing and data privacy. These can be a minefield. I particularly appreciate the practical recommendations and templates.'
Philipp Raether, Group Chief Privacy Officer, Allianz

'A masterpiece bridging data protection law and marketing. This book covers the evolution of data protection law from its inception to the most recent developments in Artificial Intelligence and marketing. Written with elegance, each chapter provides excellent key takeaways to fill the gap between data protection and marketing. Dr. Scheuing offers practical and lucid guidance for cultivating a data-protective culture to earn trust from customers.'
Professor Hiroshi Miyashita, author and Professor of Law, Chuo University, Japan

'Customer data is a key asset for the health of all businesses. As recent high-profile cases have shown, it can be extremely damaging to brands if there isn't sufficient attention/focus on safeguarding this asset and complying with evolving laws. I commend this book for providing a structure to help managers audit their use of this strategic asset and take practical steps to achieve (legal) compliance while balancing this against creating more relevant communications, including the exciting opportunities of marketing AI.'
Dr. Dave Chaffey, Digital Marketing Strategist, author of *Digital Marketing: Strategy, Implementation and Practice*

'A refreshing and practical overview of the relationship between data protection requirements and how to use customer data in marketing and advertising. The author adds her own engaging and down to earth examples to bring an otherwise complex and challenging area to life in an accessible way. A pleasure to read, with plenty of useful analogies, recommendations and summaries to guide both the novice and experienced marketing and advertising practitioner through what is becoming an increasingly difficult maze of data privacy obligations and data uses to navigate.'

Vivienne Artz, Non-Executive Director, Strategic Advisor and Expert on Data, Privacy, Financial Crime and ED&I, PICCASO Privacy Awards founder

'This book is essential reading for privacy professionals who want to become more integral to their businesses. For marketers, it's a lesson in leveraging data within the bounds of the law. As someone deeply embedded in the privacy sector, I found the book to be not only insightful but also inspiring. It doesn't just tell you how to navigate the current landscape; it encourages a shift in how we think about privacy and marketing as fundamentally interconnected worlds.'

Lauren Reid, Founder and Principal Consultant, The Privacy Pro

'This book succeeds in bringing together the worlds of privacy and marketing, and shows with a very practical approach how one can be at the service of the other to build compliant and effective marketing strategies. Like its author, this book is insightful and forward looking, it provides essential insights to understand the current landscape, but looks beyond the traditional approach to encourage readers to take on a new look at both worlds together.'

Mathilde Fiquet, Special Advisor, European Publisher Council (EPC), and Head of office Europe Analytica

How to Use Customer Data

*Navigating GDPR, DPDI and a future
with marketing AI*

Sachiko Scheuing

KoganPage

First published in Great Britain and the United States in 2024 by Kogan Page Limited

2nd Floor, 45 Gee Street
London
EC1V 3RS
United Kingdom

8 W 38th Street, Suite 902
New York, NY 10018
USA

www.koganpage.com

Kogan Page books are printed on paper from sustainable forests.

© JS Global GmbH

ISBNs

Hardback   978 1 3986 1517 5
Paperback   978 1 3986 1515 1
Ebook   978 1 3986 1516 8

British Library Cataloguing-in-Publication Data
A CIP record for this book is available from the British Library.

Library of Congress Cataloging-in-Publication Data
Names: Scheuing, Sachiko, author.
Title: How to use customer data : navigating GDPR, DPDI and a future with
    marketing AI / Sachiko Scheuing.
Description: London ; New York, NY : Kogan Page Inc., 2024. | Includes
    bibliographical references and index.
Identifiers: LCCN 2024009007 (print) | LCCN 2024009008 (ebook) | ISBN
    9781398615151 (paperback) | ISBN 9781398615175 (hardback) | ISBN
    9781398615168 (ebook)
Subjects: LCSH: Consumer profiling–Data processing. | Data protection. |
    Privacy, Right of.
Classification: LCC HF5415.32 .S327 2024 (print) | LCC HF5415.32 (ebook)
    | DDC 658.8/342–dc23/eng/20240315
LC record available at https://lccn.loc.gov/2024009007
LC ebook record available at https://lccn.loc.gov/2024009008

Typeset by Integra Software Services, Pondicherry
Print production managed by Jellyfish
Printed and bound by CPI Group (UK) Ltd, Croydon, CR0 4YY

To Joachim, Nicholas and Maria who encouraged me with 'Mama, you write your book. We will do the dishes.'

CONTENTS

LIST OF FIGURES AND TABLES

BOXES AND CASE STUDY

ABOUT THE AUTHOR

Dr Sachiko Scheuing is the European Privacy Officer of Acxiom, an IPG-Interpublic Group company, and a global leader in marketing services. She is currently serving her fourth term as the Co-Chairwoman of the trade association Federation of European Data and Marketing (FEDMA), based in Brussels. With more than 20 years' experience in the field of marketing intelligence, and as a former chief analyst, Sachiko combines theoretical and practical experience of the marketing and advertisement industries to manage Acxiom's European government affairs and compliance. She frequently shares her thoughts with clients and colleagues on all matters data protection and AI. She also contributes articles to trade magazines and academic journals. Besides FEDMA, Sachiko is active in several European and global privacy and marketing associations as well as think-tanks. She was one of the founding members of the DPO association, CEDPO.

Sachiko is passionate about empowering women and girls. She is serving as the global co-chair of Acxiom's gender equity programme, WomenLEAD. In 2020, Sachiko received the DataIQ Professor Derek Holder Lifetime Achievement Award for her contribution to and leadership in the data industry. In 2024, she was recognised by Women in Data® as one of the twenty most influential women in Data and Tech.

PREFACE

This book is written for those who know a lot about marketing and not so much about data protection, and those who know a lot about data protection but not so much about marketing. The relationship between marketing and privacy is not always harmonious. It is not your competitors but your DPO who at times seems to be the ultimate obstacle for launching the most exciting campaigns. For privacy folks, marketing departments may be those who are always challenging the border.

A privacy colleague once told me that ever since he moved to a small village, he left his hedge to grow high. One day, he trimmed the hedge dramatically, and suddenly people started to talk to him. 'Good morning!' 'Isn't it a beautiful day? The sun is shining!' 'I love your roses.' He was greeted by many, and in no time he became very much part of village life; all because his neighbours finally saw what was behind the row of tall conifers.

This book is the gardener that trims the hedge between marketers and privacy experts. I hope you will get to see the other side a bit better after reading this.

Some notes about the chapters. At the time of writing, the DPDI Bill had just passed the House of Lords, and the negotiations of the EU AI Act have reached the point of a political agreement. Both of these laws are in the final stage, which means it is unlikely that the text changes dramatically. However, I need to caveat that statements are written based on information available to me in early January 2024.

The title of the book mentions both the GDPR and DPDI Bill, so I assume that you are most likely based either in the EU or the UK, or have business interest in these geographies. Hence, I draw heavily on the opinions and comments from the European Data Protection Board (a group of EU regulators) and the UK ICO. Most court cases referred to are from the Court of Justice of the European Union. In addition, many examples come from Germany, the Netherlands and the UK. This is because I am more familiar with these three countries than others.

The book is structured in a way that the first three chapters lay the funda-
mentals of both data protection and marketing. Chapters 4 and 5 discuss
the data classification and legal grounds applicable to marketing. Chapters
6 to 11 provide practical application of the laws, and review privacy statements, subject access requests, partners and suppliers, data security, data
protection template documents and data protection officers. These six chapters can be used as a reference which you can look up when working on the
relevant topics. The book concludes with a chapter on AI and marketing.

ACKNOWLEDGEMENTS

I would like to thank the following people for generously allowing me to use their respective organizations' materials in this book: Marty Abrams, Bojana Bellamy, Philippa Donn.

My thanks also go to my colleagues Jo Robson, Tracey Turner, David Keens, Andrew Hooper and Alex Wright from Channel 4 for their help with the case study in Chapter 10.

Lastly, thank you Donna Goddard and Kogan Page for publishing this book. Special thanks go to Jeylan Ramis for her indispensable assistance in shaping the text and for her reminder emails that kept me going.

LIST OF ACRONYMS

1PD	First Party Data
2PD	Second Party Data
3PD	Third Party Data
ACL	Access Control List
AI	Artificial Intelligence
AMA	American Marketing Association
API	Application Programming Interface
BCR	Binding Corporate Rules
BYOD	Bring Your Own Device
CDP	Customer Data Platform
CHAID	Chi-squared Automatic Interaction Detection
CIA	Confidentiality, Integrity and Availability
CIPL	Centre of Information Policy Leadership
CMO	Chief Marketing Officer
CRM	Customer Relationship Management
DCMS	Department of Digital, Culture, Media and Sports
DG	Directorate-General
DPA	Data Protection Agreement
DPC	Data Protection Commission
DPDI Bill/Act	Data Protection and Digital Information Bill/Act
DPIA	Data Protection Impact Assessment
DPO	Data Protection Officer
EDPB	European Data Protection Board
EEA	European Economic Area
ENISA	European Union Agency for Cybersecurity
E-Privacy Directive	Privacy and Electronic Communications Directive
FCRA	Fair Credit Reporting Act
GDMA	Global Data and Marketing Alliance
GDPR	General Data Protection Regulation
GIGO	Garbage In Garbage Out
HR	Human Resources
ICC	International Chamber of Commerce
ICO	Information Commissioner's Office

IDTA	International Data Transfer Agreement
LIA	Legitimate Interest Assessment
MD5	Message-Digest algorithm 5
OA	Output Areas
OECD	Organisation for Economic Cooperation and Development
OLG	Oberlandesgerichte (Higher Regional Courts)
ONS	Office of National Statistics
PECR	Privacy and Electronic Communications Regulation
PET	Privacy Enhancing Technologies
PGP	Pretty Good Privacy
PII	Personal Identifiable Information
PIN	Personal Identification Number
RFM	Recency Frequency and Monetary value
RoPA	Record of Processing Activities
SaaS	Software as a Service
SAR	Subject Access Request
SCC	Standard Contractual Clauses
SFTP	Secure File Transfer Protocol
SHA256	Secure Hash Algorithm 256
SWOT analysis	Strengths-Weaknesses-Opportunities-Threats analysis
TCF	Transparency and Consent Framework
TIA	Transfer Impact Assessment
TOMs	Technical and Organizational Measures
TPS	Telephone Preference Services
TRA	Transfer Risk Assessment
TTP	Trusted Third Party
UK DMA	UK Data and Marketing Association

1

What is data protection?

An intensive private course in data protection. That was the first step in shifting my career, leaving behind the familiar terrain of marketing data analytics for the then uncharted frontier of data protection. The course massively helped me when getting started with the job, which was all about the intersection between marketing data use and data protection. Fast forward almost 20 years, I am still excited with this niche subject area.

That is why I decided to start off this book by explaining what data protection is all about, before getting into how the subject matter ties into what marketers and marketing data scientists do every day. I am also hoping that you will have a better understanding of the myriad of rules imposed by your legal and data protection departments, and that you get into a dialogue with them to look for solutions that are both compliant and effective. Let us now unlock the secrets of compliant personalization at scale, the privacy department approved use of personalized advertising.

What are data protection laws protecting?

To be compliant, it helps to understand what it is that you are trying to protect by following the instructions from your legal and privacy departments. One of the tasks you are carrying out for your privacy department may be a so-called Legitimate Interest Assessment, where you are asked to balance the benefits your company will gain in using the data in a certain way against how persons, whose data you intend to process, may be impacted. Knowing what you are supposed to be protecting can help you balance the interests of both sides in a fair and just way.

The challenge is, however, that law texts do not readily provide the answer. At first glance, UK General Data Protection Regulation does not yield much. There is a section at the very beginning that describes the background of the law called the Recital. The following clause from Recital 2 sets the scene (legislation.gov.uk, 2016):

> The principles of, and rules on the protection of natural persons with regard to the processing of their personal data should, whatever their nationality or residence, respect their fundamental rights and freedoms, in particular their right to the protection of personal data. This Regulation is intended to contribute to the accomplishment of an area of freedom, security and justice and of an economic union, to economic and social progress, to the strengthening and the convergence of the economies within the internal market, and to the well-being of natural persons.

From this, it is clear that these are the fundamental rights and freedoms, including the protection of personal data, that the law is trying to guard. Convention 108, a treaty which the 1984 Data Protection Act was based upon, says the following (Council of Europe, 2018):

Article 1 – Object and purpose

The purpose of this Convention is to protect every individual, whatever his or her nationality or residence, with regard to the processing of their personal data, thereby contributing to respect for his or her human rights and fundamental freedoms, and in particular the right to privacy.

Again, here, respecting human rights and fundamental freedoms seems to be something data protection laws defend. Let us review what these rights and freedoms are all about by looking into the Charter of Fundamental Rights of the European Union.

CHARTER OF FUNDAMENTAL RIGHTS OF THE EUROPEAN UNION

The Charter of Fundamental Rights of the European Union lists out the rights and freedoms that should be guaranteed to EU residents. It is a legally binding document, which means the rights, when contested, can be brought to court. This charter was declared in the year 2000 and came into force in December 2009 with the Treaty of Lisbon. It is important to note that the fundamental human rights in the charter are universal. The Charter itself was based on the United Nation's Universal Declaration of Human Rights, that came into force in 1953 (EU, 2000).

The key pillars of the rights are Dignity, Freedoms, Equality, Solidarity, Citizens' Rights and Justice. The right to data protection falls under Freedoms, and are expressed as follows (EU, 2000):

Article 8 Protection of personal data

1. Everyone has the right to the protection of personal data concerning him or her.

2. Such data must be processed fairly for specified purposes and on the basis of the consent of the person concerned or some other legitimate basis laid down by law. Everyone has the right of access to data which has been collected concerning him or her, and the right to have it rectified.

3. Compliance with these rules shall be subject to control by an independent authority.

Since privacy is often used interchangeably with the word data protection, you may think GDPR is based on the right to privacy, as described in Article 7, and on data protection, in Article 8 of the Charter. This is not the case as the second sentence of Recital (1) of the GDPR only refers to the first point of Article 8. Here is what the recital says (legislation.gov.uk, 2016):

Article 8(1) of the Charter of Fundamental Rights of the European Union (the 'Charter') and Article 16(1) of the Treaty on the Functioning of the European Union (TFEU) provide that everyone has the right to the protection of personal data concerning him or her.

Interestingly, the E-Privacy Directive, implemented in Britain by the Privacy and Electronic Communications Regulation (PECR), aims to protect the right to privacy, as Recital 56 specifically mentions both the right to data protection and the right to privacy (eur-lex.europa.eu, 2002).

It is also important to note that the rights and freedoms protected under the Charter are all of equal importance; no right or freedom is more important than the other (UK Government, 2017).

However, there are altogether 50 articles that spell out the rights and freedoms that are protected by the Charter of Fundamental Rights, varying from the 'right to an effective remedy and to a fair trial' to rights to 'fair and just working conditions'. Some of these rights and freedoms are more relevant to data use than the others.

Drackert helpfully identified the following risks to rights and freedom as being relevant to the processing of personal data (Drackert, 2014; Veil, 2018):

Increased individual vulnerability to crime: the handling of personal data is risky if it increases the likelihood of crimes.

Shaming and damage to public image: the publicity of information threatens the data subject with a loss of public respectability.

Selective targeting damages: through the use of legally or politically undesirable information targeting (e.g. in selection processes) the data subject is threatened by discrimination or stigmatization.

Informational permanence: the capabilities for timeless storage, availability and retrievability of information enables for the constant reconstruction of individual behaviour and thereby reduces the chances for a collective social amnesia.

De-contextualisation: the transfer of information from one aspect of life to another may negatively affect the individual.

Emergence of information: new dangers arise from the possibility of automatically gaining new knowledge from diverse sources, for example about personal aspects of the data subject.

Information inaccuracy: unstructured data sources, uncontrolled and non-transparent processing procedures and data falsifications entail the risk of poor data quality, which in turn can cause different risks.

Treatment of human beings as mere objects: in particular, through exclusively automated individual decisions, there is the danger of human beings being degraded to objects.

Heteronomy: the manipulation of individual behavior can, at the micro level, negatively influence human freedom of behaviour as well as political processes at the macro level.

Disappointment with reasonable expectations of confidentiality: the expectations of the data subject are a relevant criterion both from the point of view of the individual and from the point of view of the community (in the sense of a (consumer) criterion of confidence necessary for collective living).

Are these, then, what data protection is protecting? It is certainly more practical than evaluating the 50 rights and freedoms of the Charter. Veil (2018) considers these as risks that need to be dealt with caution. Still, not all risks listed above are in my view relevant to marketing use of personal data. Let us focus on the following risks that seem to me worthy of discussion in the context of marketing and advertising.

1   **Increased individual vulnerability to crime:** The provision of data security is important to all organizations, also for companies that are engaged in marketing and advertisement. Since data is often passed onto partners, service providers or clients, security measures such as encryption must be in place to protect personal data or, before you know it, your company's customer and prospect data can be traded on an online black market.

2   **Emergence of information**: When creating insight of your customers, you most likely are automatically generating information about them from data gathered from a variety of sources; data you have collected directly from the customers and licensed from third parties. Marketers must consciously create information that is strictly relevant for shaping the communication, selecting the channel to deliver the message or improving the services etc., and not intrusive or harmful to the customers.

3   **Information inaccuracy:** Only when data quality is maintained can marketers deliver the right message to the right person, at the right moment. Marketers have known the importance of this risk all too well. My employer has been providing data hygiene services since the advent of direct mail in the 1970s.

4   **Treatment of human beings as mere objects**: I want to make a point that marketers are doing just the opposite through automating their operational processes. Your marketing department ideally wants to tailor their communication and offerings to every single person in the file through the numerous automated decisions they make based on propensity models and clustering techniques. Speaking to customers in a way that a human call centre agent or a shop keeper can, addressing the unique needs and wants of the person, helps not only in establishing trust of your brand, but also in appreciating that every customer is a person, not just an object.

5   **Heteronomy:** There is this tendency among data protection professionals and policymakers to assume that the aim of marketing is to manipulate consumers. While trying to gain interest from consumers for a particular product, say a shampoo, can be labelled manipulation, it cannot be compared to that of engineering election results, which translates into tampering with the democratic system of our society (Hern, 2018).

Marketing campaigns are more about automated salesmanship, an act that has most likely been practised from the moment mankind engaged in trade. On the other hand, making consumers more likely to click on consent buttons or put products into a shopping cart through subtle nudging techniques, called dark patterns, may constitute behavioural manipulation. The Digital Services Act, which will be enforced in 2024, is the first piece of legislation that uses this term in the EU (Troge, 2023). The law tries to, among other things, combat dark patterns by requiring companies to be transparent about their practices (eur-lex. europa.eu, 2022).

In a very simplistic way, for marketers, protecting personal data ultimately means ensuring data security, vetting additional information created, maintaining accurate data and ensuring data use is fair and responsible.

My take on what data protection laws want us to protect

At this point, I feel that there is something tangible that I can recommend you to be on the watch out for when using personal data for marketing, be it measurement, audience creation or running a contact centre.

1 **Maintain** clean and accurate data files.
2 Develop **Responsible** apps and websites.
3 Think of all possible **Consequences** to your customers when appending attributes to your customer records to creating insights.
4 Ensure data **Security**.

Or go through the what I call the **MaRCS-protection check**. When you can tell your Data Protection Officer or your privacy department what your plan is on the above four points, you will immediately give them a great impression!

Data protection from a historical perspective

After discussing what data protection laws are trying to protect, I'd like to take a moment and showcase a brief history of data protection laws. Before data protection, there was data capture on an automated medium. The invention of the transistor in 1947 (Computer History Museum, 2023), followed by the invention of the microchip in 1956, led to the birth of the first integrated circuit (Berlin, 2006; Texas Instruments, 2020). Ever since then, computing power and data storage have been growing exponentially. Known as Moore's Law, computing power, as a rule of the thumb, doubles every two years (Intel, 2023). What happened after that is easy to predict. The cost of storing data collapsed and crumbled rapidly, making it accessible to the mass (McCallum, 2002).

It was also in the early 1960s that direct mail business began to grow, starting the golden age of direct mail (We Are MBC, 2022). Now-retired colleagues of mine once explained to me the cumbersome process of collecting and typing names and addresses onto the computer. The records were sorted out by postal codes so that advertisers could select specific areas where consumers with a higher likelihood than the national average to purchase their products or services were presumably living. What was revolutionary is that unlike mass advertising, such as TV, radio and billboard, direct mail opened up the possibility of finding out how effective advertising has been through carrying out a so-called response analysis. Being able to measure the effectiveness of campaigns had a side-effect that allowed marketers to command bonuses like salespeople. A new type of marketing information started to grow, mapping out postal code areas, then street sections, for its purchasing power, socio-demographics and lifestyle information, like the likelihood of someone living in a particular street to go on a ski holiday.

The birth of data protection laws

However, it was not the marketing use of data that ultimately gave birth to the world's first data protection law. In the late 1960s, a single article published by a political correspondent of a major German newspaper, moved the then Minister President of the German state of Hessen to start a legislative process to form the world's first data protection law (Simitis, 1996). In this article, the author articulated the danger of giving the government the power to access centralized personal data, warning that this could possibly lead the country to become a totalitarian state (Kühnert, 1969). Reading this more than 30 years after the Cold War, and after being accustomed to typing at least 20 messages a day on social media, I find myself reading the article as a matter of fact, without evoking any emotion. Perhaps there was a sense of fear among West Germans which associated totalitarianism with East Germany and communism? In any case, the day after the article appeared, the state of Hessen commenced its work to draft a data protection law, and a mere six days later the first draft of the law was ready.

The first data protection law required the establishment of a data protection authority, and so Willi Birkelbach became the first person in the world to be appointed as the head of data protection authority in 1971 (HBDI, 2021).

One key concept, informational self-determination, which forms the basic premises of the notion of opt-in, was an important principle this law embodied. The Hessian parliament explained that this right would allow individuals to determine whether people's personal data could be disclosed to or used by third parties (lagis-hessen.de, 1970).

The Greek-German Professor Simitis, hailed as the father of data protection, is known to be the main contributor to the first data protection law. In 1975, he was appointed head of the Hessian data protection authority and kept the position until 1991. He was also well known for promoting the concept of informational self-determination for the protection of personal data (Goethe Universität Frankfurt, 2023).

Swedish Data Protection Act

In 1973, three years after the data protection law of Hessen was adopted, Sweden passed a national data protection act (lagen.nu, 1973). Against the backdrop of the national census and the growing concern of government surveillance, the Royal Commission on Publicity and Secrecy made a recommendation to develop a data protection act. This law incorporated principles such as purpose limitation, data minimization and data security, as well as requiring the setting up of a data protection authority. The challenge was that every data processing needed to be approved by the regulator before being carried out.

French Data Protection Law

After Sweden, France came up with a comprehensive data protection law in 1978. Also in France, the fear of government abuse of power, or the threat of government surveillance and totalitarianism, initiated the data protection law. There was a public outrage, triggered by an article in a widely read newspaper *Le Monde*, which reported a government programme which was aimed at creating a central database of French citizens (Boucher, 1974).

Data protection in the USA

While the three European countries developed their data protection laws to protect the citizens from government's potential abuse of power, it was the financial institutions that the US lawmakers were more concerned about, how they evaluate the financial well-being of individuals. In 1970, to protect persons from becoming victims of wrongful credit information, a sector-specific data protection law, which eventually evolved into Fair Credit Reporting Act (FCRA), was enacted (govinfo.gov, 1970). With the FCRA, the USA became one of the first countries to have a data protection law. It provided for subject access rights, through which consumers were able to obtain information about the data the institution held. FCRA also gave consumers the possibility of correcting wrongful information kept by the institution. Today, both of these rights are incorporated in most data protection laws, including Japanese and Mexican laws, as well as GDPR (Japanese Law Translation, 2011; diputados.gob.mx, 2010; legislation.gov.uk, 2016).

The OECD and the Council of Europe

On an international level, two organizations' initiatives, that of the Organisation for Economic Cooperation and Development (OECD) and the Council of Europe, have been instrumental in promoting the drafting of data protection laws around the globe. In 1980, the OECD recognized an increasing concern (OECD Publishing, 2023):

> The 1970s may be described as a period of intensified investigative and legislative activities concerning the protection of privacy with respect to the collection and use of personal data. Numerous official reports show that the problems are taken seriously at the political level and at the same time that the task of balancing opposing interests is delicate and unlikely to be accomplished once and for all. Public interest has tended to focus on the risks and implications associated with the computerised processing of personal data and some countries have chosen to enact statutes which deal exclusively with computers and computer-supported activities. Other countries have preferred a more general approach to privacy protection issues irrespective of the particular data processing technology involved.

As an organization promoting international economic development, the OECD put its focus on issues arising from cross-border data transfers. *The Guidelines on the Protection of Privacy and Transborder Flows of Personal Data*, the *Declaration on Transborder Data Flows* and lastly the *Ministerial Declaration on the Protection of Privacy of Global Networks* were drawn up in the 1980s with the expectation for OECD member countries to introduce data protection laws that reflect the contents of these documents, globally (OECD, 2001).

The Council of Europe, a human rights organization, recognized a *serious danger for the rights of the individual inherent in certain aspects of modern scientific and technological development* (pace.coe.int, 1968) and recommended member states to study their laws, to determine whether they sufficiently protected the right to privacy (echr.coe.int, 1950). As they did not, the Council of Europe started their work on privacy and data protection in the late 1960s. This resulted in a treaty called Convention 108, which concerns data protection, in 1981. As a side note, despite its name, 40 per cent of their current members are non-European countries. All member countries have signed up to the European Convention of Human Rights, which means the European Court of Human Rights oversees the implementation of the treaties (coe.int, 2023). This makes Convention 108 the first internationally binding legal instrument that commits countries to develop and implement data protection laws.

As one of the Council of Europe members, the UK enacted the UK Data Protection Act in 1984 to implement Convention 108 (legislation.gov.uk, 2018). However, it is noted that the UK could have been the first country to adopt a law that protected privacy, as the 'Right of Privacy' bill was proposed but later rejected as early as 1961 (The Law Reform Commission of Hong Kong, 2004). The 1984 Data Protection Act became the first data protection law in the UK (legislation.gov.uk, 1984).

European Data Protection Directive

In 1995, with the aim of further harmonizing data protection rules within the EU, the European Union adopted a Data Protection Directive, mandating all EU member states to pass a data protection law that adopts this directive (eur-lex.europa.eu, 1995).

THE DIFFERENCE BETWEEN A DIRECTIVE AND A REGULATION

There are two types of European Union legislative acts. While directives set out goals that EU member states shall achieve, they do not prescribe a law. European member states are free to implement laws that fulfil the requirements spelt out in the directives. The advantage is that the resulting laws can be designed to fit the legal tradition of each country. The disadvantage is that there are usually differences in implementing the directive among different member states. This is why the 1995 Data Protection Directive was implemented in all countries, but every country differed in its nuances. For instance, with a few exceptions, conducting direct mail in Germany required consent from the individual receiving advertorial post, while Britain and France did not require this.

Regulations, however, are binding and are adopted word-for-word in all EU member states. GDPR is a regulation, and therefore every EU member state has to adopt it directly in its country. This is also why the phrase 'level playing field' was often used in describing the harmonization of the rules by the GDPR, compared to the EU Data Protection Directive (EU Commission, 2016).

E-Privacy Directive and opt-in

Several years later, the EU Directive on Privacy and Electronic Communications, often referred to as the E-Privacy Directive, was proposed and later adopted in 2002 (eur-lex.europa.eu, 2002). The directive was positioned as a *Rex Specialis* of the EU Data Protection Directive, among other things to protect the confidentiality of communication. *Rex Specialis* are laws that define the details of specific parts of a general law (University of Cologne, 2023). For marketers, the adoption of the E-Privacy Directive noted the start of the opt-in requirement for telemarketing (some countries), fax marketing and email marketing. In the UK, the E-Privacy Directive was implemented through PECR (legislation.gov.uk, 2003).

With the growth of online advertising, in 2009, the E-Privacy Directive was updated (eur-lex.europa.eu, 2009). The 2009 directive is dubbed as 'cookie law' and, among other things, requires opt-in from marketers to collect consent to set cookies, for instance for displaying personalized advertising. As with the 2002 E-Privacy Directive, these changes were also implemented through local laws; in the UK the implementing law was once again PECR.

Modernizing data protection laws in Europe

In the meantime, the first study by the European Commission was carried out on how the EU Data Protection Directive has been implemented across the member states (Art 29 WP, 2009). Among other things, the study highlighted the need to further harmonize the way the directive has been implemented. Then, in 2009, the commission started a process of reviewing the directive. In July 2009, a public consultation was launched, and in 2010 more targeted stakeholder consultations were concluded. In September 2010, the EU Commission announced that they would start working on revising the EU Data Protection Directive, with the aim of addressing, among other things, the following issues (EU Commission, 2010):

- addressing the impact of new technologies
- enhancing the internal market dimension of data protection
- addressing globalization and improving international data transfers
- providing a stronger institutional arrangement for the effective enforcement of data protection rules
- improving the coherence of data protection legal framework

The EU thus embarked on the legislative quest which ultimately resulted in what we know as the General Data Protection Regulation, or GDPR, today.

GDPR

On 27 April 2016 the European Union adopted the new data protection law, the EU General Data Protection Regulation or GDPR, and two years later on 25 May 2018, the law came into effect. Although this is a regulation, there is a provision, expressed in Articles 92 and 93, which allows countries to further supplement several sections (legislation.gov.uk, 2016). Every country has therefore set up a separate law that implements the GDPR. For the UK, that is the UK Data Protection Act 2018.

The group of regulators of the EU, which were called the Working Party Article 29 back then, organized so-called 'Fab Labs', inviting a wide range of stakeholders from academia, civil society and industry (including marketing and advertising industry representatives) (Art 29 WP, 2016). At the Fab Lab, the EU group of regulators focused the discussions on topics they felt required priority guidance, such as the role of the Data Protection Officer, Data Portability, Data Protection Impact Assessment and Certifications. The guidelines were subsequently published and adopted in 2017, in time before GDPR would come into effect. In the coming chapters, I will explain GDPR in greater detail, and how this affects the marketing profession.

CHANGES BROUGHT TO OFFLINE CONSUMER SURVEYS BY GDPR

In the olden days, marketing companies collected consumer data through paper surveys. They would be sent out to millions of households in the first week of January. The thinking was that, at that time of the year, many people would have taken days off work. Survey experts assumed that people would have a bit more time after Christmas and New Year's Eve festivities, and would likely fill out consumer surveys. The survey was combined with a prize draw with big prizes, like a brand new car, and came with a covering letter with contact details of the company. The following text appeared on one such survey in the pre-GDPR era (Acxiom Ltd, 2005).

> Your views count. Manufacturers and service providers depend on your input to help them offer the right products in the right way at the right price. Please take a few minutes to complete this survey.

> Just ignore any questions you would prefer not to answer. Thank you for helping us. This survey is conducted by Acxiom Limited who shall safeguard your information according to the Data Protection Act 1998. By completing this survey you agree that Acxiom Limited, its group of companies and other reputable organizations may use the information you give for the purposes of developing products/services, marketing, research and analysis, updating, validation and integration of files, identity verification and reducing fraud. If there is a change in the ownership of any of Acxiom Limited assets, it may disclose your information to the new owner. If you are responding on behalf of another person please ensure that you have their permission. If you would rather that the information you give is not used for the above purposes then please tick the appropriate boxes: you ( ) partner ( ). Certain questions have been included in the survey on behalf of: *** a list of brands that partnered in the survey *** Thank you very much for your help.

If you want to carry out a similar survey today, under GDPR, at least contact details of the Data Protection Officer (DPO), legal basis for using this data, information on transfer of files to a third country, information on data subjects' rights and the right to lodge a complaint with the Information Commissioner's Office (ICO) need to be added.

GDPR has indeed increased the amount of information that needs to be provided to the data subject.

Code of Practice

GDPR gave the EU regulators' organ, Working Party Article 29, a new name, the European Data Protection Board or the EDPB. The EDPB continued to develop guidelines. In addition, many regulators have drawn up guidelines to help companies and organizations to better understand and implement the law.

The German regulators, for instance, have published several so-called 'orientation help' documents. One was developed for marketing in February 2022 (DSK, 2022). The UK Information Commissioner's Office (ICO) published a draft Marketing Code of Practice in 2020 for public consultation. The ICO announced their intention to finalize the Marketing Code of Practice, but, perhaps because the UK government is in the process of passing a new data protection law, this has not been finalized to date (ICO, 2023).

Brexit

The renewal of the data protection laws is the direct consequence of Brexit. As of 1 February 2020, the EU GDPR is no longer applicable in the UK. Companies and organizations are, however, still subject to the UK Data Protection Act, and UK GDPR, which is identical to EU GDPR. The British government did not stand still as it recognized that tough data protection laws might be preventing the British economy from growing. In the autumn of 2021, the department of Digital, Culture, Media and Sports (DCMS) launched a public consultation to find out how to change UK GPDR in such way as to bring improvements for both consumers and businesses. The DCMS stated (UK Government DCMS, 2021):

> The proposals aim to deliver an even better data protection regime that will:

- support vibrant competition and innovation to drive economic growth
- maintain high data protection standards without creating unnecessary barriers to responsible data use
- keep pace with the rapid innovation of data-intensive technologies
- help innovative businesses of all sizes to use data responsibly without undue uncertainty or risk, both in the UK and internationally
- ensure the Information Commissioner's Office (ICO) is equipped to regulate effectively in an increasingly data-driven world

All points, perhaps with the exception of the last one, can support businesses, including marketers. The UK Data and Marketing Association (UK DMA) provided a comprehensive response, in which they see less dependence on consent, less administrative burden and the maintenance of high standard of data protection which will allow continued barrier-free data flow with Europe and internationally as changes that can help companies and marketers to go about more efficiently with their activities (UK DMA, 2021).

In total, the consultation received almost 3,000 responses. The DCMS subsequently published the findings titled 'Data: a new direction – government response to consultation' in June 2022 (UK Government DCMS, 2022). A draft law called the Data Protection and Digital Information Bill (DPDI Bill) was subsequently proposed in July 2022 (UK Parliament, 2022).

The DPDI Bill is aimed at removing unnecessary paperwork, clarifying that data used in marketing context can clearly rely on legitimate interest as its legal ground, while allowing Britain to maintain an adequate level of data protection, allowing trading relationships with the EU countries to continue as it is today. Currently, the DPDI Bill has passed the House of Commons and is in the hands of the House of Lords. The House of Lords has so far passed the first two readings, which means the content of the Bill is unlikely to be changed dramatically anymore. Once the draft passes the House of Lords, the Bill will go through the final stages and will be formally adopted as an Act of Parliament after the Royal Assent (UK Parliament, 2023).

Developments in the EU

Laws in Europe that touch marketing and data protection are changing too. Two laws, the Digital Services Act, governing online advertising transparency, and the Digital Market Act, creating a level playing field in the digital ecosystem, have both been adopted in 2022 (eur-lex.europa.eu, 2022; eur-lex.europa.eu, 2022a). The Data Act, aimed at facilitating data sharing, as well as the AI Act, a comprehensive AI law, are expected to come into effect in 2025 and 2026 respectively (EU Commission, 2022; EU Commission, 2021). There is also a new law, Political Advertising Regulation, which, as the name suggests, increases the transparency of obligations surrounding political advertising, going through the formal approval stage in 2024 (EU Commission, 2023a).

GDPR is also getting a small facelift. Legislators are working on procedural rules that will assist regulators of the EU countries to better cooperate, as well as harmonize their approaches in applying GDPR (EU Commission, 2023).

Key takeaways

1 The right to data protection is one of many rights and freedoms. The right to data protection must be balanced against other rights and freedoms.

2 Before you use personal data for marketing, go through the **MaRCS-protection check** and informally review for yourself what data protection laws are trying to protect.

3 Data protection laws emerged from the fear of potential governmental power abuse.

4 Data protection laws are evolving to adapt to technological shifts, and to improve the effectiveness of the law.

Conclusions

Data protection laws are aimed at protecting a fundamental human right. Understanding what the laws are intended to do helps marketers use personal data most responsibly to achieve their goals, whether concerned with insight, identity or measurement. Protections due in the marketing context are from crime, harmful insights, inaccurate data and heteronomy or manipulation. These can be avoided when marketers can ensure data security, carefully vet additional information created using personal data, maintain accurate data and use personal data fairly and responsibly. Data protection laws were first created from the fear of possible abuse of data by the government. Since then, through the help of international organizations, the legislative concept evolved and spread globally. Data protection laws continue to evolve today, setting new requirements for using personal data.

Bibliography

Acxiom Ltd (2005) Acxiom Research Opinion Poll, Survey Base 219 V18, 2 August 2005, Acxiom Ltd, London, UK. Internal document kindly made available from Acxiom Ltd

Art 29 WP (2009) Article 29 Data Protection Working Party, The Future of Privacy Joint Contribution to the Consultation of the European Commission on the Legal Framework for the Fundamental Right to Protection of Personal Data, https://ec.europa.eu/justice/article-29/documentation/opinion-recommendation/files/2009/wp168_en.pdf (archived at https://perma.cc/LA6U-RZT3)

Art 29 WP (2016) Article 29 Data Protection Working Party, Fablab: GDPR/from Concepts to Operational Toolbox, DIY – results of the discussion, 30 September 2016, https://ec.europa.eu/justice/article-29/documentation/other-document/files/2016/20160930_fablab_results_of_discussions_en.pdf (archived at https://perma.cc/AP7Q-ZBUM)

Berlin, L (2006) *The Man Behind the Microchip: Robert Noyce and the invention of Silicon Valley*, Oxford University Press.

Boucher, P (1974) Une division de l'informatique est créée à la chancellerie 'Safari' ou la chasse aux Français, *Le Monde*, 21 March 1974, 9

coe.int (2023) The Council of Europe at a Glance – 46 Member States – 700 Million Citizens, www.coe.int/en/web/portal/the-council-of-europe-at-a-glance (archived at https://perma.cc/PAN2-28V7)

Computer History Museum (2023) 1947: Invention of the point-contact transistor: John Bardeen and Walter Brattain achieve transistor action in a germanium point-contact device in December 1947, www.computerhistory.org/siliconengine/invention-of-the-point-contact-transistor/ (archived at https://perma.cc/8APK-EUN7)

Council of Europe (2018) *Convention 108 + Modernised Convention for the Protection of Individuals with Regard to the Processing of Personal Data – Adopted by the Committee of Ministers at its 128th Session of the Committee of Ministers*, Council of Europe, Strasbourg Cedex, France, https://rm.coe.int/convention-108-convention-for-the-protection-of-individuals-with-regar/16808b36f1 (archived at https://perma.cc/5PQM-9EQ5)

diputados.gob.mx (2010) Ley Federal de Protección de Datos Personales en Posesión de los Particulares, Cámara de Diputados del H. Congreso de la Unión, Secretaría General, Secretaría de Servicios Parlamentarios, México, 5 July 2010, www.diputados.gob.mx/LeyesBiblio/pdf/LFPDPPP.pdf (archived at https://perma.cc/3L8P-XSC7)

Drackert, S (2014) *Die Risiken der Verarbeitung personenbezogener Daten*, Max-Planck-Institut für ausländisches und internationales Strafrecht, Freiburg, Germany, 291, English translation available in (Veil, 2018)

DSK (2022) Datenschutzkonferenz: Orientierungshilfe der Aufsichtsbehörden zur Verarbeitung von personenbezogenen Daten für Zwecke der Direktwerbung unter Geltung der Datenschutz-Grundverordnung (DS-GVO), www.datenschutzkonferenz-online.de/media/oh/OH-Werbung_Februar%202022_final.pdf (archived at https://perma.cc/JQ2U-BZ2W)

echr.coe.int (1950) European Court of Human Rights – Convention for the Protection of Human Rights and Fundamental Freedoms, Rome, 4 November 1950, www.echr.coe.int/documents/d/echr/convention_eng (archived at https://perma.cc/6B68-LV5G)

EU (2000) European Union Charter of Fundamental Rights of the European Union, 2000/C 364/01, www.europarl.europa.eu/charter/pdf/text_en.pdf (archived at https://perma.cc/8SMN-PFWT)

EU Commission (2010) Communication from the Commission to the European Parliament, the Council, the Economic and Social Committee and the Committee of the Regions, A Comprehensive Strategy on Data Protection in the European Union, Brussels, COM(2010) XXX final, www.statewatch.org/media/documents/news/2010/oct/eu-com-draft-communication-data-protection.pdf (archived at https://perma.cc/8RPL-7D44), see pp 4–5

EU Commission (2016) Joint Statement on the Final Adoption of the New EU Rules for Personal Data Protection, 14 April 2016, https://ec.europa.eu/commission/presscorner/detail/en/STATEMENT_16_1403 (archived at https://perma.cc/YZA3-6SKR)

EU Commission (2021) Regulatory Framework Proposal on Artificial Intelligence, https://digital-strategy.ec.europa.eu/en/policies/regulatory-framework-ai (archived at https://perma.cc/2GLJ-7KQR)

EU Commission (2022) Data Act, https://digital-strategy.ec.europa.eu/en/policies/data-act (archived at https://perma.cc/YU5R-ZE5B)

EU Commission (2023) Data Protection: Commission adopts new rules to ensure stronger enforcement of the GDPR in cross-border cases, 4 July 2023, https://ec.europa.eu/commission/presscorner/detail/en/ip_23_3609 (archived at https://perma.cc/38GD-82L6)

EU Commission (2023a) Commission welcomes political agreement on transparency of political advertising regulation, 7 November 2023, Brussels, https://ec.europa.eu/commission/presscorner/detail/en/IP_23_4843 (archived at https://perma.cc/5EAT-GAYG)

eur-lex.europa.eu (1995) Directive 95/46/EC of the European Parliament and of the Council of 24 October 1995 on the protection of individuals with regard to the processing of personal data and on the free movement of such data, Official Journal L 281, 23/11/1995 P. 0031 – 0050, https://eur-lex.europa.eu/legal-content/EN/TXT/?uri=celex%3A31995L0046 (archived at https://perma.cc/PK9A-KU4L)

eur-lex.europa.eu (2002) Directive 2002/58/EC of the European Parliament and of the Council of 12 July 2002 Concerning the Processing of Personal Data and the Protection of Privacy in the Electronic Communications Sector, Directive on privacy and electronic communications, Official Journal L 201, 31 July 2002, pp 0037–0047, https://eur-lex.europa.eu/LexUriServ/LexUriServ.do?uri=CELEX:32002L0058:en:HTML (archived at https://perma.cc/HT58-75XT)

eur-lex.europa.eu (2009) Directive 2009/136/EC of the European Parliament and of the Council of 25 November 2009 Amending Directive 2002/22/EC on Universal Service and Users' Rights Relating to Electronic Communications

Networks and Services, Directive 2002/58/EC concerning the processing of personal data and the protection of privacy in the electronic communications sector and Regulation (EC) No. 2006/2004 on cooperation between national authorities responsible for the enforcement of consumer protection laws, https:// eur-lex.europa.eu/LexUriServ/LexUriServ.do?uri=OJ:L:2009:337:0011:0036:en: PDF (archived at https://perma.cc/73R4-EZY7)

eur-lex.europa.eu (2022) Regulation (EU) 2022/2065 of the European Parliament and of the Council of 19 October 2022 on a Single Market for Digital Services and Amending Directive 2000/31/EC (Digital Services Act), https://eur-lex. europa.eu/legal-content/EN/TXT/?uri=CELEX%3A32022R2065& qid=1703665485067 (archived at https://perma.cc/QK2U-FJXX)

eur-lex.europa.eu (2022a) Regulation (EU) 2022/1925 of the European Parliament and the Council of 14 September 2022 on Contestable and Fair Markets in the Digital Sector and Amending Directives (EU) 2019/1937 and (EU) 2020/1828 (Digital Markets Act), https://eur-lex.europa.eu/eli/reg/2022/1925 (archived at https://perma.cc/J4W4-EP45)

Goethe Universität Frankfurt (2023) Goethe Universität Frankfurt am Main: Hessischer Goethe-Universität trauert um Spiros Simitis, 22 March 2023, https://aktuelles.uni-frankfurt.de/menschen/goethe-universitaet-trauert-um-spiros-simitis/ (archived at https://perma.cc/93FG-YH86)

govinfo.gov (1970) Fair Credit Reporting Act (FCRA), 15 U.S.C. § 1681 et seq, 26 October 1970, www.govinfo.gov/content/pkg/STATUTE-84/pdf/STATUTE-84-Pg1114-2.pdf (archived at https://perma.cc/YXD7-QQRM)

HBDI (2021) Der Hessische Beauftragte für Datenschutz und Informationsfreiheit: Hessen als Vorreiter – Geschichte des Datenschutzes, https://datenschutz.hessen. de/ueber-uns/geschichte-des-datenschutzes (archived at https://perma.cc/GXV3-C7P7)

Hern, A (2018) Cambridge Analytica: how did it turn clicks into votes? The Cambridge Analytica files, big data, *The Guardian*, 6 May 2018, www. theguardian.com/news/2018/may/06/cambridge-analytica-how-turn-clicks-into-votes-christopher-wylie (archived at https://perma.cc/A5Z4-N3ZC)

ICO (2023) ICO's 2020 consultation on a draft direct marketing code of practice – summary of responses, v1, January 2023, https://ico.org.uk/media/about-the-ico/ consultations/draft-direct-marketing-code/4024327/icos-2020-consultation-on-a-draft-direct-marketing-code-of-practice-summary-of-responses-v1_0.pdf (archived at https://perma.cc/43SC-C788)

Intel (2023) Cramming more components onto integrated circuits: Moore's Law, www.intel.com/content/www/us/en/history/virtual-vault/articles/moores-law. html?wapkw=cramming%20more%20computing%20into%20circuits (archived at https://perma.cc/9B7R-EM6Q)

Japanese Law Translation (2011) Act on the Protection of Personal Information, Act No. 57 of 2003, www.japaneselawtranslation.go.jp/en/laws/view/4241/en (archived at https://perma.cc/YSS4-TDK5)

Kühnert, H (1969) Tücken der Computer, *Frankfurter Allgemeine Zeitung*, 10 October 1969

lagis-hessen.de (1970) Landtag verabschiedet das weltweit erste Datenschutzgesetz, 7 October 1970, www.lagis-hessen.de/de/subjects/xsrec/current/305/pageSize/50/mode/abstract/setmode/abstract/sn/edb?q=YToxOntzOjM6Im9ydCI7czoxMToiTGFuZCBIZXNzZW4iO30= (archived at https://perma.cc/7NDX-4JFK)

lagen.nu (1973) Datalag, 1973:289, lagen.nu/1973:289 (archived at https://perma.cc/6MXB-V2WS)

The Law Reform Commission of Hong Kong (2004) The Law Reform Commission of Hong Kong Report Civil Liability for Invasion of Privacy, December 2004. www.hkreform.gov.hk/en/docs/rprivacy-e.pdf (archived at https://perma.cc/YJ8Y-9TVL). The actual texts of the proposed bills are not available (any more) online. Discussions in the House of Lords confirm the existence of the Right of Privacy Bill and the Younger Report and are made available under https://api.parliament.uk/historic-hansard/lords (archived at https://perma.cc/N453-FXR6)

legislation.gov.uk (1984) Data Protection Act 1984, 1984 CHAPTER 35, https://www.legislation.gov.uk/ukpga/1984/35/enacted (archived at https://perma.cc/8KSB-X7S8)

legislation.gov.uk (2003) The Privacy and Electronic Communications (EC Directive) Regulations 2003, www.legislation.gov.uk/uksi/2003/2426/contents/made (archived at https://perma.cc/2N7W-4NMW)

legislation.gov.uk (2016) Regulation (EU) 2016/679 of the European Parliament and of the Council, 27 April 2016, www.legislation.gov.uk/eur/2016/679/introduction (archived at https://perma.cc/V856-CZCD)

legislation.gov.uk (2018) Data Protection Act 2018, www.legislation.gov.uk/ukpga/2018/12/notes/division/4/index.htm (archived at https://perma.cc/S4LY-994N). Background and General Processing, paras 50 and 51

McCallum, J (2002) Historical cost of computer memory and storage, https://ourworldindata.org/grapher/historical-cost-of-computer-memory-and-storage (archived at https://perma.cc/AX5J-HGMA)

OECD (2001) OECD Guidelines on the Protection of Privacy and Transborder Flows of Personal Data, www.oecd-ilibrary.org/docserver/9789264196391-en.pdf?expires=1686480974&id=id&accname=guest&checksum=BD38471E44E4C4D798E86D0C762B21F3 (archived at https://perma.cc/X6AU-BDSP)

OECD Publishing (2023) Explanatory Memoranda of the OECD Privacy Guidelines, OECD Digital Economy Papers, October 2023, No. 360, www.oecd-ilibrary.org/docserver/ea4e9759-en.pdf?expires=1703608063&id=id&accname=guest&checksum=7718BDEFB73C0F5FB569F3C80E501107 (archived at https://perma.cc/76Y5-5VMW)

pace.coe.int (1968) Council of Europe: Human rights and modern scientific and technological developments – recommendation 509 (1968), https://pace.coe.int/pdf/e8a602cbcd96bec44cbbf3c37579429e2aa263e9cf1f740533820a8ec3c53ba4/rec.%20509.pdf (archived at https://perma.cc/76Y5-zzzz)

Simitis, S (1996) Virtuelle Präsenz und Spurenlosigkeit – Ein neues Datenschutzkonzept. Kritische Vierteljahresschrift für Gesetzgebung und Rechtswissenschaft (KritV), 79(1), 99–108

Texas Instruments (2020) The chip that changed the world, https://news.ti.com/blog/2020/09/15/the-chip-that-changed-world (archived at https://perma.cc/U2YN-UBQB)

Troge, T (2023) Does AI enhance the risk of dark patterns and how does EU law regulate them? www.taylorwessing.com/en/interface/2023/ai---are-we-getting-the-balance-between-regulation-and-innovation-right/does-ai-enhance-the-risk-of-dark-patterns-and-how-does-eu-law-regulate-them (archived at https://perma.cc/8MX9-E9X9)

UK DMA (2021) UK Data and Marketing Association – Data: A new direction – consultation response, 29 November 2021, https://dma.org.uk/article/data-a-new-direction-consultation-response (archived at https://perma.cc/TQ8Q-MFEX)

UK Government (2017) Charter of Fundamental Rights of the EU Right by Right Analysis, 5 December 2017, https://assets.publishing.service.gov.uk/government/uploads/system/uploads/attachment_data/file/664891/05122017_Charter_Analysis_FINAL_VERSION.pdf (archived at https://perma.cc/9UD3-XJYD). Page 4: 'It is important that the Charter is viewed as a whole. There is no hierarchy of rights in the Charter; no one right is more important than another, and certain rights in the Charter will conflict with and have to be balanced against other rights in the Charter.'

UK Government DCMS (2021) Original consultation – Public consultation on reforms to the UK's data protection regime, www.gov.uk/government/consultations/data-a-new-direction (archived at https://perma.cc/9KVS-VA9D)

UK Government DCMS (2022) Consultation outcome: Data: a new direction – government response to consultation, updated 23 June 2022, www.gov.uk/government/consultations/data-a-new-direction/outcome/data-a-new-direction-government-response-to-consultation (archived at https://perma.cc/3G9Q-G6CC)

University of Cologne (2023) No. I.3.2 – Lex specialis-Principle, www.trans-lex.org/910000/_/lex-specialis-principle/ (archived at https://perma.cc/9ELN-9LP8)

UK Parliament (2022) Data Protection and Digital Information Bill, ordered by the House of Commons to be printed, 18 July 2022, https://publications.parliament.uk/pa/bills/cbill/58-03/0143/220143.pdf (archived at https://perma.cc/VVR3-8PMX)

UK Parliament (2023) Data Protection and Digital Information Bill, Government Bill, originated in the House of Commons, Sessions 2022–23, 2023–24, last updated 20 December 2023, https://bills.parliament.uk/bills/3430 (archived at https://perma.cc/H4X3-B94N)

Veil, W (2018) The GDPR: The emperor's new clothes – on the structural short-comings of both the old and the new Data Protection Law, *Neue Zeitschrift für Verwaltungsrecht*, 10, 686–96, Section III point 2, https://papers.ssrn.com/sol3/papers.cfm?abstract_id=3305056 (archived at https://perma.cc/UH6M-2CHY)

We Are MBC (2022) Why the 1960s was the start of the 'Golden Age of Advertising', 7 June 2022, https://wearembc.com/why-the-1960s-was-the-start-of-the-golden-age-of-advertising/ (archived at https://perma.cc/MPF5-VCXH)

2

What is marketing?

Marketing is a big topic. Before I sat in my first marketing lecture at the university, marketing for me was all about advertising on TV and billboards, created by fashionably dressed people toasting each other with champagne glasses. I now know better, as in, I think I know better. Marketing is all about using data, the new oil, to promote products and services through communicating the right way. My sister, however, working in the creative side of the industry, seems to have a very different concept of what marketing is. In this chapter, I will describe marketing to set the context for the rest of this book.

Marketing as a business discipline

Regardless of what your company is doing, be it manufacturing towels or providing consultancy services, there are certain categories of activities that are commonly required for operating a business. Organizations have functions that are creating products and services, looking at how much is spent versus how much revenue is generated, taking care of people at work, and selling the products and services. The BBC's Bitesize explains business functions to children in an easy-to-digest format. Their website says organizations typically have at least four functions, namely operations, finance, human resources and marketing (BBC, 2023). The management, which usually sits on top of these functions, is the conductor of the business, orchestrating all functions, and making sure they work in harmony. There are other functions such as IT, purchasing and research and development, though, to illustrate the point, I will stick to the four disciplines in Bitesize in a simplistic manner.

The first function, operations, may be called the production department, service department or consultancy department, depending on the nature of the business. Operations can be the function that manufactures shoes, if it is a company selling shoes. For a property maintenance services provider, operations will be plumbing or mending a window. The operations department is the raison d'être of a company, and the added value it brings to society.

Then there is finance, or I would call it the finance and accounting department, where you track how much money is made versus how much it has cost. This function prepares, among other things, profit and loss statements and balance sheets for the management.

At present, businesses have people working in the company. You need people to run a business. This in turn means you need someone to make sure that people are working happily, and productively, in an organizational environment that makes people want to stay. Where a specific skill is missing, people with these skills need to be recruited. That is the role of the human resources (HR) team.

Marketing is also one of the functions necessary for running an organization, alongside operations, finance and human resources. The role of marketing is to sell products and services, created by the operations department, which allows an organization to survive, grow or attract investors. Many organizations separate sales from marketing, seeing marketing taking a supporting role for salespeople to sell products and services.

Defining marketing

Let us look a bit more closely into how marketing is defined. Kotler (1988) defined marketing in the following way:

> Marketing (management) is the process of planning and executing the conception, pricing, promotion, and distribution of ideas, goods, and services to create exchanges that satisfy individual and organizational objectives.

Kotler's definition cited above is more than 35 years old. The definition sees the whole planning process as part of marketing activity. As satisfying the objectives of customers, individuals or organizations is set as its ultimate aim, Kotler's definition implies that organizations must understand their customers and their objectives to be successful in marketing. Accordingly, the 1988 edition of Kotler's *Marketing Management* book places great importance on market research as a source of insight. Today's marketer has access to data, captured in the course of customers interacting with the company or those that are collected by third parties, as an additional source where more accurate and deeper customer insights can be obtained.

The American Marketing Association (AMA) updates its definition of marketing regularly. The most recent definition of marketing adopted by this organization reads as follows (American Marketing Association, 2017):

> Marketing is the activity, set of institutions, and processes for creating, communicating, delivering, and exchanging offerings that have value for customers, clients, partners, and society at large.

The AMA's definition includes activities on top of processes, but does not include the word 'planning', as with Kotler's definition. It emphasizes the inclusive and interactive nature of marketing; the phrases 'set of institutions' and 'partners and society at large' are named in addition to customers and clients as integral parts of marketing. My assumption here is that when organizations are working together, information and certainly data can be exchanged among the parties involved. For instance, where two companies jointly organize a free webinar to generate leads, both companies will most likely want to share the contact details of the participants, each for their own promotional activities.

What both definitions have in common is that marketing is carried out for the good of individuals and companies. Kotler's definition requires the satisfying of individual and organizational objectives for a process to be categorized as marketing. AMA's definition requires value to be created for customers, clients, partners and society for an activity or institutions or process to be considered marketing. In other words, promotional activities relying on deception and trickery, which neither help customers to achieve objectives nor bring value to them, are not marketing. Marketers are there to commercially persuade customers and potential customers to see more value in what their company has to offer, compared to the competitors (Jobber and Ellis-Chadwick, 2024).

I will use the definition from AMA for 'marketing' throughout this book.

MANIPULATION AND COMMERCIAL PERSUASION

Particularly in the digital field, marketing data use is criticized as a manipulative tactic to trick consumers into buying something they don't need. The expression 'Surveillance Capitalism', popularized by Zuboff (2019), may leave a general impression that marketing and advertising are inherently malevolent.

Though to sell any product or service, especially if what you are offering is innovative or new, you need to inform others that your product or service is being offered. People need to know that it is out there. Digitalization brought the opportunity to advertise cost effectively, making marketing campaigns, previously only accessible to large corporations, affordable to SMEs and start-ups (Doty, 2019). Besides, selling and commercial persuasion have been around since the birth of trade some 300,000 years ago (Boissoneault, 2018).

Let's take a quick look at the difference between manipulation and persuasion. Manipulation and persuasion both aim to influence the behaviour or belief of the other. Manipulation is usually associated with moral disapprobation, characterized by unfairness and dishonesty. These negative attributes are absent in the definition of 'persuasion'. In addition, persuasion requires both the persuading party and the persuaded party to benefit as a result. When manipulation takes place, only one party, i.e. the manipulator, benefits from the changed behaviour of the manipulated (Noggle, 2018; American Psychological Association, 2023; Thompson, 1996). Nichols (1987), who was an authority in the field of listening behaviour, articulated the difference between manipulation and persuasion in the following way:

> Manipulation is the attainment of compliance based on illusion, intimidation, or fear. By contrast, persuasion is the attainment of commitment based on the reality of need, discernment and conviction.

There are political advertisements that are carried out in good faith, in adherence to a marketing industry's code of conduct. But let's take a look at an obvious case of changing voting behaviours in manipulative ways. According to Nichols' definition, putting someone under peer pressure, via social media or in person, so that the person will vote for a certain political candidate, is manipulation. Playing on someone's fear of losing their sense of belonging, by voting in a certain way, is also manipulation. It should be noted that, with both of these examples of manipulating voting behaviour, the length of time within which the manipulated is under the control of the manipulator can be relatively short. After the election is over, it may be irrelevant to the manipulator if people are still convinced by how they voted. However, the results of the votes have the potential to fundamentally change the basis of our society, namely our democracy.

How does this compare to, say, a dairy company advertising their butter or a rooftop photovoltaic business promoting their electricity-generating panel to those who might be interested in these products? In marketing, trusting long-lasting relationships with customers is important, as those customers will buy more products (i.e. repeat purchases of the same butter or trying the cheese from the same brand). Trusting relationships can also result in more persons being interested in the product or service. For instance, a satisfied customer sharing a positive experience with the photovoltaic company can influence their friends' and families' decisions in choosing a renewable energy generator supplier.

By defining manipulation as synonymous with commercial persuasion, the act of robbing the right to democracy from citizens, and, displaying one ad and not the other to a person, are being treated the same. Recognizing the difference, the European Union is about to finalize a regulation, specifically on political advertising (EU Commission, 2023).

It is helpful that ANA's definition of marketing requires it to have an element of value creation for others (customers, clients, partners and society at large), which means an action benefiting only one side cannot be called marketing. This means manipulation cannot be, by definition, considered marketing. It is just what it is – an act of manipulation!

A short history of marketing

Marketing is not static. It has evolved over the years, influenced by the available technology, as well as from learnings over the years. In this section, we will review some of the popular concepts of marketing.

Emergence of marketing

At the beginning of trading, exchanging goods against goods in what was agreed as having equal values (bartering) and later on against currencies, marketing was fairly simple. Trading posts and stalls were lined along the most-travelled streets and squares. Venders with the loudest voice were typically thought to grab the attention of passers-by most efficiently, a technique which is still in practice in many markets and by street vendors today (Rao, 2021).

Jumping through many centuries, in the 1920s the electrification of the manufacturing process drove mass production, through which products were in over-supply. This meant it became more important than ever to make the manufactured products appeal to customers, more so than competing products in the market. Hence arose the necessity to advertise and differentiate products (Beaudreau, 1996). Graphic designers and copywriters were creating eye-catching billboards, newspaper and magazine ads. Radio sponsoring and advertising flourished, as radio was the most popular home entertainment form for a long time until TV took over in the 1950s (Pope, 1983).

The marketing mix

Amidst a multitude of promotional activities, the first major strategic framework of marketing, or marketing mix as they are often referred to, was born. McCarthy (1960) introduced the 4Ps of marketing which every marketing student is taught to this date. He argued that the foundation of marketing activities can be defined by determining:

Product – What are the characteristics of your product or service? How does it differentiate itself from the competition?

Price – What is the price level that allows the product or service to be perceived the way you want it to be seen?

Place – Which distribution channel is most suited for promoting the product or service?

Promotion – How to advertise and promote to create brand awareness and stimulate customers to purchase your product or service.

In the next evolution, Booms and Bitner (1981) suggested three more 'P's to be added to create the 7Ps of marketing. They are:

People – What level of customer service and interactions, supported by employee recruitment and training activities, are necessary for the delivery of quality experiences to the customers?

Physical Evidence – What are the most appropriate facilities, equipment and other tangible properties that shape customer perceptions of the quality of experience that a company is offering?

Process – How to streamline activities, procedures, protocols, etc. to provide a smooth, efficient and customer-friendly experience?

These three Ps were particularly suitable to the service industry and consumer services, such as hotels and call centres, and were becoming integral elements of the organization's marketing activity.

The Ps, even with the added list, are inward-focused, without much attention to the customers. To better address customer needs, the 4Cs framework emerged as a customer-centric successor to the traditional 4 and 7Ps (Lauterborn, 1990). Lauterborn, the creator of the framework, places greater emphasis on understanding the needs and wants of the customer and helps companies to tailor offerings accordingly. The Cs are:

Customer – Tailoring the offering to the needs and wants of the customers.

Cost – Adopting a price which can be viewed by the consumers as being a fair cost to cover, given the perception.

Convenience – Placing the products and services in places which make it easily accessible and convenient for the customer.

Communication – Determining the way to engage in a dialogue with customers, to foster trust.

This approach also takes the cost to the customer, not that for the company, into consideration, as well as providing convenience to the customer, and fostering effective communication.

Data protection and marketing

The move towards consumer focus and the realization that long-term relationships must be established upon trust resonate with some of the principles of data protection laws. For instance, both the consumer-centric approach and many data protection laws adopt data transparency as a key principle.

With the growth of email marketing in the 1990s, the resemblance between the customer-centric approach of marketing and data protection merged into a new paradigm called permission marketing. As people's email inboxes were starting to explode with unsolicited commercial emails, Godin (1999) introduced this concept, which advocates asking for customers' consent before sending any commercial messages via email. Sending out messages that land in the junk mail folder is also not in the interest of the sender, as they have paid for sending this email message. The E-Privacy Directive made it law in 2002 that commercial emails, with minor exceptions, should be carried out only where there is an opt-in (eur-lex.europa.eu, 2002).

Today, companies are creating relevant and valuable content that consumers want to opt-in to. Some years ago, as a newly converted vegetarian, I found it very helpful to receive recipes for delicious vegetarian dishes. The online organic grocery store that sends out the 'Recipes of the Week' email newsletter benefits from subscribers like me, because they can establish a mutual benefit: they are able to keep their customers happy, and the customer gets useful information for free.

Smartphone ownership and customer journey

In recent times, digitalization evolved further, thanks to the growth in smartphone ownership. In 2022, smartphone ownership in countries like the UK, Germany, the US and France was around 80 per cent, establishing this device as a more than viable medium for commercial communication (Statista, 2023). These devices are unique, compared to other communication tools, because information can be presented to smartphone owners at their fingertips, 24/7, making us all in 'always on' mode. The accessibility of information has also influenced consumer behaviour, as well as expectations, which in turn required marketers to once again shift the way they interact with the market (Nielsen Company, 2014).

Based on the foundation of customer-centric marketing, laid out by the 4Cs framework, the concept of the customer journey emerged. The customer journey represents the entire process that a customer goes through, starting from the initial awareness phase, evolving into the evaluation and then purchase phases, and concluding the journey with the post-purchase stage (Oxford Strategic Marketing, 2014).

The approach helps marketers to consider various customer touchpoints, online and offline, when shaping the strategy within the different phases of the customer journey. For instance, when booking a hotel room, I would go to several online hotel booking sites to see which accommodation is available in the city where I want to go to. Putting a hotel marketer's hat on, it would make the most sense to make sure that the hotel is listed on the online booking portals during this initial search stage, so that potential customers, like me, will notice the hotel.

While searching for a room, I might also be engaged in looking for fun activities during the visit. The marketing department of the hotel may increase its chance to be considered as a hotel I might stay at by sponsoring an ad on the city's online destination and activity guide, or by simply displaying an advertisement on social media to people who are likely to come to the city where their hotel is.

Putting 'my' hat back on, once past the awareness stage I will compare different hotels that I like, and finally decide where to stay. After the stay, I might look back to the stay and think, 'That was a great hotel. Nice design, spacious and the staff were friendly.' When prompted by the booking site, I might give a 5-star rating, which can inform future customers of the hotel. When managed well, the customer journey can work wonders.

THE EVOLVING CONSUMER ATTITUDE

Earlier in this chapter, I explained how marketing has been evolving along with consumer expectations. The Global Data and Marketing Alliance (GDMA) has been carrying out international consumer surveys for some years (GDMA, 2022). The survey was initially launched in the UK and then was extended to include Argentina, Australia, Canada, France, Germany, the Netherlands, Singapore, Spain and the USA. In 2022 the study expanded its geographic reach to cover Belgium, Brazil, China, India, Japan and Mexico, covering 16 countries from four continents in total.

What I find interesting in this survey are the consumer segments they have created to understand the base attitude, namely:

- **Data Pragmatists:** Those who are concerned about online privacy but will make trade-offs on a case-by-case basis as to whether the service or enhancement of service offered is worth the information requested.

- **Data Unconcerned:** Those who are unconcerned about online privacy in general and characterized by lower levels of concern about the sharing of personal data.

- **Data Fundamentalists:** Those who are concerned about online privacy and are unwilling to provide personal information even in return for service enhancement.

I have studied how these segments evolved.

The findings

The study shows that consumer attitude has changed over the years, along with the accelerated speed of digitalization. Accordingly, almost half of the surveyed consumers seem to have adapted to the changes by becoming Data Pragmatists, looking for the right balance between the trade-offs of sharing data, and the benefit of doing so, on a case-by-case basis.

Slightly disappointing is the growth of Data Unconcerned, the group that is uninterested in online privacy, the second largest segment. As a privacy professional, I do want as many people as possible to be aware of their right to data protection and show interest in what is happening to their data. The more people know about how their data is being used, the better they can protect their own personal data. Unfortunately, this segment seems to have grown from 26 per cent in 2018 to 31 per cent in 2022 in the 10 countries surveyed in both 2018 and 2022 (GDMA, 2022).

The Data Fundamentalists make up roughly a fifth of the survey respondents, with France, Canada and the UK being on the top of the chart with 26 per cent, 24 per cent and 23 per cent of the total respondents respectively.

The study also shows that people are less concerned about online privacy, and are feeling more confident about data sharing; younger age groups more so than the older age groups.

Consumers across the globe responded that they are aware that data exchange is supporting the running of modern society. More than half (53 per cent) of consumers either agreed or strongly agreed with the statement 'the exchange of personal information is essential for the smooth running of modern society'. What's more, consumers are even motivated to share their personal data to help smaller enterprises gain a competitive advantage over large companies.

However, this openness to data sharing and understanding of the role of personal data in the digitalized society do not mean people are happy for companies to collect more and more personal data, on an ongoing basis. Consumers expect companies to maintain and improve the personalization of communication, without permanently collecting additional data.

Another interesting observation is that consumers are after trust, more control of their data and transparency. According to this research, trust is the most important aspect of data sharing, even more so than receiving free services or getting a discount.

Takeaways for marketers

So, what can marketers learn from this study? First of all, feel relieved! Consumers are open to data sharing, which means you do not have to revert to zero personalization via mass media to be aligned with consumer sentiment. It is okay to personalize.

The prerequisite is a trusting relationship with the consumer. If you have not done so, find out how much your brand is trusted. Marks and Spencer, Samsung and IKEA, for instance, are on the top of the list of most trusted brands in the UK, according to YouGov BrandIndex (Dean, 2022). Based on the GDMA's consumer attitude survey, these companies will have advantages over other companies when asking consumers for entrusting their data with them, making the lives of their marketers easier.

Marketing departments should also think of ways to give more control of the data to their customers, once they are collected. Data protection laws require this, and typically companies fulfil their obligations in such a manner that the consumer contacts the company, and the company will execute the request of the consumer, be it data suppression, correction or Subject Access Request. In a log-in environment, many organizations are allowing their customers to correct and delete information, such as contact details and date of birth, as well as letting them decide whether they want to continue or stop receiving email newsletters. This gives consumers more control of their data, as well as fulfilling data protection requirements. Also, it is cost-saving because you do not need to set up a department or a call centre to help consumers to control their data. The consumers do it themselves!

Lastly, when using consumer data, think about how best to make consumers understand what you are doing with their data. Is the privacy policy written in plain, clear, easy-to-understand language? Can a privacy notice be layered, so that people can read the notice in a bullet point form, and, as needed, dig down to find out more details by clicking a hyperlink? Creating a consumer-friendly privacy policy is also a great opportunity to collaborate with legal and privacy folks.

Marketing strategy, tactics and planning

After reviewing the historical development of marketing, I feel that it is appropriate to mention the two levels of marketing, namely marketing strategy and marketing tactics. Both levels of marketing can only be carried out successfully where there are good insights into information and data. Like all other disciplines within an organization, marketing is a function that supports the overall goals of the business. Hence the first step in developing a marketing strategy is to understand the overall business strategy.

Marketing strategy is then developed, and aligned to the business strategy. Kotler (1988) sees marketing strategy as an exercise of defining principles, consisting of broad resource allocation and marketing mix.

Chaffey (2023) explains that there is a hierarchy between marketing strategy and marketing tactics. Marketing strategy:

- defines competitive advantage
- allocates marketing resources at the top level
- sets long-term marketing vision and objectives
- determines priority markets, audiences and products
- defines brand positioning

- defines audience engagement
- determines roadmap for it and other major investments for marketing
- steers tactical activities through governance

Marketing tactics are all marketing activities that are guided by the strategy.

Both marketing strategy and marketing tactics require planning. Jobber and Chadwick-Ellis (2024) highlight the importance of aligning the marketing planning with overall corporate strategy. According to these authors, there are two levels of marketing planning: one on the business unit level and the other on the product level.

In both levels, the same questions are asked. Below are the four questions asked while developing marketing plans and a short explanation of the activities in the corresponding marketing planning stages:

Where are we now? Information-gathering activities take place to understand the current position of the business unit or the product in the marketplace. The company's internal aspects are also examined to develop a Strengths-Weaknesses-Opportunities-Threats (SWOT) analysis. This assessment helps marketers to form an objective view of the status quo, as well as create a set of assumptions about the future.

Where would we like to be? In this marketing planning phase, marketing objectives are set, which in turn define the future direction of the business unit or a product.

How do we get there? Operational decisions on marketing mix, discussed earlier in this chapter, and other concrete steps to implement the strategy are established during this phase of marketing planning.

Are we on course? In this phase, the performance of the implemented marketing plan is measured, for instance, through metrics and marketing audits, to evaluate and, where necessary, take corrective actions. The results then feed into the next marketing planning cycle.

Focusing on getting attention

Guided by marketing strategy, executed through marketing tactics, organizations determine how to communicate with clients and prospects most appropriately. Apart from the message content, communication can be seen as a function of audience differentiation and the communication channel.

FIGURE 2.1 Precision of audience selection

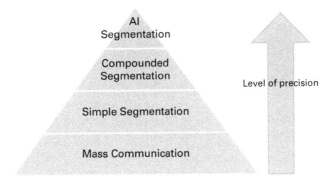

Let us take a look at the precision of audience selection through the lenses of segmentation methods (see Figure 2.1).

For many years, mass communication was the only way available to marketers. Traditional mass media are static, such as TV, billboards and radio. The same commercial messages were displayed to everyone consuming these media. Today, even these media can provide more granularity, thanks to digitalization. However, non-tailored mass advertising is still useful in some cases, for instance when trying to generate general awareness of a product or service, particularly at an early stage of the product life cycle.

Generally, the more data you have about your customer, the more effectively you can communicate with them, because you can better tailor to their wants and needs. In the beginning, when you are launching a new product or service, you have nothing more than an educated guess to go by. For instance, if you are selling car insurance, the people you are trying to reach are those who own a car. If you are selling flower-scented shampoo, most likely it is young women to which the product will appeal. These two products can be promoted with minimal tailoring. The haircare product company can place a TV advertisement on a romantic comedy show, while the insurance company can decide to advertise on billboards near a football stadium. Advertising to the mass market is, however, expensive compared to personalized ads by definition, because you cannot specify to whom you want to communicate the message, and you are charged for reaching everyone who is viewing the ad whether that person is interested in the product or not.

Once you have customers, and once you have data about them, you are able to understand who they are by learning from this data. For instance, data can be obtained through the registration process. This information can be used to narrow down the group of potential customers within the mass. The same insurance company might observe that the customers they acquired through their mass media campaign are between 18 and 30 years old. Using this information, the car insurer can create a simple segment based on age and target this age group. The company can also be more selective about which communication is best suited for reaching this age group. For instance, the insurer can choose to advertise in online magazines appealing to this group. Magazine publishers usually have information about their readership, including socio-demographics and lifestyle, which can help in choosing the right magazine to advertise in. The insurance company can also select this age group from online platforms and only display their commercial message to the selected age group.

As the insurer acquires more customers, they are able to gain more insights into this group. With more customer records, you can analyse the data to see if there are sub-groups to this simple segment. Within the 18- to 30-year-old segment, you might discover that one group owns cars that are 10 years or older, and are looking only for third-party coverage, which is the minimum required by law. Another group may be interested in a fully comprehensive coverage, and drive cars that are one or two years old. Additional insights can be gained through market research of the two sub-groups, or by enhancing the customer database with off-the-shelf lifestyle data. In addition to the purchase behaviour, you might find out that the first group like sports and love to travel abroad, while the second group enjoy the classic cultural scene and often live in big cities. The first sub-group can be displayed an advertisement on their jogging app, featuring a youngster in a training outfit, pondering about a trip abroad while driving. Another group can be shown an online video message with a strong emphasis on the extra peace of mind the insurance provides, with soothing classic music in the background.

Companies I have worked with typically have three to four customer segments per product. Efficiencies brought by AI can bring the viable number of segments to another level. With computational power and a broad range of applications, it is possible to create an almost infinite number of segments. If you would like, every customer or prospect can be assigned to a unique segment, using AI-powered predictive analytic solutions. Creatives in areas of advertising, such as videos and graphics, can also be adjusted accordingly, using AI-based personalization and recommendation engines so that everyone gets to see a different ad. This potentially gives companies the ability to achieve optimum relevance to every person they are communicating with; the right communication channel with the right message. We will discuss AI in further detail in Chapter 12.

Achieving relevance

So, why is it so important to communicate relevant messages? As I discussed earlier in this chapter, marketing is all about creating value for all parties involved. To know what value your product or service can provide your customers, you need to know who the customers are and what they want. Getting into a dialogue with them is a great way to get this intelligence. To get into a dialogue, your product and service, as well as the way you communicate about them, must trigger interest in the consumer. The relevance has to be there with every communication you have with them, morning, day or night, so that your product or service will be giving out a consistent image. On the other hand, while personalized advertising is generally more cost-effective when compared to mass media advertising with no differentiation, every delivered message has to be paid for. It is hence in the interest of organizations to minimize irrelevant messages being sent so that marketing campaign investments do not go to waste. Besides, consumers do not want to be bombarded by commercial messages that are not interesting to them.

Finding out if the communicated message was effective, or, if it was delivered to the intended audience, or how many sales it generated, are important insights that companies would like to have to improve, among other things, the relevance of their commercial messaging as well as choosing the right audience to communicate to. The feedback loop is hence essential for companies in improving their marketing activities.

Infrastructure to support marketing

Some investments need to be made to support marketing activity. First and foremost, you need a customer relationship management (CRM) database and tools. In this system, companies can capture data on customers and prospects that are relevant to marketing activities, like contact details, amount purchased, as well as socio-demographic and lifestyle information. Today, many organizations are putting their data on the cloud, referred to as the customer data platform (CDP). Unlike conventional CRMs, CDPs are used to consolidate data related to customers that may be stored in different databases within the organization like consumer interaction with the finance and customer services departments, or sometimes, even with external partners.

It is also necessary to have people who can analyse the data, so that helpful information is created from raw data which can support marketing decision making. Data analysts, data scientists or data engineers are the titles that are typically given to people who can create useful insights out of data.

Those with creative skills are also key to having a successful marketing department. Marketing campaigns must be supported by text writers who can create catchy phrases for ads and press releases. Web and app designers are also key in creating a rewarding customer experience.

Finally, there must be someone to coordinate and orchestrate all the activities. Some organizations have a manager for every product category of brands they have. Atop all the manager is usually someone who oversees the marketing activities from a more strategic level, a marketing director or a chief marketing officer.

It should also be noted that most or all of the infrastructure and human resources can be outsourced to run a marketing organization.

Personal data within the marketing channels

Because this book is about data protection, I thought it would be helpful to identify which marketing channels make use of which personal data. For all channels that enable personalization, personal data is necessary. Some are pseudonymized, such as IDs, where data on their own cannot provide much information about those in question.

Table 2.1 shows the types of data that are necessary to personalize advertising, per channel. It is also noteworthy that personal data are necessary for measuring the effectiveness of marketing campaigns once they have taken place.

These identifiers, oftentimes encrypted or turned into separate unique IDs, are used to make sure that the right commercial message is communicated to the right person, as well as understanding whether the person reacted to the advertising.

TABLE 2.1 Necessary personal data per marketing channel

Direct Mail	Name	Address			
Telemarketing	Name	Telephone number			
Email Marketing	Name	Email			
Connected TV	IP Address				
Social Media	Name	Address	Email	Preferences	Data (derived) from activities on the platform
Display Marketing	Cookies	IDs			

Working with marketing colleagues around the world

Sometimes, marketing campaigns are carried out in more than one country. They may be bundled in regions, such as Europe or the Americas, or orchestrated globally. International marketing is a topic of its own, as every country has some uniqueness to it that needs to be taken into account. For instance, popular platforms are different in some countries. In China, Google cannot be used, so its counterpart, Baidu, must be separately assessed for marketing use for that market. The difference in the dominant religion of the nation also requires the content of the ad messaging to be adjusted appropriately.

As far as it is relevant to personal data use, some organizations consolidate data from different countries for marketing purposes. For example, using a single cloud instance in a centralized location may be much more cost-effective than taking out a license for 10 different cloud storage instances. Also, for administrators, the workload will be much less when all databases are stored in one place.

When consolidating data storage, for instance, it is important to bear data protection laws in mind. Under GDPR, it is important to assess whether data is going to be transferred to countries outside of the EU or the so-called adequate countries, countries with the same level of data protection as in the EU, such as the UK, Israel, Isle of Man, Japan and Switzerland. When data will be transferred to servers outside of these jurisdictions, special care must be taken.

Key takeaways

1 Marketing is one of the business functions, and its strategy must align with the overall business strategy.

2 By definition, marketing adds value to parties involved. Marketing messages that commercially persuade consumers are different from malice-laden manipulation.

3 Approaches to marketing have evolved over the years, as consumer expectation and technology changed.

4 Achieving relevance is key to effective marketing.

5 Marketing needs to be supported by appropriate infrastructure.

Conclusions

Marketing is one of the essential functions within a business organization. Marketing by definition brings value, not only to the company selling products or services, but also to customers, clients partners and society at large. Approaches to marketing, supported by appropriate infrastructure, have evolved over the years so that communication to the consumers can remain relevant, and organizations can capture their attention.

Bibliography

American Marketing Association (2017) Definitions of marketing: What is marketing?, www.ama.org/the-definition-of-marketing-what-is-marketing/ (archived at https://perma.cc/V2SD-M2W6)

American Psychological Association (2023) Manipulation, https://dictionary.apa.org/manipulation (archived at https://perma.cc/BLS9-CQA7), and persuasion, https://dictionary.aa.org/persuasion (archived at https://perma.cc/Y4UL-QLVM)

BBC (2023) Functional areas of business, www.bbc.co.uk/bitesize/guides/zpvw3k7/revision/1 (archived at https://perma.cc/Y4UL-QLVM)

Beaudreau, B C (1996) *Mass Production, the Stock Market Crash, and the Great Depression: The macroeconomics of electrification: Contributions in economics and economic history*, Holtzbrink, Stuttgart

Boissoneault, L (2018) Colored pigments and complex tools suggest humans were trading 100,000 years earlier than previously believed: Transformations in climate and landscape may have spurred these key technological innovations,

Smithsonian Magazine, 15 March, www.smithsonianmag.com/science-nature/colored-pigments-and-complex-tools-suggest-human-trade-100000-years-earlier-previously-believed-180968499/ (archived at https://perma.cc/T2MJ-3SYY)

Booms, B H and Bitner, M J (1981) *Marketing Strategies and Organization Structures for Service Firms, Marketing of Services*, American Marketing Association, Chicago

Chaffey, D (2023) Marketing strategy vs tactics: why the difference matters, www.smartinsights.com/marketing-planning/marketing-strategy/marketing-strategy-vs-tactics-difference/ (archived at https://perma.cc/Q2FV-5WV4)

Dean, G (2022) Global Best Brand Rankings 2022: UK, https://business.yougov.com/content/44323-global-best-brand-rankings-2022-uk (archived at https://perma.cc/ML8U-6ZXF)

Doty, D (2019) It's all about pricing: Digital is winning simply because it's a cheaper way for advertisers to reach consumers: A 101 course, Forbes Leadership – CMO Network, 29 October 2019, www.forbes.com/sites/daviddoty/2019/10/29/its-all-about-pricing-digital-is-winning-simply-because-its-a-cheaper-way-for-advertisers-to-reach-consumers-a-101-course/ (archived at https://perma.cc/PS98-LKPB)

eur-lex.europa.eu (2002) Directive 2002/58/EC of the European Parliament and of the Council of 12 July 2002: Concerning the processing of personal data and the protection of privacy in the electronic communications sector (Directive on privacy and electronic communications), see Article 13, https://eur-lex.europa.eu/legal-content/EN/TXT/?uri=CELEX%3A02002L0058-20091219 (archived at https://perma.cc/928X-3YWF)

EU Commission (2023) Commission welcomes political agreement on transparency of political advertising regulation, 7 November 2023, Brussels, https://ec.europa.eu/commission/presscorner/detail/en/IP_23_4843 (archived at https://perma.cc/BZK8-AWY3)

Global Data and Marketing Alliance (GDMA) (2022) Global data privacy: What the consumer really thinks 2022, GDMA and Acxiom, Foresight Factory, https://globaldma.com/consumer-attitudes/ (archived at https://perma.cc/F826-E3HA)

Godin, S (1999) *Permission Marketing: Turning strangers into friends and friends into customers*, Simon and Schuster, New York, USA

Jobber, D and Ellis-Chadwick, F (2024) *Principles and Practice of Marketing*, McGraw Hill, Maidenhead

Kotler, P (1988) *Marketing Management: Analysis, planning, implementation and control*, Prentice-Hall, New Jersey, USA

Lauterborn, B (1990) New marketing litany: Four P's passe: C-words take over, *Advertising Age*, 61(41), 26

McCarthy, E J (1960) *Basic Marketing, a Managerial Approach*, R D Irwin, Homewood, USA

Nielsen Company (2014) How smartphones are changing consumers' daily routines around the globe, February 2014, www.nielsen.com/insights/2014/how-smartphones-are-changing-consumers-daily-routines-around-the-globe/ (archived at https://perma.cc/YN6M-VNGW)

Nichols, R G (1987) Manipulation versus persuasion, International Listening Association, www.tandfonline.com/doi/abs/10.1080/10904018.1987.10499005?-journalCode=hijl19 (archived at https://perma.cc/BS9E-2ZEZ)

Noggle, R (2018) The ethics of manipulation, *Stanford Encyclopaedia of Philosophy*, 20 March 2018, revised on 21 April 2022, https://plato.stanford.edu/entries/ethics-manipulation/ (archived at https://perma.cc/4M7D-C8P6)

Oxford Strategic Marketing (2014) Customer journey mapping: An introduction, for HM Government – Government for the United Kingdom, https://digitaltransform.org.uk/wp-content/uploads/2014/03/ESD-Customer-Journey-Mapping-An-Introduction.pdf (archived at https://perma.cc/C8C2-JGXU)

Pope, D (1983) *The Making of Modern Advertising*, Basic Books Inc., New York, USA

Rao, S (2021) Bengaluru street vendors worried as megaphone, loudspeaker banned in residential areas, *The News Minute*, 27 August 2021, www.thenewsminute.com/article/bengaluru-street-vendors-worried-megaphone-loudspeaker-banned-residential-areas-154469 (archived at https://perma.cc/75WF-VQJT)

Statista (2023) Penetration rate of smartphones in selected countries 2022, www.statista.com/statistics/539395/smartphone-penetration-worldwide-by-country/ (archived at https://perma.cc/UX24-ZEF5)

Thompson, D (1996) *The Oxford Compact English Dictionary*, Oxford University Press, Oxford

Zuboff, S (2019) *The Age of Surveillance Capitalism: The fight for a human future at the new frontier of power*, Profile Books, London

3

Data protection laws

In this chapter, we change gears and look into the other major topic of this book, data protection. What does data protection mean to you? Clicking the 'OK' button to go to the next page? Making sure that your legal and privacy departments understand that collecting opt-in is dramatically reducing the amount of data you can use for a campaign? From my experience, the words 'data protection' seem to be associated with consent for the vast majority of people. That needs to change. In this chapter, we touch on the basics of the discipline of data protection. It truly is more than an opt-in!

Key concepts of data protection

Let me start by going over some of the jargons used by the privacy folks.

PII, data subject and personal data

I often join video conference calls with my colleagues and marketers from all corners of the world. Whenever they refer to data, the term PII, short for Personal Identifiable Information is used. Someone on the call will then tell me that I am in the wrong meeting because no personal data is involved in the project. 'Oh, we don't use PII, we only use IDs and data attributes. No names and emails', I am told.

The term PII, used widely within the marketing and advertising world, comes from the United States. When marketers talk of PII, they mean records with direct identifiers such as name, address, telephone number and email address (IAB, 2000).

As a side note, the term data subject under GDPR is used to express the person to whom the personal data relates (ICO, 2023). For simplicity's sake,

I use the term data subject, consumer, customer, prospect, person, individual, etc. interchangeably.

Under GDPR and many other laws around the globe, the notion of personal data is all-encompassing. The term personal data goes beyond direct identifiers and includes a broad range of data.

In Article 4, GDPR defines the term personal data in the following way (legislation.gov.uk, 2016):

> 'personal data' means **any information relating to an identified or identifiable natural person** ('data subject'); an identifiable natural person is one who can be identified, directly or indirectly, in particular by reference to an identifier such as a name, an identification number, location data, an online identifier or to one or more factors specific to the physical, physiological, genetic, mental, economic, cultural or social identity of that natural person.

And now we get into the nitty-gritty. Here are three phrases that I want to highlight from this definition. For data to be information about a person, it has to fulfil four criteria. It must:

1 provide information
2 that information must relate to someone
3 that someone needs to be identifiable
4 that someone needs to be an individual (natural person) and not an organization (legal person)

To illustrate the point, I have created a table to show what will be considered personal data under GDPR (see Table 3.1). Postal address files contain house number, street name, postal code and city. Your marketing department can use this file to help customers auto-fill online forms, and the records within this file can identify a building, associate the street, etc., but not individuals. Postal address files are therefore not personal data. If, however, you have a client file with vehicle make and model associated to each client, this file provides information that can be related to a person who is identifiable. The client file therefore contains personal data. The last column of the table provides information of the opening hours of supermarkets. However, the information is about the supermarket, which usually is a legal entity, but not an individual or natural person. This data is therefore not considered personal data.

The regulators of the EU, several years ago, took a deep dive on this topic (Art 29 WP, 2007). Let me highlight some interesting points I picked up

TABLE 3.1 Is this personal data?

	Postal address file	Vehicle information of clients	Opening hours of supermarkets
Data provides information	yes	yes	yes
Information relates to a person (not an organisation)	no	yes	no
The person is identifiable	n.a.	yes	n.a.
It is personal data	no	yes	no

from their paper. The regulators took the position that the information in question does not have to be true or objective, it does not necessarily have to invade the right to private life, and can be both about someone's private or professional life. In plain English, this means assumptions made by marketers, such as 'this consumer belongs to this customer group' or 'this person from company XYZ will buy more products form us', count as 'information'.

Secondly, the information then needs to relate to someone. For instance, a description of a house – it has a south-facing roof, and the roof at a size of more than 20m² – describes a building and not a person. Therefore, the information is not personal data, which means GDPR is not applicable to this information. If this information can be related to an individual, for example if you know that this house turns out to be Tom Jones's property at 25 Springwell Road, then this information is related to a person, and GDPR applies.

Thirdly, if there is a possibility of pinpointing the information to a particular person, then that information becomes personal data. For instance, a car dealer carries out an informal neighbourhood survey and received a response from 100 households. The dealership does not have the names and addresses of these persons, but you can see that record number 23 in the survey response file relates to an adult male with three children driving a red Toyota in a certain neighbourhood. If the marketer at the car dealer is living in the same area, or if that marketer decided to visit this neighbourhood, then, hypothetically, it is possible to 'single out' this person, even if the red Toyota driver's name and address are not available. The combination of information – 'a specific neighbourhood, male, has 3 children, drives a red Toyota' – can point to a single person. In another instance, if you received a file consisting of hashed names, addresses and telephone numbers, and you have no means to reverse the hash, the records in these files cannot be used to identify or to single someone out.

The group of EU regulators further explained that in determining the likelihood of whether someone can be identified or singled out, cost, time and effort as well as the state of available technology need to be taken into consideration (Art 29 WP, 2007). A statement very similar to this opinion was later embedded in Recital 26 of GDPR (legislation.gov.uk, 2016). So, with the car dealer example above, if it was not a local dealer that carried out the survey, but a company located a thousand miles away, singling out the person with three children and a red Toyota as well as other data subjects in the file would be unlikely, considering the time and cost it would take to reveal the identity. In another example, let's assume that you have a file containing identifiers that are hashed using a one-way hash technique called SHA-256, which technically cannot be reverse-hashed. However, if you have a separate database that contains millions of names, addresses and phone numbers in the same format, then through hashing the data in the same way you can create identical hash values for the same name-address-phone number combination. It might then be possible to find out the identity of persons. Identifiability should therefore be carefully examined, case by case.

Anonymous data

GDPR does not apply to anonymous data. When personal data is aggregated, it becomes anonymous. When calculating the average age of five persons, and then deleting the input data used for calculating this, the resulting value can no longer be used to differentiate the individuals. There are two approaches to anonymity, namely the absolute approach and the relative approach. The absolutists claim that data cannot be considered anonymous if someone on this planet can identify the person to whom the data belongs, even if your organization is not able to do so. The relative approach, or objective approach as it is sometimes referred to, takes the position that the same file can be anonymous to one organization and personal data to another organization (curia.europa.eu, 2014).

Special categories of data

GDPR and other data protection laws call certain types of personal data sensitive as they require special protections because they can harm people's rights and freedoms. Data that falls under the so-called special categories of data are as follows (see Article 9 GDPR) (legislation.gov.uk, 2016):

- racial or ethnic origin
- political opinions
- religious or philosophical beliefs
- trade union membership
- genetic data
- biometric data (for the purpose of uniquely identifying a natural person)
- health
- sex life or sexual orientation

These types of data are seldom used in a marketing context in Europe, apart from marketing in a small number of sectors such as the pharmaceutical and medical sectors, insurance industry and religious institutions. In such cases, extra measures must be taken.

PROCESSING

'Processing' is defined in Article 4 (2) of the GDPR. There it lists out some examples of processing: collection, recording, organization, structuring, storage, adaptation or alteration, retrieval, consultation, use, disclosure by transmission, dissemination or otherwise making available, alignment or combination, restriction, erasure or destruction (legislation.gov.uk, 2016).

I think it is safe to state that processing refers to anything and everything you can do with data.

ROLES OF THE ORGANIZATIONS: CONTROLLER, PROCESSOR AND JOINT CONTROLLER

Like all other definitions, the concepts of controller and processor are given in Articles 4(7) and 4(8) of the GDPR, respectively. In summary, controllers are often data owners, and have the authority to use the data the way they want. If anything goes wrong, controllers are responsible, and it is also the controllers that regulators come after when something happens. Processors, on the other hand, are service providers. They do not have a say about what can be done with the data, and only perform work as instructed by the controller, usually in the form of a data protection agreement. Let's take a look at the concepts a bit more closely.

Controller and joint controller

GDPR defines controller as follows (legislation.gov.uk, 2016):

> 'controller' means the natural or legal person, public authority, agency or other body which, alone or jointly with others, determines the purposes and means of the processing of personal data; where the purposes and means of such processing are determined by Union or Member State law, the controller or the specific criteria for its nomination may be provided for by Union or Member State law.

The European regulators have dissected the topic so that it is clear when companies can consider themselves controller or processor, respectively (Art 29 WP, 2010).

Controller can mean both a person and an organization. A controller can decide how to use the data and what for. For instance, you can decide what to do and how to use data you have collected about your customer, stored in the CRM. It is possible to have more than one controller. In Article 26, GDPR defines joint controllers, where two or more controllers jointly determine the purposes and means of processing (legislation.gov.uk, 2016).

Think of a situation in which your company teams up with another company to hold a webinar, a popular promotional tool in the field of business-to-business. Both your company and the partnering company are interested in generating leads through this online event. You set up the registration link in such way that contact information can be captured for both, for the person to be able to attend the webinar and for the two partnering companies to independently carry out marketing activities. Say you agreed with your partner that you do the data capture and perform data hygiene, and your partner sends out the invitation. In this case, you and your partners are joint controllers because you jointly decided what to do with the data and split the tasks accordingly. However, when participant data is used to send out commercial communications, whether to do so will be decided without consulting each other. Because the two companies will be independently using the data and making their own decisions, both parties will be considered independent controllers.

Processor

Processor, on the other hand, just executes instructions. GDPR Article 4(8) defines processor as (legislation.gov.uk, 2016):

a natural or legal person, public authority, agency or other body which processes personal data on behalf of the controller.

In a marketing context, processor can be a person or a company, even a subsidiary or other affiliated company within your greater organization. Most of your processors, however, are likely to be external service providers such as agencies and cloud storage providers. These service providers are bound by instructions from you as data controller. Processor can also have another service provider, which will be acting in the capacity as a sub-processor of the controller. In this case, processor will be passing down the instructions and obligations to the sub-processor.

PROFILING

Let's be honest. What comes to mind first when you hear the word 'profiling'? Is it an audience group for a campaign? Well, not for me. The word reminds me of a TV programme that showed forensic detectives collecting circumstantial evidence of crime scenes, like a piece of fibre or dust in the carpet, to create a profile of the perpetrator. I bet many people associate profiling with crime, something scary and bad. So I do understand when I get a puzzled reaction from marketers when I say something like 'the RFM score (Recency, Frequency and Monetary value score) is a profile'.

GDPR Article 4(4) defines profiling as follows (legislation.gov.uk, 2016):

'profiling' means any form of automated processing of personal data consisting of the use of personal data to evaluate certain personal aspects relating to a natural person, in particular to analyse or predict aspects concerning that natural person's performance at work, economic situation, health, personal preferences, interests, reliability, behaviour, location or movements.

Under such a broad definition, almost all data you have captured on your CRM or elsewhere for marketing purposes can be considered profiles. Particularly so because the collected data will be used, among other things, to create consumer insight. Household income is often used by data scientists and usually expressed in terms of 'below average' 'average', 'above average' and 'more than 2x above average', evaluating someone's *economic situation*. Therefore, it is a profile. Also, understanding customer types often involves guessing areas of interests, such as tennis or online games, as well as *predicting* (purchasing) *behaviour*. To sum this up, marketing makes use of profiling in its process.

Nevertheless, GDPR in Article 22 says there are two types of profiling. One that can be harmful and can 'produce legal effects concerning him or her or similarly significantly affects him or her' and those that can't (legislation. gov.uk, 2016). The aim of marketing is to communicate relevant and interesting messages. For the data subject, the consequence of marketing data use will be that they will receive certain advertising instead of other messages. Put this through the MaRCS-protection check I introduced in Chapter 1, and find out for yourself what harm seeing one type of advertising as opposed to the other will do. Check if files containing customer profiles are properly maintained, where applicable ensure websites and apps are developed responsibly, consequences of attributing a profile to customers are considered and profile data is kept securely. I trust that you come to the same conclusion as I do. Even if marketers use profiles, it is unlikely to *produce legal effects concerning him or her or similarly significantly affect him or her*.

Principles of data protection

Now that we have covered the key data protection terms, let's take a look at the key principles that underline many data protection laws, including GDPR, namely:

- lawfulness, fairness and transparency
- purpose limitation
- data minimization
- accuracy
- storage limitation
- integrity and confidentiality (security)
- accountability

Lawfulness, fairness and transparency

LAWFULNESS

Everything you do with data must be legal. Even if all other principles are adhered to, if, for instance, data was stolen from another company through hacking, this is illegal and that makes the processing automatically unlawful. In addition, for the data to be processed lawfully, the processing must be based on one of the reasons listed in Article 6(1) of GDPR (, 2016):

(a) the data subject has given **consent** to the processing of his or her personal data for one or more specific purposes;

(b) processing is necessary for the performance of a **contract** to which the data subject is party or in order to take steps at the request of the data subject prior to entering into a contract;

(c) processing is necessary for compliance with a **legal obligation** to which the controller is subject;

(d) processing is necessary in order to protect the **vital interests** of the data subject or of another natural person;

(e) processing is necessary for the performance of a task carried out in the **public interest** or in the exercise of official authority vested in the controller;

(f) processing is necessary for the purposes of the **legitimate interests** pursued by the controller or by a third party, except where such interests are overridden by the interests or fundamental rights and freedoms of the data subject which require protection of personal data, in particular where the data subject is a child.

These reasons are what we refer to as legal grounds. For easier reference, I have displayed the words in bold, which will be used from now on to refer to a specific legal ground listed above.

For marketing, legitimate interest and consent are the most frequently used legal grounds.

FAIRNESS AND TRANSPARENCY

It is fair if consumers are made aware of how their data will be processed, what risks are associated with the processing and what measures are taken to prevent the risk. It is also important to reveal the identity of the controller. This information that explains how the data is being used is called transparency. But that is not all. To be transparent, any information or communication about the processing of personal data must be easily accessible and easy to understand, i.e. written in clear, plain language.

In my own words, fairness and transparency are about telling people what you are going to do with the data, and remaining truthful to this promise.

If the consumer does not want their data to be processed in the way you told them, then they can use their right to stop processing the data, delete the data or take away the data to some other company in a digital form. From the transparency information, data subjects can also use their right to access the data and find out what data is kept by the company.

The other side of the token is, if you want to do fancy things with the data, make sure that you do your best to describe this in an easy-to-understand way, in your privacy policy or in the text where data subjects tick the consent box, and keep the promise. That's right, information you give to your customers through a privacy policy, for example, is the enabler of your website-heatmap and marketing mix modelling. In Chapter 6, we will take a closer look at the topic of privacy policy.

Purpose limitation

The second principle of data protection is purpose limitation. This principle, like the first principle, relates to telling people what you are going to do with the data, and doing only that. 'We use your data to make suggestions and recommendations to you about goods or services that may be of interest to you', 'we use your data to enable you participate in a prize draw or complete a survey' and 'we use your data so that we can deliver relevant advertisements to you and for us to understand the effectiveness of the advertising we serve to you' can be some of the purposes that can be communicated to customers and prospects regarding your company's marketing use of the data.

There are exceptions where you can use the data for purposes other than what you have communicated to the data subjects. Article 6(4), in combination with Recital 50 of GDPR, allows companies to evaluate the compatibility of the new purposes with the original purposes for which the data was collected (legislation.gov.uk, 2016). If they are compatible, you may be able to use data for the new use case. Taking from the example above, let's say you have collected information for a prize draw or a survey, but you now want to use it for running a competition where consumers can paint pictures of your product and send it in. A jury consisting of art professors, well-known artists and your CMO will then choose a winner and that person will be invited to a private painting course from a well-known artist. It is neither a prize draw nor a survey. Provided that all other conditions remain the same, it is a competition, which is sufficiently close to a prize draw. In this case, you may be able to divert from the original purpose, namely prize draw and survey. Here is a caveat, though. The exception provided by Article 6(4) to purpose limitation is not available to data collected using consent.

Data minimization

The third principle, data minimization, is about preventing an excessive amount of data to be collected. Two questions 'is it necessary?' and 'is it proportionate?' can be used to assess whether data minimization is practiced.

NECESSITY TEST

You will pass the necessity test if there is no other alternative to using that data. For instance, there is no alternative to obtaining names and addresses if you want to send the product purchased to the customer. Otherwise, the parcel will never reach the recipient. Say, however, you wanted to make sure that the purchased product reaches the mother of the household and not the daughter, and decide to print the date of birth of the recipient on the label of the parcel. There is, however, an alternative, i.e. printing the first name or the initial of the mother/recipient on the label that will achieve the same result. You already have the name. It is hence unnecessary, and therefore goes against the data minimization principle, to process a date of birth for this purpose.

PROPORTIONALITY TEST

The use of data is proportionate if the importance of the processing outweighs the general privacy rights of the data subject, given that the necessary protective measures are in place. Let me explain this point with a straightforward example. Say you want to know what types of people your customers are. You decide to find that out by carrying out a survey, where consumers can redeem a discount code after answering some questions about them on your website. On top of questions like socio-demographics and hobbies, you also ask for the respondents to give names of their spouse and children living in the same house. These names may become useful for future marketing campaigns, but for now, for this survey, they do not serve any purpose. In this scenario, the additional data, specifically the names of other persons in the household, seem disproportionate, considering what you are trying to find out in your survey.

Now let's consider a more complicated example. Let's say your company has created a data lake, where as much data as possible, structured and non-structured, can be stored centrally. At the point of data collection, it is not known for what purpose the data will be used. However, the prised data storage structure allows marketing data scientists to test their hypothesis or understand the stages of customer journey at a later stage. Is this approach proportionate? I would say it depends on the information you can give to the data subject, as well as measures such as access control modules you can put in place to protect the right to data protection.

Accuracy

Another important concept of data protection is data accuracy. Recital 39 of GDRP requires controllers to take reasonable steps to assume that their data is accurate and, where necessary, kept up-to-date (legislation.gov.uk, 2016).

Many marketers may be painfully aware of the concept of GIGO, Garbage-In-Garbage-Out, experiencing first hand that the quality of the analytical insight depends on the quality of the data you put in. Working with many clients, I have observed that for most, if not all of them, data hygiene and maintenance is a standard step before doing anything with the data, I suppose because the effort pays back. It stops you from embarrassing yourself misspelling someone's name, eliminates waste caused by communicating the same message to the same person twice and getting them irritated. In addition to these practical benefits, having GIGO under control also helps you to adhere to an important data protection principle, data accuracy.

Storage limitation

Another important concept of data protection, storage limitation or honouring data retention period, is listed out in Article 5(1)e of GDPR (legislation.gov.uk, 2016). Firstly, obsolete data that is no longer useful can be problematic. To begin with, obsolete data can skew results of precious insights your data miners can generate, but it can also become a cause of frustration to your IT and finance departments. The longer you hold data, the larger the storage space required to keep them. A larger storage space usually translates into higher costs in hosting this data.

Secondly, GDPR does not require data stored in excess of the retention period, declared in the company policy, to be deleted. It prohibits keeping the data beyond its usefulness in a form which 'permits identification of the data subjects'. In other words, if you can make this data anonymous, you do not have to delete this. The question, however, is whether the anonymized data can bring value that is worth the effort for you, your IT and finance departments. This is a discussion beyond data protection.

Integrity and confidentiality

The last data protection concept may be the one that hits the news headlines the most. Integrity and confidentiality translate into data security, preventing unauthorized access and use of data as well as the equipment used for the data. All personal data must be protected by an information security infrastructure, appropriate for the type and use of the data. GDPR also recognizes pseudonymization and encryption as measures that improve data security. When data is encrypted, for instance, information remains illegible to third parties, even if hackers managed to access the data.

The accountability principle

Data protection often does not have a black or white answer. Just to illustrate a point, let me give you an example which describes why it is difficult to make clear-cut judgements in many instances. Names address a person, names personalize a message and so names are very often used in the marketing context. It is possible, with a certain degree of confidence, to guess the ethnicity of someone based on their first and last names. Ethnicity under GDPR falls under the special category of data, so should names only be processed with explicit consent? At the same time, names are available in the public domain and, for instance, the German Data Protection Act which was valid until 2018 considered names as one of the data types that carried lower risk, which can therefore be used for marketing purposes more freely (Bundesanzeigerverlag, 2009). You can see that there is not even a clear answer on the question of using 'names' for marketing purposes!

Beyond the question of how to treat names, aspects such as corporate culture and the context of data processing often contribute to determining the extent of precautions to be taken, necessary to ensure that personal data is properly protected.

Policymakers of data protection laws have hence looked at other sensitive fields that are heavily regulated, such as corporate financial reporting, money laundering and healthcare services. The nature of complaints in these areas are highly contextual and complex. In the USA, they have resorted to adopting organization accountability as a way of regulating these fields (CIPL, 2019).

Accountability in the GDPR

The concept of organizational accountability was then integrated in the field of data protection. It appeared in international documents, such as the APEC privacy framework (APEC, 2005). In 2016, GDPR enshrined the concept of accountability, and epitomized this in Article 5(2) (legislation.gov.uk, 2016):

> The controller shall be responsible for, and be able to demonstrate compliance with, paragraph 1 ('accountability').

Recital 85 of GDPR mentions accountability once more, where security breach notification is explained. Both sections that mention the word 'accountability' leave the readers with the impression that companies, in their capacity as controllers, should create documentary evidence, and that makes them an accountable organization.

Apart from the explicit mention of the word 'accountability', it can be argued that GDPR provides a checklist to help organizations small and large to become accountable by incorporating elements of accountability principle in the law. Let me jot these down in a checklist format:

- ☐ Have you put appropriate security measures in place? (GDPR Article 24(1))
- ☐ Do you have a privacy policy? (GDPR Article 24(2))
- ☐ Are your data products and data use developed with data protection by design and default in mind? Can you prove this by, for instance, certification? (GDPR Article 25)

☐ Do you keep a register of data processing (Record of Processing Activities (RoPA))? (GDPR Article 30)

☐ Do you carry out a Data Protection Impact Assessment? (DPIA) (GDPR Article 35)

☐ Do you have to appoint a DPO, and if so, have you appointed one? (Article 37)

Not everything on the above list must be ticked. For instance, appointing a DPO is only mandatory in certain cases. We will get into the details of these requirements in the remainder of this book.

While it becomes clear that GDPR places great emphasis in auditable documentation to promote accountability, I feel that an important unquantifiable aspect of what lies in the core of the accountability principle does not come across strongly enough. Accountability, or organizational accountability, requires the whole company or institution to act in a responsible manner, from the C-suite to the data scientists and marketers. It really is a cultural shift which organizations need to embrace, and only when this is achieved can companies claim to have adopted the accountability principle.

The accountability wheel

The Centre for Information Policy Leadership (CIPL), a leading global think-tank in the field of data protection and AI has created the accountability wheel which captures the universal elements of accountability.

Companies that have mature accountability programmes generally have seven essential elements that are represented in the accountability wheel in Figure 3.1 (CIPL, 2019):

1 **Establishing leadership and oversight for data protection and the responsible use of data,** including governance, reporting, buy-in from all levels of management and appointing appropriate personnel to oversee the organization's accountability programme and report to management and the board.

2 **Assessing and mitigating the risks** that data collection and processing may raise to individuals, including weighing the risk of the information use against its benefits. Risk assessment also means conducting periodic reviews of the organization's overall privacy programme and information uses in light of changes in business models, law, technology and other factors and adapting the programme to changing levels of risk.

FIGURE 3.1 CIPL accountability wheel

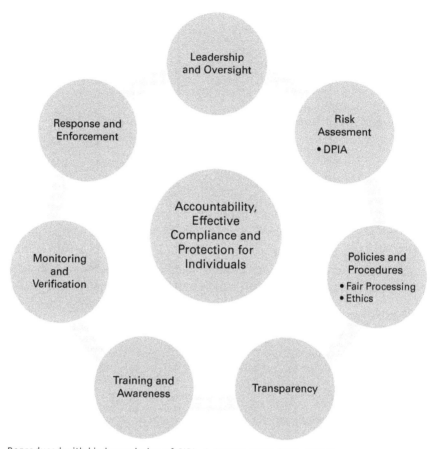

Reproduced with kind permission of CIPL, 1 August 2023 (CIPL, 2019)

3 **Establishing internal written policies and procedures** that operationalize legal requirements, create concrete processes and controls to be followed by the organization, and reflect applicable law, regulations, industry standards as well as the organization's values and goals.

4 **Providing transparency to all stakeholders internally and externally** about the organization's data privacy programme, procedures and protections, data uses, the rights of individuals in relation to their data and the benefits and/or potential risks of data processing. This may also include communicating with relevant data privacy authorities, business partners and third parties about the organization's privacy programme.

5 **Providing training for employees and raising awareness** of the internal privacy programme, its objectives and requirements, and implementation of its requirements in line with the employees' roles and job responsibilities, as well as of the importance of privacy and data protection in general. This ensures that data privacy is embedded in the culture of the organization so that it becomes a shared responsibility.

6 **Monitoring and verifying the implementation and effectiveness of the programme and internal compliance** with the overall privacy programme, policies, procedures and controls through regular internal or external audits, other monitoring mechanisms and redress plans.

7 **Implementing response and enforcement procedures** to address inquiries, complaints, data protection breaches and internal non-compliance, and to enforce against acts of non-compliance.

CAN CONSENT BETTER PROTECT DATA FOR MARKETING?

How effective can consent and the concept of informational self-determination be in protecting the right to data protection in today's world? The processing of data, also in the field of marketing, has become more and more complex, to the extent that explaining them in a clear and easy to understand manner is becoming increasingly difficult. In theory, marketers can provide transparency information, let consumers read it and have them decide if they want their data to be used in that way or not; be it for promotional purposes or for marketing analytics. There are, however, two assumptions at play.

Firstly, it is assumed that everyone, after reading the privacy policy or the consent text, understands what exactly will happen with their data. However, I challenge anyone that assumes that everyone fully understands what will happen to the data after reading the transparency statement. For instance, in a privacy statement, you can say 'we use your data to understand the effectiveness of our marketing activities' to describe a process that involves a) matching the records of campaign respondents to the file containing all persons to whom the advertising was communicated; b) enhance the file with additional information like age, degree of urbanization and frequency of purchase; c) aggregate the results into cross-tabulations using machine learning software tools in the cloud. While the description of the purpose of processing is accurate, will a non-marketer like a schoolteacher, baker, lawyer or dentist be able to associate 'measuring the effectiveness of marketing effort' to describe this process?

Secondly, the informational self-determination concept gives the data subjects, or in the marketing context, customers and consumers the ability to make a decision and assume the consequences of it, for instance, by clicking the OK button. While it seems decisions are made under the control of the data subjects, this mechanism unwittingly puts the responsibilities on the shoulders of the data subjects and not the company. When the use of their data then turns out to not be something they want, it becomes their own fault. After all, they decided to click the OK button and agreed to the data use.

One way of looking at the informational self-determination and the accountability principle is that the latter, as the word suggests, makes the data controller accountable and not the consumer. In particular, in cases where the processing is complicated, it would make sense for the controller to carry the responsibility.

It needs to be acknowledged that with the implementation of organizational accountability, the responsibility to protect personal data shifts away from consumer-data subjects to the controller. Considering the complexity of modern marketing, compounded by AI, as well as the interdependency of our digital eco system, will it not be fairer to have companies shoulder the legal responsibilities, rather than pushing this over to consumers under the banner of informational self-determination and consent?

From the accountability wheel, it is also clear to see that the pillars of the accountability principle are interdependent and designed in such a way that they can evolve with technological and procedural changes in synergy. Shifts in the organization and the technological environment are a given in the marketing industry. As an example, direct activation through a customer data platform (CDP) was unthinkable just a decade ago. Shifting from one technology to another requires a round of risk assessment, with its accompanying documentation in the form of a DPIA, which we will talk about later on in this book. The level of risk may then trigger policies to be adjusted, which also means the content of awareness training to employees must be updated. When a structure and culture that embraces the seven pillars are firmly adopted in the organization, the interrelated nature of the elements of the accountability wheel will automatically and continuously allow organizations to adjust to new states of compliance.

The risk-based approach

Closely related to the accountability principle is the risk-based approach. Measures taken to protect the rights to data protection must commensurate the inherent risk of the processing. You will find the following qualifying text in GDPR, several times (legislation.gov.uk, 2016):

> Taking into account the nature, scope, context and purposes of processing as well as the risks of varying likelihood and severity for the rights and freedoms of natural persons. (see Articles 24(1), 25(1), 32(1) and 35(1) of the GDPR)

In repeating this expression, legislators must have realized that a 'one-size-fits-all' approach will not work in data protection. After all, it would be disproportionate to ask a suburban hairdresser to have the same security infrastructure to protect their client file as large hospitals that are protecting their centralized patient files. The inherent risk in a small contact data base and a detailed medical record of tens of thousands of patients are vastly different.

Another look at the repeated phrase '*Taking into account…*,' mentioned above, reveals that the wording underpins the understanding that GDPR does not prohibit high-risk processing. If the data use carries with it an elevated level of risk, then measures to protect the data must be more robust so that the chances of the risks occurring are minimized, hence making the processing risk acceptable. In the hospital and hairdresser example, the hospital may require a full-fledged data security department with comprehensive access control, robust encryption and several layers of cyber security tools so that it becomes acceptable, under GDPR, to process the patient files. Installing an antivirus software, training employees and having strong passwords may be all that the hairdresser needs.

Understanding the level of risk

If you are processing data in a manner listed below (created from Recital 75 of the GDPR) you know that extra precautions need to be taken:

1 processing may give rise to discrimination;

2 processing may give rise to identity theft or fraud;

3 processing may give rise to financial loss;

4 processing may give rise to damage to reputation;

5   processing may give rise to loss of confidentiality of personal data protected by professional secrecy;

6   processing may give rise to unauthorized reversal of pseudonymization, or any other significant economic or social disadvantage;

7   data subjects might be deprived of their rights and freedoms or prevented from exercising control over their personal data;

8   personal data reveal racial or ethnic origin;

9   personal data reveal political opinions;

10 personal data reveal religion or philosophical beliefs;

11 personal data reveal trade union membership;

12 genetic data is processed;

13 data concerning health is processed;

14 data concerning sex life is processed;

15 data concerning criminal convictions and offences is processed;

16 data related to security measures is processed;

17 personal aspects are evaluated, in particular analysing or predicting aspects concerning performance at work, to create or use personal profiles;

18 **personal aspects are evaluated, in particular analysing or predicting aspects concerning economic situations, to create or use personal profiles;**

19 personal aspects are evaluated, in particular analysing or predicting aspects concerning health, to create or use personal profiles;

20 **personal aspects are evaluated, in particular analysing or predicting aspects concerning personal preferences or interests, to create or use personal profiles;**

21 **personal aspects are evaluated, in particular analysing or predicting aspects concerning reliability or behaviour, to create or use personal profiles;**

22 personal aspects are evaluated, in particular analysing or predicting aspects concerning location or movements, to create or use personal profiles;

23 personal data of vulnerable natural persons, in particular of children, is processed; and

24 **processing involves a large amount of personal data and affects a large number of data subjects.**

Out of the list of 24, four items seem to be most relevant for marketing, namely:

18 personal aspects are evaluated, in particular analysing or predicting aspects concerning economic situations, to create or use personal profiles;

20 personal aspects are evaluated, in particular analysing or predicting aspects concerning personal preferences or interests, to create or use personal profiles;

21 personal aspects are evaluated, in particular analysing or predicting aspects concerning reliability or behaviour, to create or use personal profiles;

24 processing involves a large amount of personal data and affects a large number of data subjects.

Let us examine this one by one. Number 18 speaks of predicting economic situations. As mentioned earlier in this chapter, income level is often an important information for marketers to decide how to, for instance, determine the price of a certain product. Because marketers want to make their messages relevant and interesting for their customers and customers-to-be, it is important to understand their preferences. This is why number 20 above is in bold. Similarly, understanding customer behaviour, listed under number 21, is often a key customer insight needed to create the right message and communicating this through the right channel. Lastly, I have put number 24 in bold, particularly for marketers in the B-to-C market with many customer records on file. I assume the number of records kept inhouse by large B-to-C companies to be in the region of tens of thousands to millions of records, depending on the market they are in.

The risk shall then be evaluated in combination with the severity of the harm, for instance, using the MaRCS framework introduced in Chapter 1. Appropriate protective measures can then be taken before deciding to use the data the way you want.

The decision of whether or not to accept the residual risks, after taking precautionary measures, should be taken by persons with appropriate authorities within the organization, usually the senior management.

Other data protection laws for marketing

As though GDPR is not enough, marketers need to be aware of additional laws that govern data use.

E-Privacy Directive and Privacy and Electronic Communications Regulations (PECR)

As discussed in Chapter 1, the E-Privacy Directive, or the EU Directive on Privacy and Electronic Communications, is the cause of the opt-in requirement when using most marketing communication channels, arguably except direct mail and mass marketing channels.

TELEMARKETING

Although the E-Privacy Directive does not impose an opt-in requirement for telemarketing, some countries, like Germany, Austria and Hungary, have adopted an opt-in requirement for telemarketing. In countries where telemarketing can be conducted on an opt-out basis, marketers must first scrub the telephone list against a so-called telephone preference services (TPS) or the 'do-not-call-register'. For instance, in the UK, consumers can register on the TPS through their website www.tpsonline.org.uk.

EMAIL MARKETING, SMS MARKETING, MMS MARKETING, ETC.

The E-Privacy Directive defines electronic mail thus (eur-lex.europa.eu, 2009):

> 'electronic mail' means any text, voice, sound or image message sent over a public communications network which can be stored in the network or in the recipient's terminal equipment until it is collected by the recipient.

Which means it encompasses all types of electronic communication. In general, consent must be available. However, a soft-opt-in option, where messages can be sent on an opt-out basis, is available when contact details were collected in the context of the sale of product or service, for promoting similar products and services. Furthermore, the possibility to opt out has to be provided to the consumer. This possibility must be given at the moment their email address, etc. are collected, and subsequently, each time a marketing communication is sent.

ONLINE BEHAVIOURAL ADVERTISING AND OPERATING A WEBSITE

E-Privacy Directive's Article 5(3) requires consent from the data subject if you are storing information on a device, or reading information stored on a device. This has caused the industry to develop a mechanism called TCF (Transparency and Consent Framework) as many ad-tec companies in the digital eco system, typically small in size and newly established, never have direct contact with device users. The framework provides participating companies to obtain opt in and/or provide transparency information to the users through a standardized interface (IAB Europe, 2018). In that respect, marketers that have direct contact with their customers and prospective customers can collect consent, for instance, the minute they visit the website, through a cookie banner.

Your company's website is an online business card or a flagship store equivalent. To ensure this important interface is compliant, a consent collection mechanism, like a cookie banner, cookie notice or cookie popup, must be displayed when a user first visits your website. The notice should then inform them about cookies and other means the site uses, and asks for the user's consent to store cookies, and from then on to read them, on the devices.

LOCATION DATA AND LOCATION-BASED MARKETING

Using the location of the device, or as the E-Privacy Directive states the 'geographic position of the terminal equipment', requires consent (eur-lex. europa.eu, 2009). This requirement applies if you are providing a free app, say a weather app that gives you the default forecast based on the location of your device, or when providing WiFi access points to your customers. Right to withdraw consent, as well as transparency information, is required for lawful marketing use of location data, according to Article 9 of the E-Privacy Directive (Art 29 WP, 2011).

Key takeaways

1 Understand the key concepts of data protection: data subject and personal data, processing, controller, processor and profiling.

2 Seven principles of data protection are: lawfulness, fairness and transparency; purpose limitation; data minimization; accuracy; storage limitation; integrity and confidentiality; and accountability.

3   Fostering an accountable organization, embedded also into corporate culture, enables companies to better adjust to technological and procedural changes.

4   GDPR takes a risk-based approach. The higher the risk the higher the importance for preventative measures to be put in place for the data use to remain compliant.

5   The E-Privacy Directive, or PECR in the UK, is another major data protection law that marketers need to comply with.

Conclusions

The definition of personal data covers more than just PII. Personal data can be any data that can be related to an individual. Terms such as processing and profiling have special meanings in the context of data protection. GDPR has seven principles, namely; lawfulness, fairness and transparency; purpose limitation; data minimization; accuracy; storage limitation; integrity and confidentiality (security); and accountability. The regulation takes a risk-based approach, the higher the risk the higher the obligation attached to using the data. Marketers must also adhere to data protection rules in the E-Privacy Directive and PECR that govern marketing data use.

Bibliography

APEC (2005) APEC Privacy Framework, www.apec.org/docs/default-source/publications/2005/12/apec-privacy-framework/05_ecsg_privacyframewk.pdf?sfvrsn=d3de361d_1 (archived at https://perma.cc/Q4Q6-H94B)

Art 29 WP (2007) Article 29 Data Protection Working Party, WP 136: Opinion 4/2007 on the concept of personal data, adopted on 20 June 2007, https://ec.europa.eu/justice/article-29/documentation/opinion-recommendation/files/2007/wp136_en.pdf (archived at https://perma.cc/YJ84-P2S3)

Art 29 WP (2010) Article 29 Data Protection Working Party, WP 169: Opinion 1/2010 on the concepts of 'controller' and 'processor', adopted on 16 February 2010, https://ec.europa.eu/justice/article-29/documentation/opinion-recommendation/files/2010/wp169_en.pdf (archived at https://perma.cc/P36K-NBEB)

Art 29 WP (2011) Article 29 Data Protection Working Party, WP 185: Opinion 3/2011 on geolocation services on smart mobile devices, adopted on 16 May 2011, https://ec.europa.eu/justice/article-29/documentation/opinion-recommendation/files/2011/wp185_en.pdf (archived at https://perma.cc/PS85-PGJH)

Bundesanzeigerverlag (2009) Bundesdatenschutzgesetz (BDSG) Gesetz zur
Änderung datenschutzrechtlicher Vorschriften Vom 19 August 2009, www.bgbl.
de/xaver/bgbl/start.xav#__bgbl__%2F%2F*%5B%40attr_id%3D%
27bgbl109s2814.pdf%27%5D__1693732955257 (archived at https://perma.cc/
RV8C-T2YP), see §28 paragraph 3 (3)

CIPL (2019) Centre for Information Policy Leadership: Organisational
accountability – past, present and future, 30 October 2019, www.
informationpolicycentre.com/uploads/5/7/1/0/57104281/cipl_white_paper_-_
organisational_accountability_%E2%80%93_past_present_and_future__30_
october_2019_.pdf (archived at https://perma.cc/XF48-WQQ3)

curia.europa.eu (2014) Patrick Breyer v. Bundesrepublik Deutschland, 2014,
European Court of Justice, Case C-582/14, https://curia.europa.eu/juris/
document/document.jsf?text=&docid=184668&pageIndex=0&doclang=en&m
ode=req&dir=&occ=first&part=1&cid=1130557 (archived at https://perma.cc/
Y6Z9-CDBQ)

eur-lex.europa.eu (2009) 2002/58/EC of the European Parliament and of the
Council, 12 July 2002 with amendment on 2006 and 2009, https://eur-lex.
europa.eu/LexUriServ/LexUriServ.do?uri=CONSLEG:2002L0058:20091219:-
EN:HTML#tocId4 (archived at https://perma.cc/7QB3-M3V6). Conditions on
electronic mail are listed under Article 13 'Unsolicited Communication' and
Article 9 deals with location data

IAB (2000) WAA Guidelines on Privacy and Spam, WAA Privacy Committee WAA
General Assembly, 7 November 2000, www.iab.com/news/waa-guidelines-
privacy-spam/ (archived at https://perma.cc/9RYV-Y6PH)

IAB Europe (2018) TCF Transparency and Consent Framework, https://iabeurope.
eu/transparency-consent-framework (archived at https://perma.cc/W4US-TR8A)

ICO (2023) Legal Definitions, https://ico.org.uk/for-organisations/data-protection-
fee/legal-definitions-fees/ (archived at https://perma.cc/KT8T-UAB8)

legislation.gov.uk (2016) Regulation (EU) 2016/679 of the European Parliament
and of the Council, 27 April, 2016, www.legislation.gov.uk/eur/2016/679/
article/4 (archived at https://perma.cc/FZK3-KUHZ)

4

Classifying personal data

The context in which personal data is used varies quite a bit. Personal data is used by a logistics company for assigning shifts to lorry drivers, by pharmacists to prescribe medicines to a patient and by an immigration office to decide whether someone can enter a country. In marketing, we can, among other things, use personal data to choose which ad to display in a particular app. In this chapter, we take a closer look at the different types of personal data used by marketers.

Use of personal data in marketing

In Chapter 2, I said personal data helps achieve relevance in communication, through which it improves the effectiveness of marketing. Concretely, data is used to support the following activities of the marketing department.

Communication

Ideally, marketers want to have tailor-made communication with every customer and prospect. To communicate, you need contact details (see Table 2.1) such as name, address, email address, (mobile) phone number, IP address, cookies and IDs of all kinds. Without this contact information, delivering personalized communication, such as sending coupons ahead of Mother's Day, is not possible.

Data hygiene

To avoid embarrassment, like misspelling your loyal customers' names or displaying an ad for hearing aids to youngsters, data, particularly contact information, must be in top form. Apart from the routine normalization and standardization, files are corrected against external reference files to check that street names are spelled accurately, or that the postal code provided by the customer is correct. Taking utmost care to prevent GIGO is also an important preparatory step of data analysis.

Insight generation

The generation of insights may be the main use of marketing data. The information you gain about clients and prospects can be both descriptive and quantitative. For instance, 'customer XYZ purchases our products once a year, and that is on day one of the annual sale, with a discount we exclusively offer to bonus programme customers' is a description of a particular customer. This insight helps marketers to communicate ads that highlight other discounts offered throughout the year, by the bonus programme, instead of a generic ad that encourages people to join the loyalty programme. Other information, such as how many new people became customers after viewing a particular TV ad, also helps marketers better understand how best to communicate in the marketplace.

Strategic decision making

Data can be used to shape marketing strategy, which allows the company to decide which market to enter, or on which groups of clients to focus its efforts and allocate resources accordingly. For example, a group of frequent shoppers may feel that the most important factor for choosing a supermarket is its vicinity to home. Since the company traditionally has a strong logistic infrastructure and supplier network in the British Midlands, the marketers (and the senior management) of the company may decide to give priority to opening stores in this region. To create this intelligence, personal data is typically aggregated and summarized in a report.

Data source

Both internal and external data are used to support marketing decisions. To differentiate the type of data source, first-party, third-party and second-party data are used.

First-party data

First-party data, usually abbreviated to 1PD, refers to data that is collected internally, directly from the data subjects, and owned by the company. This can include financial transaction data, such as the total sum of the last invoice, and IDs and cookies that are set on the user's device. As the *owner* of this data, the company is the data controller. As such, the company is responsible for fulfilling all data protection requirements, from the provision of transparency to ensuring information security.

Third-party data

Third-party data, or 3PD in short, is data collected by someone else and made available to the marketer's organization. There are a variety of third-party data sources. They can be, for instance, data suppliers, specializing in consumer lifestyle data, data management platforms (DMPs) offering online behavioural and contextual data, or public bodies offering geo-spatial data. 3PD is typically used in conjunction with 1PD.

Second-party data

Second-party data, or 2PD, also comes from another organization. The difference between 3PD and 2PD is that the data in question is not usually licensed to other organizations for a fee. Rather, client data of that third party is made available to your company under strict conditions. For instance, automobile manufacturer A and national classical music foundation B decide to jointly organize a concert which launches a new limousine line of A. To promote this event, the classical music foundation B is offered use of the contact details of all clients that are in A's CRM system. As a side note, when using 2PD, data sharing usually takes place in a protected environment, such as a data clean room. This means data does not flow from auto company A to music foundation B. Instead, company A sends the data to an independent service provider, and music foundation B sends the same service provider the creatives to be communicated with. The service provider then communicates the ad creative to B's clients.

Getting to know your customers through data

I felt that we could not skirt around the topic of how marketing data scientists create insights out of the available data. Let me take a moment and talk about the different approaches and what their implications are for data protection.

Explorative analyses

Data analysis is not all the same. Analytical studies can be divided into two general categories, namely, explorative and conclusive studies. Used in the marketing context, the former provides marketers with new ideas and clues as to which area to focus the next studies. Particular answers this type of study can address include questions like 'Why are we selling fewer products ever since we changed the packaging?' or 'What makes these companies use our services and not that of our competitors?' An exploratory study aims to identify the next course of investigative actions, through a better understanding of the situation. Exploratory analysis is often used as a preparatory stage for further studies that shape the direction of insight gathering in the next phase.

In conducting explorative analysis, limiting the type of data to be included in the study is counterproductive. This is because you don't know what type of data can be key to finding out the answer to your open-ended questions. Where you can tap for information also varies; information can be obtained from industry experts, 'mystery shoppers' or interviews with clients, as well as overlaying additional data to the CRM. For exploratory studies, ideally, you want to be able to make use of as much data as you can. Some data might be in native format, in your company's data lake.

Can explorative analysis be considered to be in line with one of the data protection principles, 'data minimization'? Whether it is truly necessary or proportional in this case is determined only after the analysis has been carried out. However, without using whatever piece of information as part of the studied universe, you cannot be sure that that particular data is of relevance or not; in a way, it is a chicken-or-egg dilemma.

Conclusive analyses

The other type of study, the conclusive analysis, is used by data scientists for testing hypotheses such as 'If we change parameter A (lower the price of the service), will it positively influence behaviour B (frequency of purchase)?' or 'Are our customers active volunteers in their communities?' Conclusive studies have two sub-categories, namely, causal studies and descriptive studies.

In conclusive studies, analyses are typically carried out with more structure than that of explorative studies because you already know that the result will be one of the two outcomes: confirmation or rejection of the assumption. For a conclusive study, it is important that marketers can apply the findings to the general population. This translates into having a sample size, or number of data subjects, which is large enough that the findings of the study are statistically significant. For that reason, the absolute number of records that flow into conclusive studies are often much larger than that required by explorative studies. On the other hand, only limited types of data attributes may be necessary to test the hypotheses.

CAUSAL STUDIES

Causal studies are used for establishing cause-and-effect relationships. This can be purely measured using as little as two to three data elements. For instance, if you want to find out if the colour of the packaging affects purchase behaviour, the attributes you need are 'original packaging (yes/no)', 'new packaging colour (yes/no)' and 'product sold (yes/no)'.

DESCRIPTIVE STUDIES

As the name indicates, this type of conclusive analysis allows data scientists to describe the studied persons as a group, such as campaign respondents. One way to do so is to append an off-the-shelf consumer lifestyle database to the CRM and campaign databases and find out what characteristics are over-represented or under-represented, compared to the national average, or compared to all the customers in the CRM system. It might surface that campaign respondents are much younger than other customers in the CRM, enjoy different disciplines of sports and tend to prefer active holidays compared to both the national average and an average person in the CRM.

In conclusive studies, analyses are typically carried out with more structure than that of explorative studies because you already know that the result will be one of the two outcomes: confirmation or rejection of the assumption.

Statistical techniques and data protection

Just as the types of insight you are looking for have data protection implications, the statistical techniques applied when seeking the answers of the marketing department also have effects on how the study impacts the right to data protection of the data subjects. Also here, the point of concern of your data protection office would be that of data minimization. Statistical techniques can be categorized into two groups, namely, univariate techniques and multivariate techniques.

Univariate techniques

As the name implies, univariate techniques analyse a single element at a time. A shoe shop may want to know how many sneakers were sold online on a given day. The data attributes you need for this analysis are the 'date of purchase' for selecting that particular day and the 'number of sneakers bought' so that the sum of all sneakers sold can be calculated.

Multivariate techniques

Multivariate techniques, by definition, require more data. Multivariate statistical techniques analyse two or more data elements in one go. Using the shoe store example, say the marketing team wanted to find out if gender plays a role when purchasing a particular sneaker. In that respect, they are also interested if age or the time of the day the purchase was made had any influence. Perhaps looking at age in combination with the time of the day the purchase was made gives some further insights. And to what extent does gender influence purchasing behaviour, in combination with the moment of purchase and age? Marketers can ask for countless cross-tabulations and regression analyses. These techniques can be deployed to find out combinations of data attributes that are of importance in sneaker purchasing decisions. The more data attributes studied, the more insight the technique can provide the marketer. Marketing analysts can, to a certain degree, guide the process and predetermine which limited set of attributes will give the most sought-after answers.

Another example comes from cluster analysis, a technique often used to develop customer segments that studies the interdependence or underlying similarities of the data, and group the records to a number specified by the data scientist. This means that, before conducting a cluster analysis, it is not known which attributes are likely to determine the grouping of records. In addition, to a certain degree, it makes sense to use many records and different attributes, as permitted by memory storage and computing power, to determine the clusters. For instance, so that campaigns are manageable, you decide that you want to find three customer groups in your database. The marketing data scientists then put together all attributes collected for marketing, including 3PD, and run a cluster analysis. The three clusters turned out to be in groups that can be labelled 'time savers', 'healthy lifestyle' and 'discount hunters'. The segments would not have been discovered had the analysis omitted attributes that fed into the analysis, taken from the campaign response data and 3PD consumer lifestyle data.

Hitting the right balance

Just because it is not ideal to feed in many data attributes to the analysis, to me it does not seem a good idea to ban your data scientists from using multivariate techniques. In fact, results of data-intensive multivariate analyses are often used to minimize data that is required in a later stage, when the study results are operationalized.

Let me explain this by telling you a real-life story from outside of the marketing field. A couple of years ago, I was trying to organize house contents insurance. At the office of the insurance company, I asked how much it would be to cover my belongings at home. The young lady sitting across the table opened her laptop and said, 'I have your postal code here, so I can type that in. Hmm, what is the highest academic degree you hold? How old are you? How many persons live in your household?' I gave her the answers and, in a split second, she gave me a quote. 'Amazing!' I thought. Last time I organized my house contents insurance, I had to list out everything that I owned, and on top of that explain all the anti-theft measures at home. 'We don't need that', answered the clerk politely. 'From our experience, we can quite accurately predict the coverage requirements with postcode, academic degree, age and number of persons in the household. We don't need other information. It's in the interest of data protection, you know?' she said, and gave me a wink.

What I have experienced there with my insurance can be applied to assigning customer groups to new customers and prospects for marketers. Yes, some analytical techniques require many variables to create customer groups. However, once the analysis is complete, it may be that you only need three to four data elements – 'age', 'gender', 'type of dwelling' or whatever, to put this person in the right customer group so that the messages are more relevant and are communicated in a suitable tone of voice. In other words, without the multivariate analysis, economizing on the number of attributes in operation would not have been possible.

Market research

Generating insights often involves market research. The marketing department might have its own in-house research team. In most companies, market research is contracted out, either entirely or partially, to research institutions.

Phases of market research

The process is similar to any analytical projects that are carried out in-house, so you might note that some sections of the description below sound familiar. The concrete stages of formal market research, while they might differ in detail, typically have the following stages (Malhotra, 1993):

Stage 1: **Problem recognition and drawing up a research proposal** – identifying the information required and writing up a business case for budget allocation.

Stage 2: **Exploratory research** – first round of study to shape the research. Apart from carrying out a literature review, experts in the fields can be consulted. Qualitative studies of the data subjects using panels, interviews or the observation of (online) activities can also be used as input for this phase.

Stage 3: **Main data collection phase** – in this phase, the research questions that were formulated in the exploratory phase are examined. Hypotheses are usually tested, collecting data through online or mobile surveys, as well as through interviews.

Stage 4: **Drawing conclusions and reporting** – findings in stage 3 are then analysed and put together in a report, with which the research question is answered.

Use of personal data in market research

In stages 2 and 3, both qualitative and quantitative methods are used, with stage 2 making heavier use of qualitative data.

Personal data collected through qualitative means are often unstructured and are likely to contain contextual information, peculiar to the data subject, so much so that it can reveal the person's identity. In some cases, the phrases and expressions used by the person might reveal the identity of the interviewee. Hence, it may be challenging to anonymize raw qualitative data.

In quantitative research, information is collected in a structured manner and is processed in a uniform way. Some techniques can be used to anonymize these records. However, similar to data collected through qualitative means, the combination of attributes, such as city of residence and profession, can already reveal the identity of the person when the city is small. This means, regardless of the type of study, qualitative or quantitative, or a mixture of both, raw data in most cases should be treated as personal data, and it is best to assume that GDPR applies.

Using research exceptions in GDPR

There are provisions within GDPR that give privileges to 'scientific or historical research' and the processing of personal data 'for statistical purposes' (legislation.gov.uk, 2016). For instance, when using personal data for scientific research, you can be exempt from the requirement of providing research subjects the right to data access, rectification, erasure and, in some cases, objection. Imagine a situation where people who participated in market research massively opt out of it. The research results will be skewed and, even worse, the number of records may no longer be large enough to establish statistically significant findings. Scientific and statistical data use is also exempted from purpose limitation, one of the basic principles of GDPR we discussed in Chapter 2. The so-called research exemptions allow researchers to 'recycle' data collected for other unrelated studies.

In discussing research exceptions, two expressions must be closely examined. One is whether the research can fall under the category of 'scientific and historical research' or whether it can be considered to be carried out for 'statistical purposes'. The answer is, as is often the case, 'it depends'.

Whether a study can be considered scientific or not depends on the aim of the research. By all means, commercial organizations can be carrying out scientific research. However, ICO requires many of the following criteria to be met (ICO, 2023):

ACTIVITIES
- formulating hypotheses, isolating variables, designing experiments
- objective observation, measurement of data
- critical exposure to scrutiny, including peer review
- publication of findings
- sampling populations
- designing and conducting surveys
- integrating and analysing data
- drawing inferences about populations from samples
- qualitative research activities

STANDARDS
- ethics guidance
- committee approval
- peer review
- compliance with pre-existing policies and procedures
- adherence to relevant codes of conduct and regulatory frameworks
- compliance with recognized standards of research ethics and integrity
- compliance with rules on researching animals or human participants
- compliance with rules on involving the public in your research
- supporting diverse and inclusive research
- ensuring safeguarding and preventing bullying and harassment in the conduct of research
- findings do not lead directly to decisions about individuals

ACCESS
- publication of results, and commitment to sharing findings of research
- does not need to be Open Access – can be in an academic journal with paid access

When many of the above criteria can be ticked off, your market research can most likely be considered scientific research. It is to be noted that using renowned research institutions for your market research may be a worth-while investment, as they should have standard policies and procedures in place, as well as follow codes of conduct applicable for the market research sector, such as the ESOMAR Code of Conduct (ICC/ESOMAR, 2016). Among other things, this code of conduct requires institutions to provide robust protection of the data, as well as safeguard research subjects' identities from being revealed.

Similarly, marketers can examine whether the market research can be seen as having statistical purposes. Recital 162 of GDPR clarifies the concept as follows (emphasis added in bold) (legislation.gov.uk, 2016):

> Where personal data are processed for statistical purposes, this Regulation should apply to that processing... Statistical purposes mean any operation of collection and the processing of personal data necessary for statistical surveys or for the production of statistical results. Those statistical results may further be used for different purposes, including scientific research purposes. The statistical purpose implies that the result of processing for statistical purposes is not personal data, but aggregate data, **and that this result or the personal data is not used in support of measures or decisions regarding any particular natural person.**

Here too, ICO recommends examining the following aspects in concluding whether the market research should be considered for statistical purposes (emphasis added in bold) (legislation.gov.uk, 2016):

Activities
- designing surveys
- sampling populations
- interpreting and analysing data
- drawing inferences about populations from samples

Outputs
- **not used to make decisions or justify measures about people**
- anonymous data, not personal data

Standards
- compliance with pre-existing policies and procedures
- adherence to relevant codes of conduct and regulatory frameworks
- where part of a wider research project, this should adhere to recognized standards of research integrity – ethics committee approval, peer review

One knock-out criterion from market research to be considered for being carried out for statistical purposes is, in bold above, if research results are used to append information to records, for making personalized decisions. Imagine a situation where a group of 'high net value customers' were identified in market research. If you decide to identify who in your CRM system belongs to this segment, you would create an extra column called 'high net value customer' and assign a 'yes' or 'no' depending on the information about each and every person. In this case, the market research cannot be categorized as having 'statistical purposes', and as a result research exemptions of GDPR cannot be applied.

Working with research institutions

If the market research requires your organization to transfer personal data to the marketing research institution, one important requirement under Article 28 of the GDPR is that proper safeguards are given to the entrusted data (legislation.gov.uk, 2016). If you are working for a multinational brand, it may be your privacy and security departments, together with legal and compliance, that would insist on robust measures and water-tight contractual languages to be in place before a research institute can be appointed.

DPDI Bill and research exemptions

The DPDI Bill makes some changes to the research provisions of UK GDPR. A particular change that helps marketers is the new definition of scientific research. The revised definition explicitly mentions that scientific research includes privately funded studies, or those being carried out as a commercial activity (UK Parliament, 2023).

Types of data under GDPR

Now let me take a moment to explain the way GDPR categorizes data. It does so according to the perceived risk associated with the categories of data; very appropriate for a law with a risk-based approach at its core. A list of general data taxonomy in data protection laws, compiled by the OECD, can be applied one-to-one to GDPR. Let me introduce their data taxonomy (OECD, 2014).

Data categorization by the sensitivity of the data

GDPR and many other laws around the world have a so-called special category of data, which, when in the wrong hands or when processed with malicious intentions, can lead to discrimination (legislation.gov.uk, 2016). Examples of such data include data related to religion, health and political opinions. It is possible to use such data for marketing. For instance, a church's marketer may have an email list of parishioners, so that they can send an invitation to an Easter event. The prerequisite is that explicit consent is obtained, and measures are taken to protect the data to reduce the processing risk.

Data categorization by the data subject to whom the data refers

Just as consumer protection laws protect 'vulnerable consumers', such as minors, the elderly and those with a disability, data protection laws have come up with their own idea of who vulnerable data subjects are (Šajn, 2021). Employees, for instance, are protected under Article 88 of GDPR (legislation.gov.uk, 2016). This is because, among other things, consent needs to be given freely. However, when the employer approaches you and says, 'We want to introduce this performance evaluation tool. Can you consent?', you most likely will agree to allow the use, out of fear that a refusal may leave a negative impression on your boss. There is a whole article, for instance, in the German delegated act, i.e. national law that determines certain details of GDPR, where a section is dedicated to the protection of personal data in the employment context (German Federal Office of Justice, 2022).

For marketing, it is most important to acknowledge that children need to be protected, particularly when online (legislation.gov.uk, 2016). Say a toy manufacturer develops an app to support the augmented reality features of a toy spaceship. Marketers must collect consent for data collected through the app use. In the case of children below the age of 16, the consent of their parents is necessary.

Data categorization by the purpose for which the data is collected

Data used for scientific research or statistical purposes are treated differently, with exemptions here and there, as we discussed earlier in this chapter (legislation.gov.uk, 2016). Even when it is personal data, when data is collected for private use, the law does not even cover it (legislation.gov.uk,

2016). GDPR applies to business use of personal data, which is why marketers need to consider data protection compliance when using customer or prospect data.

Data categorization by the context in which the data is collected

The context of data collection can be online or offline. In the case of online data collection, electronic communication, in a *lex specialis* of GDPR, is given extra protection. Generally, the E-Privacy Directive requires an opt-in for setting cookies or sending email messages (eur-lex.europa.eu, 2009). Marketing, too, is recognized as a specific context. In Recital 47 of GDPR, legitimate interest is called out as a suitable legal ground when using personal data for marketing purposes. Rights to opt-out from commercial communication and personalized ads, i.e. in a marketing context, are also mentioned in the same law (legislation.gov.uk, 2016).

Data categorization by degree of identifiability

GDPR as well as other data protection laws categorize data by the ease of identifying a person in the database. Some data directly identifies persons, like names and addresses. Also, the law recognizes the existence of data that can be used to single out a person through, for instance, a combination of attributes (legislation.gov.uk, 2016). Then there are pseudonymous data that require a secret key or a crosswalk to associate the record to a person.

With anonymous data, such as one-way hashed data and aggregated data, GDPR does not apply. The concept of aggregated and hence anonymous data, frequently used by marketers, might require extra explanation. Aggregated data cannot be decomposed to individual level information, once the aggregation has taken place. There is a well-written guideline published by the Singaporean regulator, which includes a section on anonymization (PDPC, 2022).

Data categorization by direct or indirect collection of data

How the data has been collected is also used to categorize personal data in GDPR. When collecting data directly, the transparency obligations of Article 13 apply. When you license data from another company, i.e. indirectly collect data, then the transparency requirements of Article 14 apply (legislation.gov.uk, 2016).

TABLE 4.1 Data categories based on origin

Category	Sub-Category	Level of Data Subjects' Awareness
Provided Data	Initiated	High
	Transactional	High
	Posted	HIgh
Observed Data	Engaged	Medium
	Not anticipated	Low
	Passive	Low
Derived Data	Computational	Medium to Low
	Notational	Medium to Low
Inferred Data	Statistical	Low
	Advanced Analytical	Low

Adapted from Abrams (2013)

Data categorization based on the data subject's awareness

Personal data can also be differentiated based on the level of awareness of the data subjects. Data protection experts from the school of information self-determination would argue that the less data subjects are aware of the processing, the fewer chances they will have to control their data, which makes the processing present a higher risk. The awareness level often depends on how the data is collected, which is why there is a classification that is based on the origin of the data (Abrams, 2013).

Abrams recognized four general categories of data origin (Abrams, 2013) (see Table 4.1):

PROVIDED DATA

This type of data is obtained as a result of direct actions taken by the consumer, and they are hence highly aware that this type of data is created.

There are three sub-categories to provided data:

- **Initiated data:** Initiated data is created at the beginning of the relationship. Registration data, when a consumer opens an account or prospects sign up for your newsletter, falls under this category.
- **Transactional data:** This type of data is created when customers are involved in a transaction. Examples include payment for a purchase, responding to a prize draw campaign or answering a customer satisfaction survey.

- **Posted data:** This type of data includes blogs, vlogs and online reviews of products and services. Posted data, except that by company-sponsored influencers and online reviews, are usually not used by marketers.

OBSERVED DATA

The second category of data, as the name implies, is collected through companies observing and recording the information. Compared to the provided data, the consumer is less aware of observed data being created. The sub-categories of this data type are engaged data, not anticipated data and passive data. According to Abrams, data subjects have medium awareness of engaged data and low awareness of the other two sub-categories of observed data.

- **Engaged data:** With engaged data, consumers are informed ahead of the data collection, but with time may become less aware of the data capture. Online cookies and loyalty card information are two examples of such data.

- **Not anticipated data:** Not anticipated data is data observed and captured where data subjects may be aware of the data collection, but are not entirely clear that the collected data is being associated with them. Automobile manufacturers make use of information collected from connected cars, just as household appliance manufacturers collect and use product use data from, for instance, high-end air fryers. As a side note, information compiled through direct observation of cookies in browsers would have fallen under this category, had it not been for the consent requirement under the E-Privacy Directive.

- **Passive data:** This sub-category of observed data is usually captured without individuals noticing the pertinence of collected data to them. Data used for marketing rarely come from this category, however, examples given by Abrams include WiFi readers in buildings that establish location and facial images from CCTV.

DERIVED DATA

Derived data is straightforwardly created from other data. Data in this category is considered to have a medium to low awareness level of the individuals. This category also has sub-categories, namely computational-derived data and notational-derived data.

- **Computational data:** Computationally, as in mathematically, derived data are created by feeding data into a fixed formula. For instance, you want to calculate the total number of orders in a year. A formula adds up the sum of the orders per month per customer, and the answer is shown in a new column. This additional insight available in the new column falls under computational data.

- **Notational data:** Notational data is new information created that assigns persons in a data file to a particular category. The assignment of customer group membership is determined by certain characteristics (e.g. age is below 30, student = 'yes', clicked website more than 10 times before purchase = 'yes', then the person is assigned to the customer group 'search engine savvy') and falls under this sub-category of derived data.

INFERRED DATA

Inferred data is a mathematically and probabilistically formulated 'educated guess' about a person. The awareness level of data subjects of the two sub-categories, statistically inferred data and inferred data, calculated using advanced analytical techniques, are low.

- **Statistical data:** To create statistically inferred data, you need to follow two steps. In the first step, data is analysed, mainly using counts and frequencies, to establish a rule of thumb, such as 'persons with character-istics X and Y are likely to be Z'. In the second step, all records in the database that show certain combinations of characteristics X and Y are assumed to be Z (in database terminology, column Z gets a value '1'). For instance, a pet food manufacturer establishes that persons who 'have a big dog' and 'do not live in urban areas' are likely to be 'interested in large-sized dog food'. It is to be noted that this is an educated guess, and does not necessarily have to be true.

- **Advanced analytical data:** The second sub-category of inferred data differs from statistical data in that it makes use of a more diverse set of data, and presumably makes use of multivariate analytical techniques. A larger, more diverse source of data, from online click-through behaviour and third-party lifestyle information to purchase records kept in-house, are consolidated to generate the data universe for the analysis that creates this type of data. Creating of customer segments, like 'business travellers' and 'tourist families', are examples of advanced analytical data. Segmen-tation of customers and prospects are performed using techniques such as cluster analysis, factor analysis, regression and CHAID.

Conscientious curation of data

After going through the taxonomies of data and analytical techniques, and their data protection implications, you may be wondering what is next. The answer is, now that you have this knowledge, you can choose what type of data you use for your analyses and which techniques you want to use to study these. Arguably, analytical techniques will continue to develop, particularly given the advance of AI use in the field, increasing the analytical efficiency by severalfold. Putting restrictions on techniques you can use to mine insights out of data is counterproductive. Bear in mind that your competitors may continue to use advanced data interrogation methods regardless of what you do.

On the other hand, more care can be given to the data side. Accountable marketers should be more conscious about which data is feeding into the analysis. As an example, marketing data scientists may prioritize the use of 1PD for analyses, not only because its predictive power is usually greater than external data, but also because the company has the means to directly inform customers and prospects of the way data is being used.

But what about data that you can license from third parties? Are there different aspects that you can consider so that you are being more responsible in curating third-party data files? External data that are more data protection-friendly are those that come from low-risk sources, such as telephone directories and registers that are already in the public domain, and the awareness level of consumers that this data is out there is high. On the other end of the spectrum is online behavioural data, collected through setting cookies, about which consumers may be less aware despite cookie banners. It is also fair to the consumer to use data that comes from surveys, prize draws or market research, where people are clearly made aware of the marketing use of their data. Lastly, using anonymized data in your analysis may be the most data-protective approach. Data elements such as 'presence of a pet' or 'plays tennis' are aggregated and made available on micro-geographic, neighbourhood levels. An accurate description of such data elements would be 'there is a high probability of this person owning a pet because this group of five households have a higher occurrence of persons owning a pet than the national average' and 'there is a high probability of this person playing tennis because this group of five households have a higher occurrence of persons enjoy playing tennis than the national average'. While the information is probabilistic, micro-geographic files usually have national coverage and can be appended with geo-location information like address and latitude-longitude.

Key takeaways

1 Marketing makes use of personal data to accomplish different tasks, such as data hygiene and the creation of customer insights.

2 Personal data used for marketing can be 1PD, 3PD or 2PD.

3 Insights can be gained through explorative or conclusive studies. Data requirements differ between the two types of studies.

4 Different statistical techniques, univariate or multivariate in nature, have different data requirements. Data protection aspects, such as data minimization, should be carefully examined.

5 GDPR classifies the data, based on the perceived level of risk. Another approach, creating a taxonomy based on data origin, considers the level of data subject awareness. With this knowledge, marketers are empowered to be more conscientious when deciding which data to use for any given analysis.

Conclusion

Personal data used in the marketing context can be categorized in several ways. Types of data also determine how much risk the data inherently carries, which informs organizations of the scale of precaution that has to be put in place.

We reviewed classification methods based on data use, data source and the different types of analytical techniques for studying personal data. The field of data protection also puts data into different categories, based on sensitivity, identifiability and collection method of personal data etc. Lastly, data can be classified according to the awareness of data subjects, which is closely related to where the data originates from.

Bibliography

Abrams, M (2013) The origins of personal data and its implications for governance, The Information Accountability Foundation, https://secureservercdn.net/192.169.221.188/b1f.827.myftpupload.com/wp-content/uploads/2020/04/Data-Origins-Abrams.pdf (archived at https://perma.cc/L2CT-DH35)

eur-lex.europa.eu (2009) 2002/58/EC of the European Parliament and of the Council, 12 July 2002 with amendments on 2006 and 2009, https://eur-lex.europa.eu/LexUriServ/LexUriServ.do?uri=CONSLEG:2002L0058:20091219:EN:HTML#tocId4. (archived at https://perma.cc/7K9Y-J5DF) Conditions on electronic mail is listed under Article 13 'Unsolicited Communication' and Article 5 'Confidentiality of Communication' (3)

German Federal Office of Justice (2022) Federal Data Protection Act (BDSG(neu)), www.gesetze-im-internet.de/englisch_bdsg/ (archived at https://perma.cc/7ZBW-K7SZ) See §26 for processing employee data

ICC/ESOMAR Code of Conduct (2016) International Code on Market, Opinion and Social Research and Data Analytics, Paris, France and Amsterdam, the Netherlands

ICO (2023) UK GDPR Guidance and resources: What is research related processing?, https://ico.org.uk/for-organisations/uk-gdpr-guidance-and-resources/the-research-provisions/what-is-research-related-processing/#criteria-statistical (archived at https://perma.cc/M53D-37C7)

legislation.gov.uk (2016) Regulation (EU) 2016/679 of the European Parliament and of the Council, 27 April 2016, www.legislation.gov.uk/eur/2016/679/contents (archived at https://perma.cc/3XWV-JLBU). Research exceptions are found in Articles 89, 17(3)d and 21(6) / special categories of data found in Article 9 / protection of children Article 8(1) on minors and consent / personal data use is not covered by GDPR Article 2(1) / rights to opt-out from commercial messages in Article 21(2) and (3) / for identifiability as an element of defining what is personal data see Article 4(1) / definition of pseudonymized data Article 4(5)

Malhotra, N (1993) Marketing Research: An applied orientation, Prentice-Hall Inc, Englewood Cliffs, New Jersey, USA

OECD (2014) Summary of the OECD privacy expert roundtable, Protecting privacy in a data-driven economy: Taking stock of current thinking, working party on security and privacy in the digital economy, 21 March 2014

PDPC (2022) Personal Data Protection Commission Singapore: Advisory guidelines on the personal data protection act for selected topics, issued 24 September 2013, revised 17 May 2022, Singapore, www.pdpc.gov.sg/-/media/Files/PDPC/PDF-Files/Advisory-Guidelines/AG-on-Selected-Topics/Advisory-Guidelines-on-the-PDPA-for-Selected-Topics-17-May-2022.pdf (archived at https://perma.cc/QRF3-36Q8). See section on anonymization

Šajn, N (2021) Vulnerable consumers, European Parliamentary Research Service, Members' Research Service, PE 690.619, May 2021, www.europarl.europa.eu/RegData/etudes/BRIE/2021/690619/EPRS_BRI(2021)690619_EN.pdf (archived at https://perma.cc/A27Q-Q5N9)

UK Parliament (2023) Data Protection and Digital Information Bill, Government Bill, Originated in the House of Commons, Sessions 2022–23, 2023–24, last updated 20 December 2023 at 09:33, https://bills.parliament.uk/publications/53287/documents/4126 (archived at https://perma.cc/FX4T-CRVF), pp 3 and 4

5

Legal grounds for marketing

Is it possible that we are somewhat conditioned to believe that consent is considered the golden standard of legal ground in protecting personal data? Familiarity, fostered through the daily ritual of clicking the 'ok' and 'accept' buttons, may be contributing to holding this belief. In this chapter, we take a closer look at the legal grounds used for marketing, and how they differ from each other to help you decide which legal ground is most suitable for the marketing activity you are trying to carry out.

Legal grounds for marketing

If you are using personal data, then you must have a legal ground, or it is illegal. Legal ground is like completing a sentence that goes 'I am allowed to use this personal data because…', by choosing one of the six options, listed in Article 6(1)f of GDPR. The six options are often abbreviated as 'Consent', 'Contract', 'Legal Obligation', 'Vital Interest', 'Public Task' and 'Legitimate Interest'. If none of the six options is applicable, then what you are doing with the data is illegal.

GDPR treats all six legal bases equally, which means there is no hierarchy among the legal grounds. No one legal ground is superior to the other, which means, Consent is not by default a better legal ground than, say, Legitimate Interest.

At the outset of the GDPR era in 2018, three legal grounds were considered to be appropriate for basing marketing data uses upon, namely Contract, Consent and Legitimate Interest.

Contract

Let me start with Contract. GDPR Article 6(1)b says

> processing is necessary for the performance of a contract to which the data subject is party or in order to take steps at the request of the data subject prior to entering into a contract. (legislation.gov.uk, 2016)

As an upfront comment, I don't think it is going to be easy to base your data use on this legal ground. Here is why:

Presence of a valid contract

Firstly, there must be a contract concluded between the organization and the data subject. The concluded contract must be lawful and valid.

Secondly, you need to check if your contract is fair. For this, the contract must describe the data use transparently and be sufficiently detailed in the agreement. Regulators seem to think that Terms and Conditions are not the right place to do this, because they are usually written very generally for a variety of situations to be covered. To fulfil the fairness criteria of a valid contract, the processing must be described in detail in the written agreement itself. That way, it can be argued that the consumer signing the agreement had a reasonable expectation of how the data would be used (EDPB, 2019).

General necessity

When using Contract as the legal ground, companies must be able to prove that the processing is absolutely necessary. In other words, you have to be sure that there is no other less invasive way to achieve the same results. For example, a consultancy firm asks visitors to their website to enter into an agreement to receive a report. The firm offers this, provided that people sign an agreement that requires their date of birth to be made available to the consultancy company. The date of birth data will be used to create a unique password for downloading the report. However, the consultancy firm can also create a password using an order number they assign to each client instead. This makes the collection of date of birth unnecessary, and the consultancy firm will hence not be able to use Contract as the legal basis for processing this information.

Necessary for executing the agreement

Using Contract as a legal ground further requires that data is not only generally necessary but also necessary for *the performance of the contract*. EDPB, the data protection regulators of the EU member states, suggests using the following checklist to find out if Contract can be used as the legal ground for the processing you have in mind (EDPB, 2019):

- What is the nature of the service being provided to the data subject? What are its distinguishing characteristics?
- What is the exact rationale of the contract (i.e. its substance and fundamental object)?
- What are the essential elements of the contract?
- What are the mutual perspectives and expectations of the parties to the contract? How is the service promoted or advertised to the data subject? Would an ordinary user of the service reasonably expect that, considering the nature of the service, the envisaged processing will take place to perform the contract to which they are a party?

The regulators have a restrictive view on determining if data is truly necessary for executing the agreement. Consider a situation in which a credit card was used to purchase a product. It is arranged so that the customer will pick up the parcel at a physical store. EU regulators in such situations will not permit the collection of customers' addresses because the product will not be sent to a certain address. To use address data in this scenario would in their opinion require another legal ground.

There is a general question when applying this criterion to data used for marketing purposes. Personalized communication and advertising are seldom part of a contract. Consumers typically do not enter into a contractual agreement with an organization for the sole purpose of receiving marketing material. This makes it very difficult to use Contract as the legal ground for marketing data use for most organizations.

Another drawback of using Contract is the lack of legal certainty. OLG Vienna, the Viennese court of appeal in Austria, concluded that in the case of Facebook there is a contractual necessity for processing personal data. The court explained that the social media company has contractually agreed with their customers to provide content personalization services, for both private and commercial content. To tailor contents for each customer, personal data is necessary. OLG Vienna hence ruled that Contract is the appropriate legal ground for this particular marketing activity (OLG Wien, 2020). However, in 2023, EDPB issued a decision that Meta, an operator of several social media platforms including Facebook, among other things, cannot base its use of personal data for behavioural advertising purposes on Contract (EDPB, 2023).

What about prospect data?

Going back to the law text of GDPR Article 6(1)b, it also mentions '*processing is necessary… in order to take steps at the request of the data subject prior to entering into a contract*', which in the first instance sounds like something to justify choosing Contract as a legal ground for using data of potential customers (legislation.gov.uk, 2016). The reason why this phrase will not be of too much use is because the law says there has to be a request from the potential customer. EDPB has clearly stated that unsolicited marketing communication initiated by advertisers cannot base its legal ground on Contract (EDPB, 2019).

Last but not least, the termination of the contract marks the end of Contract as the legal base. A logical first thought when a contract *expires* is to use Legitimate Interest as the new legal ground. However, the guidance note of the regulators explains that it would be unfair to the ex-customers to do so. On the other hand, knowing who terminated the agreement can provide extremely useful insights. Data protection authorities suggest consent to be collected if, for instance, marketers want to conduct churn analysis after the contract is terminated (EDPB, 2019). Let us pause for a moment and think about this recommendation for a second. Realistically, why would someone who has terminated a relationship be bothered reading a text requesting consent for churn analysis, let alone giving an opt-in to the company? The message between the lines seems to be 'do not use Contract as a legal base for marketing'.

The verdict on Contract as a legal ground for marketing

Contract may not be the best legal base for marketers to base the data use upon. First of all because marketing activities are often not provided in the course of executing a contractual agreement for most companies. Secondly, because you cannot be legally certain, even when your marketing activity and hence the use of personal data is for the purpose of fulfilling the agreement with your customer.

By the way, the regulators are not saying that using data for personalizing communication is prohibited. They explicitly acknowledge, for instance, that the use of customer groups or 'look-alike' modelling is permissible. It is just that the legal ground, Contract, in their opinion is not the right legal ground to base these activities (EDPB, 2020).

Now, then, let us look at the two other legal grounds that are more suitable for marketing data use.

Consent

The ICO thinks that Consent, along with Legitimate Interest, is one of the two legal grounds most suitable for marketing. These two legal grounds have one thing in common. They can both be used in a variety of contexts, including marketing. The other four legal grounds, on the other hand, can only be used in a specific context.

The legal ground Consent is deeply rooted in the concept of informational self-determination we discussed in Chapter 1. You can say that a person's self-determination, namely their own will, is what gives Consent its legitimacy. There are some requirements for consent to be valid under GDPR, and as a matter of fact most data protection laws around the world.

In Article 4 of GDPR, consent is defined as (legislation.gov.uk, 2016):

> 'consent' of the data subject means any freely given, specific, informed and unambiguous indication of the data subject's wishes by which he or she, by a statement or by clear affirmative action, signifies agreement to the processing of personal data relating to him or her.

Articles 7 and 8 set additional conditions for using Consent as a legal ground.

Let us break down this definition into small, digestible chunks.

Freely given

Consent for data protection purposes must be a genuine free choice, without coercion, intimidation or deception. Consent cannot be conditional to other benefits offered, like free reports or 20 per cent discount coupons, because otherwise there is an element of conditionality in making that choice of opting-in (legislation.gov.uk, 2016). EDPB (2020) suggests that for the choice to be free, companies shall, for instance, offer services that use additional data, collected using consent and a separate offer that provides the same or comparable services, which does not use additional data.

Organizations also have to make arrangements so that consent can be withdrawn. Withdrawal of the consent must also not lead to detriment. Furthermore, using Consent as legal ground means that you need to work with your IT department to set up an opt-out system that makes withdrawing consent as easy as giving it (EDPB, 2020).

Specific

Consent needs to be specific. The policymakers and data protection authorities want to prevent a so-called function creep. Function creep is the gradual widening or blurring of purposes for which data is processed after the data subject has agreed initial collection of the data (EDPB, 2020). Often there are several reasons why you want to collect data. One reason may be to send promotional materials, and another to improve the quality of communication. The regulators expect all purposes for which you want to use the data to be listed out, and separate opt-in collected for each of them. Strictly speaking, if you want to collect names and addresses, mobile phone numbers and email addresses for marketing purposes, you would need at least three separate tick boxes. The challenge here is that many marketers fear that the more the number of tick boxes the less the number of people who will tick them, limiting, for instance, the number of new contact details that can be collected by a lead generation campaign. Needing to be specific also means Consent is not a flexible legal ground. For example, Article 6(4) spells out the exceptional cases where data can be repurposed for another use-case. Data processed based on Consent is excluded from this exemption (legislation.gov. uk, 2016). In other words, data collected based on Consent for the purposes of measuring the effectiveness of campaigns cannot be recycled for training AI performance measurement tools. If, however, the same data was collected based on Legitimate Interest, the reuse of this data for training the said AI tool becomes a possibility.

To be specific, consent must be clearly separated from other matters. ICO's Direct Marketing Detailed Guide recommends companies to have the so-called consent language, separated from the privacy policy (ICO, 2022).

Informed

In Chapter 1, I explained how consumers can make a decision about their data only when they are properly informed about what will happen to the data. There are two requirements to fulfil to prove that consumers were indeed properly informed.

Firstly, the consent language, describing what consumers are agreeing to, must be easy to understand (see Recital 42) (legislation.gov.uk, 2016). Long run-on sentences, full of legal jargon, need to be changed to everyday English if you want people to understand what you are going to do with the data. One tactic recommended by the EDPB is to use a layered approach, putting detailed information on a link, to help the readability of the consent language (see EDPB, 2020, p 16, No. 69).

Secondly, at least the following information must be provided to consumers to be able to give meaningful consent. I have adapted the list from the EDPB on page 15 of its guidance document on Consent so that it is more relevant to most marketing contexts (EDPB, 2020):

- who you are, who the data controller(s) is (are)
- the purpose of each of the processing operations for which consent is sought
- what (type of) data will be collected and used
- the existence of the right to withdraw consent

Unambiguous indication of wishes

There must be an unmistakably clear indication from the person that it is OK to use the data, in your case, most probably for marketing. There must be an element of proactiveness, which means methods that can provide no more than a passive display of willingness, like pre-ticked tick boxes, are not fit for this criterion. You may have also noticed that websites are no longer announcing 'By scrolling down this page, you consent to xxx' or 'By swiping this page, you give your consent to yyy'. This is because these forms of agreement are not considered affirmative action. Currently, ticking an empty tick box or giving a signature are considered acceptable clear indications of consumers saying 'yes' to the processing.

It must be also noted that an opt-in or consent must be given before you start using the data (Art 29 WP, 2011).

Additional requirements for using consent as your legal ground

Once you have an informed, freely given, specific and unambiguous consent, you are almost there. One last task before settling down on Consent is to make sure that you can prove that consent was given. It is equally important to make sure that a system is in place to facilitate the withdrawal of consent. In most cases, you will be keeping a minimum amount of data for the suppression file so that if this person's data was coincidentally licensed from a data supplier, the record will not flow from that new file to the CRM. Article 20 of GDPR further requires organizations to enable data portability (allowing customers to download data about them from your system and upload it to another service provider) when using Consent, as a legal base (legislation.gov.uk, 2016).

Consent fatigue

You may have experienced it yourself. After clicking on so many 'OK' and 'accept' buttons, it starts becoming a routine. This often leads to consent fatigue where people automatically click to consent merely to progress to the next page online. Choi et al (2018) found that research participants experiencing consent fatigue are more cynical and less willing to consider data protection concerns. More problematically, persons experiencing consent fatigue show disengaging behaviour and avoid facing privacy problems at hand. Informational self-determination, upon which Consent is based, is aimed at achieving the opposite, namely allowing data subjects to be empowered and take control of their data!

The Data Protection and Digital Information (DPDI) Bill tackles this problem in two ways. The new UK law encourages processing of personal data to be based on Legitimate Interest. In addition, a range of exemptions to consent for cookies and opt-in requirements for email messaging are introduced (UK Parliament, 2023).

The EU Commission is developing a voluntary framework to tackle consent fatigue called the Cookie Pledge. It is the consumer protection wing of the EU Commission that is tasked with this topic. They are working on a solution within the current legal framework, i.e. without changing GDPR or the E-Privacy Directive. The emphasis of Cookie Pledge is on cookie consent, required for online advertising. In December 2023, the first draft pledging principles were published, and the Commission's working group is expected to finalize the work by April 2024 (EU Commission, 2023).

Consent and children

Marketers, particularly those who are in the market of providing services that are heavily used by youngsters below the age of 16, such as online games and social media service providers, must be aware of the additional care that needs to go into collecting consent. Children, like the elderly and disabled, are considered vulnerable, and less aware of potential risks, especially when interacting with organizations online. Children younger than 16 cannot by themselves give a valid consent. Recital 38 of GDPR calls out the use of the personal data of minors for marketing, including the creation of marketing intelligence, about needing special care. That means, marketers must figure out a way to find out if the person interacting through a website or an app is below the age of 16.

The verdict on Consent as a legal ground for using data for marketing

One clear advantage is that people are familiar with this legal ground called Consent. 'You received this advertising because you gave us your consent to use your data' with a proof of opt in will satisfy a disgruntled consumer complaining about your using the data. However, obtaining water-tight consent remains a challenge. The list of processing purposes must cover all that you envisage doing, before getting hold of any data. In addition, as mentioned earlier, your customers and prospects may be overwhelmed by the number of tick boxes when you have many use cases, and decide not to tick any of them. That obviously leads to a very small number of records you can use for your marketing activity.

Besides, additional work is attached to using Consent as a legal ground. Consumers have the data portability right, which means they can ask you to give them all the data provided by them. They can then bring this data and upload it to your competitor's portal. Data processed based on Legitimate Interest does not have this requirement. Consumers can also withdraw consent, and that can trigger data to be erased. In practice, this does not make Consent a less desirable legal ground because people have the right to data erasure in most cases when data is used for marketing (see Article 17(1) in combination with Article 21(2) of the GDPR) (legislation.gov.uk, 2016).

Consent is also an inflexible legal ground. Article 6(4) of GDPR gives the possibility of using data for purposes other than what it was originally collected for. Consent-based data is excluded from benefiting from this exemption (legislation.gov.uk, 2016).

Last but not least, Consent is legitimized by the self-determination of the consumers. That means, if the data is used in an undesirable way, where marketers have used the data exactly for the purposes for which it was envisaged, consumers have no one but themselves to blame.

The question is, is Consent still the Holy Grail for marketers?

Legitimate Interest

Legitimate Interest is probably the most versatile lawful base for data processing. Article 6(1)f of GDPR describes the legal ground as follows (legislation.gov.uk, 2016):

> processing is necessary for the purposes of the legitimate interests pursued by the controller or by a third party, except where such interests are overridden by the interests or fundamental rights and freedoms of the data subject which require protection of personal data, in particular where the data subject is a child.

The ICO suggests Legitimate Interest be used when you cannot or do not want to give the consumers full upfront control, or bother them with disruptive consent requests when they are unlikely to object to the processing anyway (see ICO, 2018, section 'When can I rely on legitimate interests'). When marketers feel uncertain about using Legitimate Interest, it is helpful to look at Recital 47 of GDPR. This recital generally states that data can be processed for marketing based on Legitimate Interest.

On the other hand, Legitimate Interest is perhaps the most difficult legal ground to use. To begin with, a lot of thinking needs to be put in, and these thoughts need to be documented before finally deciding if Legitimate Interest is the right legal ground to use.

Can I use Legitimate Interest as the legal ground?

Let me take you through the thinking that you need to go through before settling for Legitimate Interest. The following six-step assessment was adjusted from the framework developed by the pre-GDPR EU data protection authorities' group, Article 29 Working Party (Art 29 WP, 2014).

STEP 1: IS WHAT I WANT TO DO LEGITIMATE, AND WHY DO I HAVE AN INTEREST IN DOING THIS? (PURPOSE TEST)

If what you want to do with the data is prohibited by law, it is also illegal to process this under GDPR. It may sound obvious, but, for instance, a criminal organization, stealing credit card data to sell on the dark net, can never base their data use on Legitimate Interest. Another factor regulators recommend considering includes examining if the processing is ethical.

Then there is a need to be an interest in using the data in a particular way. Regulators, by the way, differentiate *interest* from *purpose*. They understand *purpose* as a specific reason why data is used, such as for carrying out churn analysis. *Interest* is seen as something having a broader scope. There is usually a benefit that the organization can enjoy, for instance, finding new customers and increasing company revenue; this can be an *interest*.

Interestingly, any *interest* can become a legitimate interest, in the sense that the *interest* does not have to be compelling. 'I am interested in finding out how consumers will react if we change the colour of the packaging from orange to purple so that I know how to sell more products and earn more money' can be a legitimate interest.

Also, the interest does not have to be that of your organization. Data suppliers of the marketing ecosystem, for instance, are curating data, not because they are interested in using it themselves, but rather to license them to brands that have an interest in better understanding their customers. The curation of the data is hence carried out in the interest of the customers, a third party.

The interest, used for Legitimate Interest, has to fulfil two conditions (adjusted from page 25 of the Legitimate Interest paper of Art 29 WP, 2014):

1 **The interest must be clearly articulated**: Only when it is articulate can your organization's interest be balanced against that of the data subject.

2 **The interest at stake pursued needs to be real and present**: For instance, if you are interested in increasing your online sales, you can substantiate your interest by hiring online marketing specialists. Important here, I believe, is that the interest is not hypothetical, illusional or unrealistic.

STEP 2: IS THE PROCESSING NECESSARY TO ACHIEVE THE PERSONAL INTEREST? (NECESSITY TEST)

The word *necessary* is defined in a particular way in data protection as we have seen, for instance in the section on Contract of this chapter. If there are other less intrusive ways to achieve the same end-result, then the processing is not considered necessary. In that case, the data used in question cannot be based on Legitimate Interest.

STEP 3: DO EITHER THE INTERESTS OR FUNDAMENTAL RIGHTS OF THE DATA
SUBJECTS OVERRIDE MY INTEREST? (THE FIRST BALANCING TEST)

After you understand your interest clearly, the possible interests, both positive and negative, data subjects may have, shall be listed. In addition, it should be examined if their fundamental human rights, enshrined in the EU Charter of Fundamental Rights, can possibly be infringed.

A great way to start this thinking process is to list out all the interests, as a result of the processing, like sending tailor-made promotional materials to customers. Techniques such as mind mapping may help in the process as the thinking can lead in many directions. As an example, you can brainstorm about a situation where customers receive personalized promotional materials. As a plus, they will be able to benefit from a discount price. As a minus, they might decide to buy the advertised product, instead of saving that money for other use.

Once you have completed this exercise, you need to review the negatives, if they impact the rights and freedoms of the data subject, described in Recital 75 of GDPR (legislation.gov.uk, 2016). The ICO has helpfully summed up the critical points into three elements.

These are (ICO, 2018):

1 Inability to exercise rights, including data protection rights

2 Loss of control over the use of personal data

3 Any social or economic disadvantage

For marketers, the second element, loss of control over the use of personal data, may be most important. The concern related to loss of data control seems to be firmly rooted in informational self-determination. Regulators believe that when people have their data under control, whatever the data use is, it is within what they can reasonably expect. To be precise, it presumes a reasonable expectation of an average person, not a data expert. Normally, when transparency information is available in the privacy policy, it is fair to state that there is a reasonable expectation of an average person about how the data will be used.

Expectations of an average person, or an average consumer, also change over time. Just as moving around in a vehicle not pulled by horses was unthinkable 200 years ago, imagining that your personal data would be used by companies for marketing was beyond the wildest imagination in the early 1970s. Since then, the world has moved on. In today's digitalized world, most consumers around the world believe that data exchange is essential for the smooth running of modern society. Furthermore, the majority of the consumers believe that sharing personal data can encourage organizations to better meet the needs of a diverse society, and a more inclusive commercial offering (GDMA, 2022). This means the use of data by companies for marketing purposes is widely expected by consumers, and the increased awareness translating into better control over the data than in the past.

In discussing the third element, related to social or economic disadvantage, we should think about the different categories of persons to which the data belongs. In particular, when using Legitimate Interest to use data of minors, an increased level of protection is required. However, it is less likely to have a significant social or economic impact on persons acting in their business capacities. Consider a situation where Suzan the IT manager received an ad, crafted and personalized using this person's personal data at work by your marketing team, for a cloud-based file transfer tool. Companies, particularly when they are large, typically have internal purchasing policies which necessitate permissions from different stakeholders before anything can be bought. So, the data transfer tool is then put through a security assessment, as well as the approval process of the finance department, before the IT department can place an order. Imagine, then, a situation where after a month or two a new internal data transfer policy makes the newly purchased file transfer tool incompatible. Economic damage is made to the company. But is your personalized advertising and Suzan, who was motivated by the ad, to be blamed? Will she suffer a social disadvantage as the person who initiated the purchasing process? Most likely not, because the decision was made jointly, and approvals from different departments were obtained, following the internal purchasing policy. That means, Suzan does not directly suffer social or economic disadvantage, even though a personalized ad was sent using her personal data was the trigger. I am not saying that in a business-to-business setting there will never be social or economic damage to a person. However, the likelihood of a severe negative impact on an individual will be less likely than when using data of persons in their private capacity. When using personal data in a business-to-business environment, it is generally easier to use Legitimate Interest, because there will be fewer factors that will override the interest of the marketers.

DID GDPR INCREASE THE DIFFICULTY IN USING LEGITIMATE INTEREST?

Under the predecessor of GDPR, the EU Data Protection Directive, the definition of Legitimate Interest was slightly different (lex.europa.eu, 1995):

Article 7(f) processing is necessary for the purposes of the legitimate interests pursued by the controller or by the third party or parties to whom the data are disclosed, **except where such interests are overridden by the interests <u>for</u> fundamental rights and freedoms of the data subject** which require protection under Article 1(1).

The bold part sentence in GDPR reads 'except where such interests are overridden by the interests <u>or</u> fundamental rights and freedoms of the data subject' (legislation.gov.uk, 2016).

Changing 'for' to 'or' makes a huge difference. While the EU Directive definition requires a narrow range of interests, namely what relates to fundamental rights and freedoms, GDPR makes you think about a full range of interests consumers or business contact persons might have.

When implementing the EU Directives into national laws, countries like France, Italy and Germany have indeed translated the words 'interest for' as 'interest or'. In the UK, no translation was necessary. Nevertheless, legislators opted for the 'or' variation in the 1998 Data Protection Act (legislation.gov.uk, 1998):

by reason of prejudice to the rights and freedoms <u>or</u> legitimate interests of the data subject

Thus, to these countries, the new wording in the GDPR does not make any difference.

STEP 4: WHAT ADDITIONAL SAFEGUARDS CAN I PUT IN PLACE? (SAFEGUARDS AND THE SECOND BALANCING TEST)

As the risk-based approach goes, the higher the risk, the more important it is to take protective measures so that the level of data protection risk is acceptable. The regulators, in their guidance document for using Legitimate Interest, listed the following examples of protecting the data (Art 29 WP, 2014, p 42):

- technical and organizational measures to ensure that the data cannot be used to make decisions or other actions concerning individuals
- extensive use of anonymization techniques
- aggregation of data
- privacy-enhancing technologies, privacy by design, privacy and data protection impact assessments
- increased transparency
- general and unconditional right to opt out
- data portability and related measures to empower data subjects

Once additional protective measures are in place, check if the balancing exercise in Step 3 has tilted in favour of your interest, so that you can move on with using Legitimate Interest as the legal ground for your data use.

STEP 5: DOCUMENTATION AND TRANSPARENCY

In this phase, you document all the activities or thinking you did through Steps 1 to 4. In Chapter 10, we will go through the document specifically for using Legitimate Interest, namely the Legitimate Interest Assessment.

Speaking of documentation, your privacy policy may need to be updated to provide transparency for the new data use. Privacy policy is an ideal place to provide data protection information because people expect that you have one, just as they expect you to have your terms and conditions on your website. We will cover privacy policy in further detail in the next chapter.

STEP 6: BE PREPARED TO FACILITATE DATA SUBJECTS EXERCISE THEIR RIGHTS

As with Consent, the possibility of opting out, as well as access, correction, etc. are prerequisites for using Legitimate Interest as your legal ground. The right to stop processing and deletion also has a function as an expression of your customer having a clear and strong interest against your use of that person's data, on top of exercising the right to data protection. Such expressions help marketers suppress or delete the record. When the interest and rights to data protection of the customer overrides your interest, Legitimate Interest can no longer be used as the legal basis for that data.

Legitimate Interest and the DPDI Bill

The DPDI Bill brings greater legal certainty for marketers to base the data use on Legitimate Interest, compared to GDPR. As mentioned earlier in this chapter, the DPDI Bill names *direct marketing* as an explicit example of situations where Legitimate Interest can be used as a legal ground in the article. In GDPR, *direct marketing* is mentioned as an example where Legitimate Interest can be an appropriate legal ground, in Recital 47. However, recitals are mere explanatory notes of the articles (Publications Office of the European Union, 2023). By bringing in the notion of direct marketing as part of an article strengthens the case for Legitimate Interest for marketing related data use.

Choosing the right legal ground

Table 5.1 shows a simple list of pros and cons of using Consent versus Legitimate Interest in using data for marketing data use.

Considering the pros and cons, my suggestion is, for marketing use, to base the processing on Legitimate Interest wherever it is possible. Where Legitimate Interest cannot be used are situations where, for example, the E-Privacy Directive or PECR restrictions apply. These typically occur when communicating messages through digital and telecommunication channels such as email and SMS, as well as, for digital advertising, where you are directly reading information from the users' devices or storing information like cookies and tags on these devices.

Key takeaways

1 It may be challenging to use Contract as a legal ground for marketing.

2 Consent can be used to base marketing data use upon. Consent has to be freely given, informed, specific and given with affirmative action. However, the legal ground lacks flexibility.

TABLE 5.1 Consent vs Legitimate Interest: pros and cons

Consent		Legitimate Interest	
Data can only be used for specific purposes	☹	Data can be used for more generally described purposes	☺
Purpose of processing cannot be changed	☹	Purpose of processing can be changed under certain circumstances	☺
Documentation required	☺	Heavy documentation required	☹
Data portability applies	☹	Data portability does not apply	☺

3 There are marketing data uses that require consent, such as email marketing where the E-Privacy Directive (PECR) applies.

4 Legitimate Interest can be used as a legal base for marketing data use. While it requires a thorough and documented thinking process, before putting it to use, Legitimate Interest provides companies with more flexibility than Consent.

5 Regardless of the legal basis, data belonging to children needs to be given more care and protection.

Conclusion

There are three potential legal grounds for using personal data for marketing. They are Contract, Consent and Legitimate Interest. Contract, is a difficult legal ground to use because rarely is marketing necessary for executing an agreement. In addition, Contract comes with more legal uncertainty compared to the other two legal grounds. Consent is widely used, and in certain situations, such as setting cookies and sending email newsletters, the E-Privacy Directive or PECR require the use of consent. The drawbacks of Consent include its lack of flexibility and consent fatigue. Legitimate Interest may be the most appropriate legal base for a variety of marketing use cases. Legitimate Interest requires the interest of your organization, specifically that of the marketing department, to be balanced against the rights and freedoms of the customers and prospects. Only when your organization's interests weigh higher can the legal ground be used.

Bibliography

Art 29 WP (2011) Article 29 Data Protection Working Party, Opinion 15/2011 on the definition of consent, adopted on 13 July 2011, https://ec.europa.eu/justice/article-29/documentation/opinion-recommendation/files/2011/wp187_en.pdf (archived at https://perma.cc/6AUF-6KSF), see pp 30–31

Art 29 WP (2014) Article 29 Data Protection Working Party, Opinion 06/2014 on the notion of legitimate interests of the data controller, 844/14/EN WP 217, adopted on 9 April 2014, https://ec.europa.eu/justice/article-29/documentation/opinion-recommendation/files/2014/wp217_en.pdf (archived at https://perma.cc/7BSD-E2T3)

Choi, H, Park, J and Jung, Y (2017) The role of privacy fatigue in online privacy behavior, *Computers in Human Behavior*, Elsevier ScienceDirect, 5 December

EDPB (2019) European Data Protection Board Guidelines 2/2019 on the processing of personal data under Article 6(1)(b) GDPR in the context of the provision of online services to data subjects, Version 2.0, 8 October 2019, https://edpb.europa.eu/sites/default/files/files/file1/edpb_guidelines-art_6-1-b-adopted_after_public_consultation_en.pdf (archived at https://perma.cc/9P53-AWMW)

EDPB (2020) European Data Protection Board Guidelines 05/2020 on consent under Regulation 2016/679 Version 1.1 adopted on 4 May 2020, https://edpb.europa.eu/sites/default/files/files/file1/edpb_guidelines_202005_consent_en.pdf (archived at https://perma.cc/4PWH-XHDL), see p 14

EDPB (2023) European Data Protection Board, EDPB publishes urgent binding decision regarding Meta; 7 December 2023, https://edpb.europa.eu/news/news/2023/edpb-publishes-urgent-binding-decision-regarding-meta_en (archived at https://perma.cc/9UE6-VMEC)

EU Commission (2023) Cookie Pledge: A reflection on how to better empower consumers to make effective choices regarding tracking-based advertising models, https://commission.europa.eu/live-work-travel-eu/consumer-rights-and-complaints/enforcement-consumer-protection/cookie-pledge_en (archived at https://perma.cc/K5LG-8T3K)

GDMA (2022) Global Data and Marketing Alliance, Global Data Privacy: What the consumer really thinks 2022, https://globaldma.com/wp-content/uploads/2022/03/GDMA-Global-Data-Privacy-2022.pdf (archived at https://perma.cc/MEB6-5V6K)

ICO (2018) UK Information Commissioner's Office: The General Data Protection Regulation Lawful basis for processing Legitimate Interests, 22 March 2018, https://ico.org.uk/media/for-organisations/uk-gdpr-guidance-and-resources/lawful-basis/legitimate-interests-1-0.pdf (archived at https://perma.cc/Q9QD-L4LA)

ICO (2022) UK Information Commissioner's Office: Direct Marketing Detailed Guideline, 5 December 2022, https://ico.org.uk/media/for-organisations/direct-marketing-guidance-and-resources/direct-marketing-guidance-1-0.pdf (archived at https://perma.cc/7NWD-T8K8)

legislation.gov.uk (1998) Data Protection Act 1998, 1998 Chapter 29, An Act to make new provision for the regulation of the processing of information relating to individuals, including the obtaining, holding, use or disclosure of such information, 16 July 1998, www.legislation.gov.uk/ukpga/1998/29/contents/2000-03-01 (archived at https://perma.cc/ZW6V-RTBM)

legislation.gov.uk (2016) Regulation (EU) 2016/679 of the European Parliament and of the Council, 27 April 2016, www.legislation.gov.uk /eur/2016/679/contents (archived at https://perma.cc/9JAS-2XGE)

lex.europa.eu (1995) Directive 95/46/EC of the European Parliament and of the Council of 24 October 1995 on the protection of individuals with regard to the processing of personal data and on the free movement of such data, Official Journal L 281, 23/11/1995, pp 0031–0050, https://eur-lex.europa.eu/legal-content/EN/TXT/HTML/?uri=CELEX%3A31995L0046 (archived at https://perma.cc/WCQ9-H9DK)

OLG Wien (2020) Oberlandesgericht Wien, Urteil vom 07.12.2020 – 11 R 153/20f, 11 R 154/20b, Beck Online die Datenbank, Beck RS, https://beck-online.beck.de/Dokument?vpath=bibdata%2Fents%2Fbeckrs%2F2020%2Fcont%2Fbeckrs.2020.49348.htm&anchor=Y-300-Z-BECKRS-B-2020-N-49348 (archived at https://perma.cc/FA36-YCUX)

Publications Office of the European Union (2023) Europa Institutional Style Guide, last updated 1 October 2023, https://publications.europa.eu/code/en/en-120200.htm (archived at https://perma.cc/M5T2-EWHR)

UK Parliament (2023) Data Protection and Digital Information Bill, Government Bill, Originated in the House of Commons, Sessions 2022–23, 2023–24, last updated 20 December 2023 at 09:33, https://bills.parliament.uk/bills/3430 (archived at https://perma.cc/CJ4Z-YWYG)

6

Explaining what you do with data with privacy statements

Several years ago, my daughter developed allergies. She had to avoid wheat products, milk, refined sugar, etc. – practically everything children enjoy and everything served at birthday parties. 'Mom, can I eat this?' Time after time, she would bring me a package of gummy bears, cookies or crisps from her favourite aisle of the supermarket, urging me to check the ingredients. It was really not until that time that I noticed how practical it is that every packaged food has an ingredient list printed on it. This can be said about privacy statements, too. When, for some reason, your customers become extra sensitive to data protection matters, perhaps because they had an escalated consumer complaint or because the purchasing department introduced a new internal guideline, privacy statements become their nutrition information labels where they seek assurance from you. Your privacy statement is the first place they look to get a glimpse of how compliant you are.

Why do I need a privacy statement?

Do you use personal data? I bet you do, because otherwise you would not be reading this book. If your company uses personal data for marketing, accounting, HR or whatever other purposes, you need a privacy policy. The traditional approach to data protection and informational self-determination suggests that meaningful control of your own data is only possible if you were informed about how the data will be used. One of the first rules

GDPR lays down in its text, after clarifying the scope of the law and the different definitions, is Article 5 (legislation.gov.uk, 2016):

1 Personal data shall be:

(a) processed lawfully, fairly and in a transparent manner in relation to the data subject ('lawfulness, fairness and transparency')

This very requirement triggers the need for a privacy statement.

As discussed in Chapter 3, companies, in particular when they are data controllers, must be accountable for their data use and have a privacy statement. This requirement is also spelled out in Article 24(2) of the GDPR (legislation.gov.uk, 2016).

In any event, a privacy statement is an important document. GDPR dedicates two articles to list out the precise information you need to communicate; Article 13 sets out the requirements in case you collect data directly from consumers, and Article 14 those for situations where data is collected indirectly (legislation.gov.uk, 2016).

Who will read your privacy statement?

In the case of food labelling, it is me as a customer checking for a particular ingredient that reads this. Have you ever wondered who reads your privacy statement? Customers and prospects are one obvious group of stakeholders who are concerned about what is happening with their data once it's in your hands. Privacy activists and consumer protection organizations may also be going through your privacy statement. Authors and academic researchers in the field of data protection find it a great source of information learning how companies are using personal data. Regulators, judges and lawyers who are working on a case that involves your company also take great interest in your privacy notice.

Your corporate image is shaped by how your privacy statement reads. Customers, both in business-to-business as well as business-to-consumer markets, pay great attention to your privacy practice. Business partners and suppliers to your company often formalize the review of your company's data protection compliance, asking questions about your privacy statement in their due diligence questionnaires.

Whoever the readers are, it is another 'touch-point' for a variety of stakeholders, including revenue-generating parties like customers and partners. You want them to have a good impression of your privacy practices, and the first chance you have to showcase this may be your privacy statement. Borrowing the words of the ICO, a good privacy statement *helps you build trust, avoids confusion and lets everyone know what to expect* (ICO, 2023).

Things you want to know before drawing up a privacy statement

Before diving into writing your privacy statement, it will be useful to understand some of the key considerations that are important to data protection.

How long should my privacy statement be?

GDPR expects you to draw up a privacy statement long enough so that you can properly explain which data is collected, used and stored. This makes your privacy statement transparent. At the same time, your privacy statement must be concise, according to Article 12(1) of GDPR (legislation.gov. uk, 2016). These two requirements seem to contradict each other at first glance. The EU regulators therefore give some explanations in their guidelines on transparency (Art 29 WP, 2018).

While a privacy statement aims to give the necessary information so that consumers can make decisions about their personal data, regulators are also aware of the phenomena known as 'information fatigue' or 'information overload'. The hypothesis is that human beings have a limited capacity to digest information. When too much information is presented, people become overwhelmed and either ignore the information or make illogical decisions to cope with the psychological stress they experience (Simmel, 1950; Milgram, 1969). There are two strategies to avoid this and at the same time still provide all details required.

HAVE A CLEAR STRUCTURE
Before starting to write a privacy notice, list out all the information you need to provide in it. Then, think how you want to present it to your customers and other data subjects in a logical manner. In doing so, you might want to read the privacy statements of big consumer brands and governmental

organizations and find out how their privacy statements are structured. There is a good chance that their privacy notices are prepared by experienced in-house lawyers or by law firms that specialize in data protection. The idea is to get the feeling of what great privacy statements look like. You might also want to read up on the privacy statements of your competitors, as well as those of your partners in your business field. Ask your privacy person which competitors have good reputations with regard to their data protection practices, or perhaps you already know who they are. Just take a look at how their privacy notices are structured. You can also simply adopt the structure of ICO's privacy policy template. Whatever you do, the key is to improve the readability of your privacy statement by giving it a logical structure.

PREPARE PRIVACY NOTICES IN LAYERS

Another approach, endorsed by the regulators, is the so-called layered approach (Art 29 WP, 2018). Assuming that the privacy notice is going to be online, you can make your privacy policy interactive by using links, so that users can click on them when they want more information, or skip them and stay on the first-level summary information if they so wish, just as you would use an online encyclopaedia. This way, the key messages are simplified and readers of your privacy statement will have a good overview of the first layer of the statement.

Regulators recommend the following information should be visible on the first layers of the privacy notice (Art 29 WP, 2018, p 19):

1 Details of the purposes of processing
2 The identity of the data controller
3 Description of the data subjects' rights
4 Information on the processing which has the most impact on the data subject
5 Information on the processing which could surprise them.

Where do I post my privacy statement?

GDPR requires that privacy statements should be easily accessible (see Article 21(1); legislation.gov.uk, 2016). Regulators expect organizations with a web presence to put the privacy notice on their websites. A link to the

FIGURE 6.1 Consent language is separated from a privacy statement

We offer monthly newsletter that brings exclusive thought leadership from our MMM experts and latest developments in measurement techniques directly to your inbox.

[ ] yes, I want to sign up for XYZ Ltd's monthly newsletter

Name: _____

Company: _____

Email address: _____

Your personal data will be processed in accordance with our Privacy Notice.

privacy statement is usually found on the home page at the very bottom, next to the link to Terms and Conditions. Regulators also want to see your company's privacy statement in the app store so that users can read this before downloading your app (legislation.gov.uk, 2016).

Organizations must make sure that the privacy statement is clearly separated from the consent. If you are collecting data with consent, there must be a consent language, the text that describes what users are agreeing to and perhaps a link to your privacy notice (see Figure 6.1).

When do I have to present the privacy statement?

Consumers must be informed what data is collected for, for instance marketing purposes, as early as possible. When you are collecting data directly from your customers, you must present your privacy notice the moment you are collecting the data (see Article 13(1) GDPR; legislation.gov.uk, 2016). In a scenario where you license the data from other organizations, such as from public sources or marketing data providers, Article 14(3) requires the privacy information to be provided in the following manner (legislation.gov. uk, 2016):

(a) within a reasonable period after obtaining the personal data, but at the latest within one month, having regard to the specific circumstances in which the personal data are processed;

(b) if the personal data are to be used for communication with the data subject, at the latest at the time of the first communication to that data subject; or

(c) if a disclosure to another recipient is envisaged, at the latest when the personal data are first disclosed.

In short, for licensed data that is not contact detail data, the privacy notice must be communicated within a month. If you are using contact data like names, telephone numbers, email addresses and physical addresses, you need to communicate the privacy statement the first time you send a commercial message to them. In practice, companies embed a link to the privacy statement in email messages or print that link on direct mail pieces to fulfil this requirement.

Are there any rules about the tone of voice?

The whole point of a privacy statement is to write it in a way that people understand it. Article 12(1) of GDPR uses two expressions, namely 'intelligible' and 'clear and plain language', to set the expectation of how your privacy notice should sound like.

INTELLIGIBLE PRIVACY STATEMENTS

By intelligible, the legislators wanted the privacy statement to be understandable by an average person in the intended audience. For instance, if most of your intended privacy statement readers are specialists in mar-tech solutions, feel free to use terms and expressions like CDPs, Data Clean Rooms and 'breaking the silos' in your privacy statement – if they are relevant, that is. But if your clientele are marketing generalists, you may want to elaborate on what CDPs are and for what you are using them, as well as explain what Data Clean Rooms are and that you use this for added protection of personal data, before using these terms in your privacy statement.

WRITING A PRIVACY STATEMENT IN CLEAR AND PLAIN LANGUAGE

Writing your privacy statement without jargon is perhaps the most obvious way to make it *clear and easy to understand*. The European Commission believes that writing clearly only makes documents easier to read and can be understood quickly (Field, 2012). The document explains that, apart from dropping legal and technical jargon, there are several other tips and tricks you can use to develop clear and effective documents.

EU regulators provide the following additional recommendations on this topic (Art 29 WP, 2018):

- where possible, avoid qualifiers like 'may', 'might', 'some', 'often' and 'possible'

- write in active voice
- (when translating privacy statements to multiple languages) ensure that the translation is accurate

---

LESSONS FROM THE EU COMMISSION ON WRITING CLEARLY

As a mammoth administrative organization, the EU Commission must introduce hundreds, if not thousands, of official documents every week. To complicate the matter, documents are often translated into the different official languages of the member-states. To make sure that information is understood uniformly, writing clearly is imperative for European institutions.

The European Commission's mantra for clear writing is neat, 'Keep it short and simple', abbreviated to KISS (Field, 2012). Some of the tips can very well be applied when writing a privacy statement.

Shorten the length
The Commission recommends documents should be no longer than 15 pages in
    length. When it comes to sentences, the EU Commission's DG for
    Translation recommends an average of 20 words per sentence. Long run-on
    sentences can always be broken down into two or more shorter sentences.

Use simple words and expressions
You might say that I am guilty of using complicated words too. Texts you write
    give an impression to the readers. Using uncommon expressions or mixing
    in Latin words can give readers the impression that the author is well
    educated. That is all well and good, and there are certainly contexts where
    it is necessary to use specialist terms and foreign words. But when you
    want to make yourself understood, the focus really should be on readability
    and not on giving out impressions through your writing style. When you
    want your text to convey clear, simple messages, avoid ambiguities in your
    sentences. Use a positive and active voice that promotes easier reading.

Position important messages at the end of the sentence
Readers remember what is said at the end of the sentence more than what was
    said at the beginning or in the middle of the sentence. Using this
    knowledge, you can form your sentence in such a way that the Data
    Protection Officer's email address is better emphasized.

The original sentence:

> Contact our Data Protection Officer at *privacy@xyz.com* if you have further questions about the way we use your data.

can be improved by re-writing it this way:

> If you have further questions about the way we use your data, contact our Data Protection Officer at privacy@xyz.com.

What do I have to do when I change or update the privacy statement?

There is no requirement under GDPR to take action when privacy notices are changed or updated. The Article 29 Working Party once recommended, nevertheless, to explicitly and proactively inform the data subjects, well in advance when changes are made to your privacy notice. This recommendation only applies to situations where fundamental changes are made to the privacy notice. In all other cases, notifying customers and business contacts about the changes in your company's privacy statement is not necessary (Art 29 WP, 2018).

Understanding the information requirements of a privacy statement

Now let us move on to what information needs to be provided in a privacy statement. The key aim of a privacy statement is to tell the data subjects what you are going to do with the data in advance, so that there are no surprises. Article 5(1) and Recital 39 of GDPR states this pretty clearly.

Since a large part of the required information is listed out under Articles 13 and 14 of the regulation, I will pick up sections that are likely to be relevant for marketers.

Also, I would like to caveat that, although my focus in this section is on marketing and data protection, a company's privacy policy usually contains information on data processing that is not related to marketing as well. For instance, data used for invoicing or recruiting can also be described in the privacy policy.

*Who you are and how you can be reached (GDPR Article 13(1)a
and Article 14(1)a)*

You need to disclose your identity in your privacy notice. The EU regulators expect this information to be comprehensive enough so that consumers can easily identify who you are, or who your organization is. This usually means disclosing your company's name and statutory address, plus its legal form. In the UK that would be XYZ Ltd, ZYX Plc and so on. In addition, they expect you to provide a general email address, often an info@ email address, and/or the central telephone number. Some companies might also consider providing a chat function that allows many general data protection questions to be answered quickly without making people wait. However, since GDPR does not specify which contact information must be given on the privacy notice, in real terms you can choose the contact information you want to use (Art 29 WP, 2018).

*How to contact the Data Protection Officer (GDPR Article 13(1)b,
Article 14(1)b and Article 37(7))*

If your organization has a DPO, your privacy statement needs to include information about how this person can be contacted. You can publish the name and the personal work email address of your company's DPO, but it is not necessary. You can also publish a specific email address which DPO uses, such as dpo@xyz.com or privacy@xyz.com. Installing a dedicated telephone hotline or putting up an online contact formula are also considered as ways to allow consumers, customers and prospects to contact the DPO, which means they are also good alternatives (Art 29 WP, 2016).

*Purposes and legal basis for processing personal data (GDPR
Article 13(1)c, Article 13(1)d, Article 14(1)c, and Article 14(2)b)*

Your privacy statement must include information on what you use personal data for, and what the legal ground is. In Chapter 4, I outlined four main types of data processing purposes in the field of marketing, namely;

- communication
- data hygiene
- insight generation
- strategic decision making

One way of providing processing purposes is to elaborate these four types of data use, specifically to activities of your marketing department.

For each of these marketing purposes, a legal ground should be named. Based on the analysis in Chapter 5, in most cases, it would be Legitimate Interest or Consent.

In addition, when using Legitimate Interest as your legal ground, the marketing department's interest in using personal data needs to be explained. As a best practice, you can even publish the balancing test you have carried out on your Legitimate Interest and the rights and freedoms of your customers, before settling down on Legitimate Interest as the legal ground (Art 29 WP, 2018).

Which types of personal data are used (Article 14(1)d)

Some personal data used for marketing may be collected indirectly. In such cases, you are most probably sourcing the data from partners or specialist marketing data suppliers. In this case, there is an obligation to state the categories of data you license from third parties on your privacy notice (legislation.gov.uk, 2016).

The assumption here is that if data is not collected directly, the level of awareness about the data use among customers and prospects is low. In other words, mentioning the types of data in the privacy notice works as a reminder.

Even though this requirement does not apply to data you have directly collected, many companies list out the categories of data for both data collected directly and indirectly from third parties on their privacy notice.

Who are the recipients of your data (Article 13(1)e and Article 14(1)e)

Your privacy statement must have a list of either named recipients of personal data your company controls or, if not, the categories of such recipients. It is not important in which capacity (as a controller, a processor or a joint controller) the recipient receives data from you. If the data is sent to, or access is granted to, a company, that organization is considered the data recipient. The data protection authorities prefer the names of the recipients to be published in the privacy policy (Art 29 WP, 2018). In practice, this might not be an easy decision. Consider a situation where the marketing department decided to switch from using one market research institution in favour of another, necessitating the named market research company on the privacy notice to be changed. Since many research works are carried out on a project basis, every time a new project starts you would potentially need to update the corporate privacy statement. In larger organizations, there can be several brand managers carrying out studies simultaneously, which would make the changes that need to be made on the privacy statement even more frequent. The other issue may be that your competitors as well as other research institutions can find out who you are working with when publishing the names of data recipients.

While naming the parties is more transparent to data subjects, if you believe that exposing the names of organizations may harm your organization, the interests of both sides shall be weighed up. After all, Recital 4 of GDPR clearly states that the right to the protection of personal data is not an absolute right and needs to be balanced against other rights (legislation. gov.uk, 2016). This includes the freedom to conduct business (europarl. europa.eu, 2000). One factor that might help argue this point is the Subject Access Right (SAR) laid out in Article 15 of the GDPR. Customers or prospects wanting to know whom exactly the marketing department shared the data with can request this information based on this article (legislation.gov. uk, 2016).

In any case, if your organization decides to publish the category of recipients, regulators want you to include information on the types of recipients, their detailed industry sector as well and their geographic locations (Art 29 WP, 2018).

If data is transferred abroad or not (Article 13(1)f and Article 14(1)f)

For EU countries, international data transfer takes place when data crosses the borders of the European Economic Area (EU countries plus Iceland, Liechtenstein and Norway). In other words, countries located outside the EEA are considered 'third countries' or abroad. For the UK, UK GDPR in Article 4(27) defines 'third country' as a country or territory outside the UK (legislation.gov.uk, 2016).

For the cross-border transmission of data to qualify as a data transfer to a third country, it must fulfil all three of the following conditions (EDPB, 2022):

(1) the data exporter (a controller or processor) is subject to the GDPR for the given processing;

(2) the data exporter transmits or makes available the personal data to the data importer (another controller, joint controller or processor);

(3) the data importer is in a third country or is an international organization.

Your marketing manager, working from Egypt during a business trip, accessing customer data does not constitute an international data transfer because (2) is not fulfilled. The data is not made available to another company because the marketing manager is accessing the data as part of your company. In case you make use of a centralized global infrastructure, because your company is part of a global organization, or an external cloud storage service located in a third country, this information needs to be published on the privacy notice. In this case, your privacy statement needs to mention (a) to which country the data is transferred and (b) which legal instrument was used to legalize the transfer.

LEGAL REQUIREMENTS FOR TRANSFERRING DATA TO THIRD COUNTRIES

Personal data is transferred abroad, for instance, by sending a file or giving access to data to an organization located in a third country. International data transfer or restricted transfer, as it is called in the UK, takes place when you send your customers' email addresses to an organization located in India, from which emails are sent out for your email campaign. Using a cloud-based CRM system hosted by a company based in New Zealand also constitutes international data transfer.

The idea behind requiring additional legal precautions for data transferred to a third country is to ensure that EU and UK citizens' data is protected, even when processed abroad. There are several legal arrangements you can organize so that it is permissible to use an email fulfilment company in India or have your CRM hosted by a company in New Zealand.

Adequacy

Currently, the European Commission considers the following countries as having comparable data protection standards as the EU: Andorra, Argentina, Canada (for commercial organizations only), Faroe Islands, Guernsey, Israel, Isle of Man, Japan, Jersey, New Zealand, Republic of Korea, Switzerland, the United Kingdom under the GDPR and the LED, the United States (for commercial organizations participating in the EU-US Data Privacy Framework only) and Uruguay (EU Commission, 2023).

The UK considers the following EEA countries to have an adequate data protection standard: Austria, Belgium, Bulgaria, Croatia, Cyprus, Czech Republic, Denmark, EU institutions, Finland, France, Germany, Greece, Hungary, Iceland, Ireland, Italy, Latvia, Liechtenstein, Lithuania, Luxembourg, Malta, Netherlands, Norway, Poland, Portugal, Romania, Slovakia, Slovenia, Spain, Sweden. In addition, the following countries and territories outside the EEA are considered adequate by the UK Government: Andorra, Argentina, Canada (partial), Guernsey, Israel, Isle of Man, Japan, Jersey, Faroe Islands, New Zealand, Gibraltar, Switzerland, Uruguay (DCMS, 2021).

If the country to which you are transferring the data is an adequate country, there is no additional work necessary. You can send the data as though sending it to a domestic organization. In the example of a New Zealand-based CRM hosting company, no additional legal documents or procedures need to be put in place.

Binding Corporate Rules (BCR)

BCR allows inter-company data transfer of multinationals so that data can be freely transferred within the global organization. Companies can apply for BCR by committing to an extensive list of data protection requirements, which in effect makes GDPR applicable to all global entities, regardless of where they are located. This way, you can, for instance, centralize resources in a country of your choice. An example would be creating a Customer Insights Centre of Excellence where analytical talents are brought together in one country. This Centre of Excellence, say in Singapore, can develop analytical expertise and generate customer insights for all of the offices around the globe. The only downside is that, with this instrument, you cannot transfer your marketing data to a company which is not part of your global organization.

Standard Contractual Clauses (SCC) and International Data Transfer Agreement (IDTA)

SCC is perhaps the most preferred data transfer mechanism. It is a template contract, drawn up by the European Commission (EU Commission, 2021). Since 2022 the UK has a data transfer template document called IDTA. So that it is not necessary to repeal SCCs signed before Brexit, an addendum to SCC has been created (ICO, 2022). The rule for using SCCs or IDTAs is that you are not allowed to alter the template, or it will become invalid. Both the SCC and IDTA basically bind the recipient organization in a third country to abide by rules that strongly resemble GDPR. Marketers can use an SCC or IDTA, depending on where your organization is based, to transfer their emails to the email fulfilment company in India by simply signing the SCC or IDTA – and abiding by it!

Other instruments

It is also possible to transfer data to a third country by setting up effective safeguards. This can be provided, for instance, by approved industry codes of conduct or certifications. Otherwise, an approval from the competent data protection authority is required. In the absence of a GDPR-approved globally valid marketing industry code of conduct, so far I have not come across cases where an organization is using *appropriate safeguards* to transfer data, internationally.

How long the data will be kept (Article 13(2)a and Article 14(2)a)

Your privacy statement needs to publish information about how long data will be kept. In the field of marketing, old data can also become useful. For instance, marketers may want to study consumer trends over the past 20 years, which can create useful insights. However, just because it might come handy one of these days, you cannot hold on to the data forever. Perhaps there are ways to extract the necessary intelligence after data is anonymized. In that case, GDPR does not apply so the data can be kept as long as the marketer wishes. Otherwise, a fixed period needs to be set when the data expires and is deleted or anonymized. GDPR also gives the option for companies to publish the logic used in determining when data should be deleted, in case it is difficult to name the exact duration of data retention. Since it is the exact logic that you follow for deleting data that needs to be communicated, publishing a general statement such as 'your data will be kept as long as it is necessary' will not be considered compliant (Art 29 WP, 2018).

Companies often publish their retention period per type of data or by how the data is used. For instance, you can say 'for data hygiene, data is kept for X years' and 'communication data is kept for Y years'.

Inform people of their rights to data protection (Article 13(2)b, Article 13(2)c, Article 14(2)c, Article 14(2)d and Article 7(3))

Every privacy statement must clearly state that data subjects have the right to access data, rectify wrongful information, have data erased, restrict processing of data, object to processing and, in case the legal ground is Consent, the right to data portability as well as the right to withdraw the consent.

Inform people of their right to complain to the Data Protection Authority (Article 13(2)d and Article 14(2)e)

Another obligatory notice in every privacy statement is the information that people have the right to complain about your company to the regulator. A complaint can be made at the data protection authority of where the person is living, where the alleged infringement was made or at the competent authority of your organization. Many companies provide the contact information of their competent regulator on their privacy statement.

Where did we get the data from (Article 14(2)f)

If the personal data you are using for your marketing efforts were not collected from the customers or prospects directly, you would need to either name the specific source of the data or the types of organizations from which the data is obtained. The same considerations as naming the recipient of the data also apply here. If you decide not to mention the specific data source, it is expected that you at least name the nature of the source (i.e. public institutions or commercial organizations) and the industry sector.

Is your personal data used for automatic decision making? (Article 13(2)f and Article 14(2)g)

If data is used for automatic decision making, then this needs to be mentioned on the privacy statement. You might have an automated rule that says 'if the person is not our client but requested a brochure, send an invitation email to have a chat with our sales representative', and execute the command without the intervention of a marketer.

Article 13(2)f and Article 14(2)g specify that profiling that can potentially harm persons (i.e. profiling that falls under the definition of Article 22 of the GDPR) must be mentioned in the privacy policy. The same articles do not exclude mundane profiling from this requirement, for instance, for making marketing messages more relevant. This means any profiling that marketers use should be published on the privacy notice.

Points of consideration

Separate privacy policy for websites

Many organizations have more than one privacy statement; a typical example would be to have one privacy statement for general purposes, and another specifically for data captured and used on websites.

Separate privacy notices are also created for different types of data use, such as for job applicants and employees. Employee privacy policies are often available as part of your company's employee handbook or on the intranet. Certainly, there are also organizations that have incorporated data processing of employee data, job applicant data and website data in one general privacy statement.

My personal preference is to maintain a separate privacy statement for the website, if anything because I somehow got used to reading information about how specific cookies are set for which purpose and are sent to which companies. Some organizations even call them 'cookie policies' rather than 'privacy policy for the website'.

Options for generating privacy statements

There are three ways of creating privacy policies. The first way is to create a privacy notice using the templates provided by the regulators; in the case of the UK this will be the privacy policy template from the ICO (ICO, 2023a). The advantage of using this template is that there is a sense of assurance because the framework is from the regulator. On the other hand, there are several generic and intentional omissions that users of the template must be aware of. For instance, the publication of the contact details of the DPO and international data transfer are absent. This is most likely because the regulator intended to help small organizations when developing this template for which in many cases the appointment of a DPO is not mandatory (ICO, 2023a).

The second way of generating privacy statements is to use automatic privacy statement generators. Using such tools is even easier than using the

ICO template, and many such tools are often available online free of charge. For generating specific privacy policies for cookies and apps, which tend to be uniform, these tools are quite useful. On the flip side, it is difficult to adjust details that are, for instance, specific to your marketing use. If you are curious, I suggest you type in 'privacy policy generator' in a search engine and examine some of the tools that pop up as a result.

The third and perhaps the preferred option for many medium to large organizations is to create a privacy notice from scratch. This option will require either an in-house legal or privacy department, or, if not, external advice from speciality data protection consultancy organizations and law firms, or both. Developing a privacy statement from scratch has the advantage that, particularly when working with experts with a good understanding of your (marketing) activities, the resulting statement will better fit your organizational needs. The downside is that you may need to be patient if the ones who are drafting the privacy statement are not familiar with marketing data use, and do not fully understand what your marketing team is doing with the personal data (and vice versa; lawyers and advisors might get frustrated that marketers don't understand the questions they are asking). Another obvious disadvantage is that this option comes with a higher price tag, particularly if you engage external advisors for the task.

Using a familiar structure

At the beginning of this chapter, we discussed the importance of having a good structure. I would like to add that using a structure with which the readers are familiar is as important as having a good structure. Remember, it is not only customers and prospects who read your privacy notice; regulators, judges, clients' and partners' lawyers may be studying it too. I believe it helps the latter two groups of readers in particular if your privacy statement uses a widely accepted format. In Germany, for instance, the template of the Association of Data Protection and Data Security (GDD) is widely used (GDD, 2020). In the previous section, I mentioned the ICO's privacy statement. This template presents the information in the following order (ICO, 2023a):

1 Our contact details
2 The type of personal information we collect
3 How do we get personal information and why do we have it
4 How we store your information

5 Your data protection rights

6 How to complain

While it is developed with physiotherapists and plumbers in mind, the structure of the document is universal. Next time you read a privacy statement of a well-known organization, you might be able to recognize this structure.

I find it very easy to understand and would like to see this format spread beyond the British borders.

Key takeaways

1 Privacy statement is a key document for transparency that supports the principle of informational self-determination, as well as enabling your organization to be accountable.

2 Privacy statements must be concise, transparent, intelligible and easily accessible.

3 Your privacy statement is a 'customer touch point' of your company. Also, regulators, judges, privacy advocates, lawyers of clients, partners and competitors, as well as data subjects, are among those who may study your privacy statement.

4 Information needed on privacy statements is mainly provided in Articles 13 and 14 of GDPR.

Conclusion

Your privacy statement is a very important document that makes your marketing data use compliant. The statement must provide information transparency by making it easy for an average person of your intended audience to read. Having a robust and familiar structure and avoiding jargon are two of the many factors that can improve the readability of your privacy notice. Most of the information requirements of a privacy notice are listed out in Articles 13 and 14 of GDPR.

Bibliography

Art 29 WP (2016) Article 29 Data Protection Working Party, WP 243 Guidelines on Data Protection Officers ('DPOs'), adopted on 13 December 2016, https://ec.europa.eu/information_society/newsroom/image/document/2016-51/wp243_en_40855.pdf?wb48617274=CD63BD9A (archived at https://perma.cc/AH36-XP8W)

Art 29 WP (2018) Article 29 Data Protection Working Party, WP260rev.01 Guidelines on transparency under Regulation 2016/679, adopted on 29 November 2017, last revised and adopted on 11 April 2018, https://ec.europa.eu/newsroom/article29/items/622227 (archived at https://perma.cc/4HWY-URKL)

DCMS (2021) Ministry of Digital, Culture, Media and Sport, Guidance – International Data Transfers: building trust, delivering growth and firing up innovation, published 26 August 2021, www.gov.uk/government/publications/uk-approach-to-international-data-transfers/international-data-transfers-building-trust-delivering-growth-and-firing-up-innovation (archived at https://perma.cc/B66L-KYC7)

EDPB (2022) European Data Protection Board Guidelines 05/2021 on the interplay between the application of Article 3 and the provisions on international transfers as per Chapter V of the GDPR, Version 2.0, adopted on 14 February 2023, https://edpb.europa.eu/our-work-tools/our-documents/guidelines/guidelines-052021-interplay-between-application-article-3_en (archived at https://perma.cc/NE8Z-6Y5X)

EU Commission (2021) Commission Implementing Decision (EU) 2021/914 of 4 June 2021 on standard contractual clauses for the transfer of personal data to third countries pursuant to Regulation (EU) 2016/679 of the European Parliament and of the Council, https://eur-lex.europa.eu/legal-content/EN/TXT/HTML/?uri=CELEX:32021D0914#d1e32-37-1 (archived at https://perma.cc/M8GH-Q2EC)

EU Commission (2023) Adequacy decisions: How the EU determines if a non-EU country has an adequate level of data protection, last updated on 11 April 2023, https://commission.europa.eu/law/law-topic/data-protection/international-dimension-data-protection/adequacy-decisions_en (archived at https://perma.cc/KXM2-W2S6)

europarl.europa.eu (2000) Charter of Fundamental Rights of the European Union (2000), 2000/C 364/01, www.europarl.europa.eu/charter/pdf/text_en.pdf (archived at https://perma.cc/9YWG-VYV9)

Field, Z (2012) Directorate-General for Translation (European Commission): How to write clearly, https://op.europa.eu/en/publication-detail/-/publication/bb87884e-4cb6-4985-b796-70784ee181ce/language-en (archived at https://perma.cc/M9T7-YB26)

GDD (2020) Gesellschaft für Datenschutz und Datensicherheit e.V.: Überarbeitetes Muster zur Auftragsverarbeitung gem. Art. 28 DS-GVO, www.gdd.de/wp-content/uploads/2023/06/GDD-Praxishilfe-DS-GVO-Mustervertrag-zur-Auftragsverarbeitung-gemaess-Art.-28-DS-GVO-Vers.-2.1.pdf also in English (archived at https://perma.cc/ZJF3-YT4N)

ICO (2022) Standard Data Protection Clauses to be issued by the Commissioner under S119A(1) Data Protection Act 2018, International Data Transfer Agreement, VERSION A1.0, in force 21 March 2022, https://ico.org.uk/media/for-organisations/documents/4019538/international-data-transfer-agreement.pdf (archived at https://perma.cc/P599-NX8E)

ICO (2023) UK Information Commissioner's Office: Transparency direct marketing detailed guidelines, https://ico.org.uk/for-organisations/advice-for-small-organisations/frequently-asked-questions/transparency-cookies-and-privacy-notices/ (archived at https://perma.cc/K3ZR-T7E5)

ICO (2023a) UK Information Commissioner's Office: Transparency (cookies and privacy notices), https://ico.org.uk/for-organisations/advice-for-small-organisations/frequently-asked-questions/transparency-cookies-and-privacy-notices/ (archived at https://perma.cc/K3ZR-T7E5)

legislation.gov.uk (2016) 'Regulation (EU) 2016/679 of the European Parliament and of the Council, 27 April 2016, www.legislation.gov.uk/eur/2016/679/contents (archived at https://perma.cc/NVG6-PXBQ)

Milgram, S (1969) The experience of living in cities, *Science* 167, 1461–1468

Simmel, G (1950) The metropolis and mental life, in K H Wolff (ed.), *The Sociology of Georg Simmel*, Free Press, New York, USA

7

Data protection requests

I was once at a conference of call centre agencies, companies that run call centres on behalf of brands, manning hotlines and customer service numbers. A now retired regulator and myself were the only ones presenting data protection topics there. All other presenters were sharing their best practices on how to prepare and train call centre agents. One speaker discovered that their induction training course doubled its effects when they followed it up with a mentorship programme, pairing experienced agents with newcomers. Another discussed IT systems that supported efficient routing of calls, and another logically structured scripts that improved the speed of call handling. The biggest emphasis of the conference, however, was on how to keep the employees happy. The amazing impact of creating attractive lounge areas and team-building trekking trips were some of the conversations that captured participants' attention, leading the conversation to continue at the dinner table. Why are preparation and happy employees so important to call centre agencies? Customers calling hotlines usually have problems, and some let out their frustrations on the agents. The only way to help the callers is to remain professional and correct but empathetic, regardless of the callers' attitude. When employees are well prepared and have a gentle smiles on their faces, they are ready to lend their helping hands, even to the grumpiest callers. In this chapter, we discuss the data protection rights of your customers, and how you can prepare to correctly handle the requests when they come in.

What data protection rights do your customers have?

We all have seven different types of rights under GDPR.

1 Right to be informed
2 Right to rectification

3 Right to erasure

4 Right to restrict processing

5 Right to data portability

6 Right to object and rights related to automated to individual decision making, including profiling

7 Right to data access

These rights are listed under Chapter 3 of GDPR titled 'Rights of Data Subjects' (legislation.gov.uk, 2016). Since we have already extensively covered the right to be informed, especially on the topic of privacy statements, this chapter will focus on the six remaining rights.

The general flow of handling data protection requests

The general flow of handling data protection requests is as follows:

Step 1: Keep a record of when the request was received by your organization

Step 2: Check the identity of the requestor

Step 3: Search if your organization has any data about the requestor

Step 4: If the data of the requestor is kept by your organization, action the request

Step 5: Inform what has been actioned, and provide a copy of personal data if a Subject Access Request (SAR) was raised

Step 6: Archive the correspondence

To carry out these steps, appropriate infrastructure, as well as a robust organizational structure, must be in place. Training and template documents will also help your company to respond to data protection requests effectively. In the following section, I will discuss what is generally expected from your organization when a data protection query from your customer is raised.

General considerations of data subjects' rights

Before diving into the details of the rights, let me begin by highlighting some norms that need to be respected when your customers exercise their data protection rights.

Verification of identity (related to Article 12(6) GDPR)

Data subjects' rights are personal rights. It is therefore appropriate to ensure that the person exercising the data protection rights is indeed the person the requestor claims to be. Hence, one of the first actions after receiving a data protection request is to confirm the identity of the requestor.

In the spirit of helping customers with their data protection rights, a telecommunication company disclosed quite some personal data over the phone, where the only information to verify the identity was orally provided names and date of birth. This proactiveness backfired and the disclosing of personal data was labelled a security breach (BfDI, 2019). The lesson here is, even if you think it would irritate the already irritated customer further, verifying the identity is a must.

Confirming the identity is also important to find out where best to send the SAR response. There are several methods to transmit the information to the right person. If your company has an online log-in section, like a customer account page, this may be a good place to deliver your response.

Another rudimentary way may be to ask for the names and addresses and send the SAR and other responses by post to that address. The assumption here is that if the customer lives there, then the letter you send should reach that person. If not, it will be returned to you with an 'Unknown Recipient' stamp on it.

Since sending an email is more cost-efficient and faster, your organization might want to respond to the data access request by email instead. In that case, some kind of a link between an email address and the person needs to be established, because email addresses can be created quite easily. It sounds a bit disproportionate to ask for a copy of an ID card or a passport to prove identity, particularly if the only data you have is about preferences and contact details for marketing purposes. That's why many companies nowadays ask for a copy of a recent utility bill or something similar, where the person's name and address can be seen. Once you can establish that the sender of the email lives at the particular address, the email address can be associated with the person, and a copy of personal data can be sent via the email address provided.

Establishing the association between name plus address with email address can also be outsourced to an identity verification service provider. The advantage here is that the service company will take over the responsibility that your data protection correspondence is reaching the right person. The disadvantage is that using such a service may be pricey.

Manifestly unfounded or excessive requests (Article 12(5) GDPR)

The rights enshrined in chapter 3 of the GDPR must be fulfilled except when the request is either 'manifestly unfounded' or 'excessive'. Personally, I believe *manifestly unfounded behaviour* would rarely become a problem for marketers. The EDPB gives an example where someone puts forward an SAR to the wrong company. This can happen because some companies have similar names, or a group of companies have different subsidiaries carrying the same logo. If this is the case, a simple reply informing the requestor that they have contacted the wrong company will solve the situation (see EDPB, 2020, p 59).

The other case, *excessive* behaviour, is a little harder to deal with. There are two examples below, provided by the EU regulators (see EDPB, 2020, p 59).

The first example goes as follows:

- an individual makes a request, but at the same time offers to withdraw it in return for some form of benefit from the controller

I am guessing that some of you have received an email requesting data access, and at the same time offers not to do so if you pay a small fee; a fee small enough that it does not make sense for your organization to take legal action. Typically, these requests end with a line that says they will go to the regulator and complain, and that GDPR can carry a maximum fine of 4 per cent of your global annual turnover.

This is another example given by the regulator:

- the request is malicious in intent and is being used to harass the controller or its employees with no other purposes than to cause disruption, for example, based on the fact that:
  o the individual has explicitly stated, in the request itself or other communications, that it intends to cause disruption and nothing else; or
  o the individual systematically sends different requests to a controller as part of a campaign, e.g. once a week, with the intention and the effect of causing disruption.

No doubt, some people are very upset that your marketing department is using data about them to support the revenue growth of your company. As a side story, I once had a furious consumer on a phone. After making it clear that he was not fond of my employer, or the entire marketing services industry, he said, 'I know how to find you. Remember, accidents happen' and hung up the phone. The next morning, on my way to work, I had a flat tyre. The car dealership where my car was towed informed me that someone must have stabbed the tyre and that I must report the incident to the police. Was it a coincidence? These things do happen and I think the regulators recognize that data protection officers and other employees can be targets of harassment. While it is caveated that exceptions must only apply in limited cases, if excessive behaviour is observed, companies are entitled to either refuse the request or charge a small fee.

In both cases of exemptions, the regulators do recommend everything be documented. Your organization is made accountable and would need to provide proof in case of a dispute.

MITIGATING MISUSE OF DATA SUBJECTS' RIGHTS AND THE DPDI BILL

Under the DPDI Bill, or better said under DPDI Act, UK marketers will be better protected from the misuse of the rights, SAR in particular. The DPDI Bill replaces the expression 'manifestly unfounded' of Article 12 GDPR with 'vexatious and excessive'. The new UK data protection law explains that a request 'intended to cause distress', 'not made in good faith' or 'an abuse of process' may be considered vexatious. In addition, the DPDI Bill gives companies the opportunity to charge a fee to offset administrative costs associated with responding to a request, when the nature of the request is vexatious or excessive. These improvements will hopefully continue to allow genuine SAR and other requests while preventing organizations from falling victims of the abuse of legislation (UK Parliament, 2023).

CONSUMERS EXERCISING THEIR RIGHTS VIA AN ONLINE SAR PLATFORM

There are online service providers that offer to raise opt-out and SAR requests on the consumer's behalf. To my surprise, some of these service providers charge for their service, and, even more surprisingly, some consumers are paying them!

There are serious service providers who genuinely want to assist consumers and to make them more aware of their data protection rights. These are organizations that are very helpful in increasing data protection awareness among the general public. Unfortunately, some platforms clearly express their motivation of eradicating the marketing industry and global brands, appealing to consumers to join the movement. Those platforms weaponize SARs against the marketers.

The right to data protection is a very personal right. Whatever the motivation, if an online SAR platform is representing a consumer in exercising their rights, a proper authorization, such as a valid power of attorney, must be presented to your organization. Furthermore, the response does not have to be sent to the platforms as they would usually request. Instead, it can be sent directly to the consumer (see EDPB, 2020, p 30).

When sending the response back to consumers using SAR platforms, it would be best practice to inform them that in the future, they can directly contact your company and their SAR response will be provided to them free of charge, in line with GDPR.

Facilitating the data protection requests (Article 12(2) GDPR)

To marketers, maintaining positive relationships with customers and prospects is perhaps second nature. When receiving data protection requests, companies are expected to be helpful and proactive. The first sentence of GDPR's Article 12(2) says (legislation.gov.uk, 2016):

> The controller shall facilitate the exercise of data subject rights under Articles 15 to 22.

A well-known German commentator on data protection law, Professor Gola, suggests (1) appointing someone to be in charge of ensuring that the rights of customers can be exercised at your company, and (2) appointing a contact person that customers can go to for data protection requests, to efficiently facilitate the requests (see Gola, 2017, p 320, no. 13). Having an online contact form, or a link that opens up an email, addressed to your data protection team will also be very helpful for your customers.

Timing (Article 12(3) GDPR)

GDPR also sets a deadline for responding to data protection queries from your customers. In the first instance, a response as well as an action need to take place within a month. This can be further extended by two months, which may be necessary if providing a copy of personal data turns out to be laborious. If you do want to make use of an extension, you need to first inform the customer in question that your response will take longer and the reason why (legislation.gov.uk, 2016).

Also, make sure you record the moment you received the request, particularly when it comes by post. Get them time stamped as the date the request was received by your organization is when the clock starts ticking. The deadline can be put on hold, for instance, while you wait for the requestor to give you additional information necessary for verifying the requestor's identity (EDPB, 2020).

Lastly, responding to a data protection request usually involves not just the data protection and marketing departments, but many other parts of the organization too. This means there has to be a process in place to execute the request to send a response letter to the requestor on time.

Rights of data subjects in detail

As with the previous chapter, my focus in this section is on topics that are relevant to marketers. Needless to say, when your legal and privacy colleagues respond to data protection queries, they will also have to consider data uses that lay outside the realm of marketing, in areas such as finance, logistics and human resources.

Right to rectification (Article 16 GDPR)

Your customers are entitled to correct data, in line with the accuracy principle of the GDPR's Article 5(d) (legislation.gov.uk, 2016). In addition, people can complete incomplete data under the right to rectification. Interestingly, the definition of what accurate data is absent in GDPR. The UK Data Protection Act 2018 defines inaccurate data as data that is inaccurate or misleading (legislation.gov.uk, 2018). Using this definition, an incorrect email address is 'inaccurate', so a customer can request this to be corrected.

There are also cases where marketers believe that the information that is provided by the data subject, and not the information that the marketers have, is wrong. For instance, a cashmere product manufacturer receives a request to rectify incorrect information on the online account page. This customer claims that the discount code box on the account page, where you log in, should not be displaying 'used' because it did not work when using it to buy the company's bestselling cashmere scarf. Your accounting department checks this and confirms that the particular customer has used the discount code, and a reduced amount was charged as a result. In such cases, you can explain your findings in writing and tell the customer that you will not correct the data as requested (ICO, 2023).

It becomes slightly more complicated when customers complain about your opinion. Let me use a very unlikely, hypothetical example to explain this point. Let's say the same cashmere product manufacturer has assigned the customer segment 'winter sports enthusiast' to a particular customer. This customer gets to see advertising of this cashmere company, featuring people enjoying downhill skiing and snowboarding. Upon finding out about this segment assignment, the customer requests the incorrect information to be rectified, because another segment, 'fashion conscious', sounds more suitable to this person. Assignment of a segment is, in a way, the opinion of the marketing department. Since opinions are subjective, they cannot be inaccurate. (There is no such thing as an inaccurate opinion!) In this case, the cashmere company can explain that since the customer purchased four items from the winter sports line of products, the 'winter sports enthusiast' segment has been assigned as an appropriate way to describe this customer. The cashmere company's marketing department does not have to correct the assigned segment, because it is an opinion so it cannot be corrected. On the other hand, it might be a good idea to assign 'fashion conscious' to this person because tailoring communication based on affinity will also work. But that decision will be outside of data protection considerations.

The right to data rectification applies to all data that your company holds, including that on backups. I will elaborate on the topic of backup in the next section which discusses the right to erasure.

Right to erasure (Article 17, GDPR)

Your customers and prospects have the right to have their personal data deleted in the following situations (relevant points for marketing data use of Article 17(a) to (f) in a simplified manner) (legislation.gov.uk, 2016):

a. the personal data are no longer necessary;

b. the legal ground is Consent and the consent is withdrawn;

c. the legal ground is Legitimate Interest and the legitimate interest of the customers or prospects weighs more than that of the marketing department/company, or, there is an objection to personal data being used for marketing;

d. the personal data have been unlawfully processed;

e. the personal data have to be erased for compliance with a legal obligation;

f. the personal data have been collected to offer information society services, such as social media, to a child.

When responding to data erasure requests, it is important to inform the requestor that, even after all data are erased, the correspondence between the customer and your organization will be kept for a certain period. The period may vary depending on the legal requirements of the country.

PERSONAL DATA IN YOUR BACKUP

To respect the right to erasure, all data relating to the customer raising this request must be erased. Requesting backup data to be erased will most likely raise the eyebrows of your IT and security colleagues. However, thankfully, the UK ICO adds some additional nuances to interpret this requirement. According to the ICO, the key to honouring the right to erasure is to ensure that data is put beyond use, within a month (ICO, 2023). That means if companies set their backup cycle to 28 days, newly created backups will replace the previous backups within the one-month-deadline, so there is no need to delete the data from the backup.

However, this poses another question. What if backups are not deleted every time a new backup is created? There may be situations where a full backup can only be made once a quarter, and incremental backups are created every day or even every hour. That's plenty of backup files to go through to see if that particular customer's record can be found. Also, usually, it is not easy, or even possible, to search through a backup file. You need to restore it first before searching the record, which means pouring in a lot of man-hours and processing capacity for fulfilling just one deletion request. Now imagine receiving several data erasure requests a day!

Searching for one record in a backup is bound to be a manual operation, which means it is prone to error. In the process of deleting one record, a record belonging to another customer can be accidentally altered or deleted. You can say that deleting records in the backup defeats the accuracy principle, as well as the integrity principle of the GDPR (see Article 5(1)d and 5(1)f respectively, as well as Article 32(2)) (legislation.gov.uk, 2016).

In examining the law text and regulators' recommendations closely, a different picture emerges. Both the ICO and the EDPB recognize that the right to erasure is not an absolute right (ICO, 2023; EDPB, 2020). Article 17(3)b even says that, if data erasure cannot be carried out because of other legal obligations, it is not necessary to fulfil the data deletion request. Since the operation of erasing data on a backup potentially conflicts with requirements under the GDPR itself, it can be argued that erasing data from a backup is not necessary. If you are going to argue that data in backups will not be erased, the explanation behind it must be documented and clearly communicated to the customer raising this request.

SUPPRESSION FILES

Another challenge of the data erasure right, particularly in marketing, is that organizations often acquire new files. If the data is deleted, there is a chance the data of the person who has just requested data erasure is included in that file. Let me explain with a short example. Samantha Satsuma from 25 Mozart Avenue requested that her data be deleted. So, you delete her record from your file. A few weeks later, your data supplier delivers a new batch of data, collected using Legitimate Interest. One of the records is from Samantha, but since you have deleted the data, there is no way for you to know that she requested data deletion. Samantha then gets a direct mail from you and becomes very irritated, remembers her right to complain to the regulator, and does just that. It is a bit of a dilemma because the deletion request is causing unwanted data use!

Maintaining a suppression file is an industry solution that has been around for more than 50 years. When new data arrives from suppliers and partners, the suppression file is used to filter out persons who have requested deletion or opted out from your marketing data use. The idea is to keep a minimum amount of information, just enough for you to identify the customer, or ex-customer, who has requested that you delete the data or no longer use the data. Indeed, suppression files are also used when the person objects to you using the data for marketing. I will discuss the topic of right-to-object processing later on in this chapter.

The legal ground for maintaining in-house suppression files can be based on Article 6(1)c 'processing is necessary for the compliance with a legal obligation to which the controller is subject', where the legal obligation is Article 21 of GDPR. Alternatively, it can be based on Article 6(1)f, Legitimate Interest, where your company's legitimate interest is to enable deletion or honour objection of data used by customers (legislation.gov.uk, 2016).

My way of dealing with this dilemma is to explain to the requestor that deleting all personal data will make it impossible to prevent new personal data from that person from flowing into our database when we get new data delivery. I then recommend that the request be changed, so that it is possible to save a minimum number of identifiers in the suppression file. If, however, the person insists on deletion, I respect that and delete the relevant personal data.

Right to restrict processing (Article 18 GDPR)

Customers and prospects can restrict the marketing department from processing the data when (legislation.gov.uk, 2016):

- the accuracy of the data is contested by a customer;
- data has been unlawfully processed and a customer wants data use to be restricted rather than deleted;
- the marketing department no longer needs the data but the customer needs you to keep it for a legal claim; or
- a customer objects to your marketing team using the data, but your team wants to evaluate if your company's legitimate grounds override those of the customer. (rephrased Article 18 GDPR).

When a customer requests to restrict the use of its personal data, all you can do is store the data, unless you have obtained consent for the purpose of using the record for a specific marketing use. Other conditions under Article 18 of GDPR can restrict the use of data, such as for legal claims, as mentioned above, but I am omitting it here as it is highly unlikely to be relevant in the marketing context (legislation.gov.uk, 2016).

Unlike other rights of data subjects, found in chapter 3 of GDPR, this right seems to be a temporary right, used until a definite decision is made on other issues. In terms of how to restrict data use, Recital 67 suggests that the relevant records be temporarily removed so that marketers and marketing data scientists cannot access the data, not even accidentally. When the decision is made, it is recommended that the restriction on data processing be lifted (legislation.gov.uk, 2016).

In case the requester's data has been passed on to another organization, they need to be informed that that person's data cannot be used.

Right to data portability (Article 20 GDPR)

If you are using either Consent of Contract as your legal base, the data subject is given the right to data portability. Concretely, it means that all data given to your company by the requestor-customer needs to be transmitted back to that person. You must know someone who was stuck with a particular music streaming service provider due to the fear of losing the playlist cultivated over the years. Well, this right was originally designed to promote platform interoperability, so that consumers can, for instance, switch more easily between streaming services (OECD, 2021).

Article 20 also specifies that data must be packaged in a 'structured, commonly used and machine-readable format' (legislation.gov.uk, 2016). Let us take a quick look at what this means. The ICO often turns to the Open Data Handbook when it comes to computing terminologies. According to this handbook, 'structured data' and 'machine readable' are explained as follows (Open Knowledge Foundation, 2023):

> **Structured data** – All data has some structure, but 'structured data' refers to data where the structural relation between elements is explicit in the way the data is stored on a computer disk. XML and JSON are common formats that allow many types of structures to be represented. The internal representation of, for example, word-processing documents or PDF documents reflects the positioning of entities on the page, not their logical structure, which is correspondingly difficult or impossible to extract automatically.
>
> **Machine readable** – Data in a data format that can be automatically read and processed by a computer, such as CSV, JSON, XML, etc. Machine-readable data must be structured data. Compare human-readable.
>
> Non-digital material (for example, printed or hand-written documents) is by its non-digital nature not machine-readable. But even digital material need not be machine-readable. For example, consider a PDF document containing tables of data. These are definitely digital but are not machine-readable because a computer would struggle to access the tabular information – even though they are very human-readable. The equivalent tables in a format such as a spreadsheet would be machine-readable.
>
> As another example, scans (photographs) of text are not machine-readable (but are human-readable!) but the equivalent text in a format such as a simple ASCII text file can [sic] machine-readable and processable.
>
> Note: The appropriate machine-readable format may vary by type of data – so, for example, machine-readable formats for geographic data may differ from those for tabular data.

That makes 'structured, commonly used and machine-readable format' understood as .cvs, .xml or .json files but not .pdf, .docx or .xlsx files.

In addition to the format, the requestor reserves the right to ask you to transfer the file to another organization, perhaps even to your competitor.

Remember, when Legitimate Interest is your legal ground, this requirement does not apply!

Right to object and rights related to automated decision making including profiling (Article 21 and Article 21(2) GDPR)

The right to object can be considered as some sort of veto that can stop marketers from using their data for marketing purposes. It can be a blanket 'no' or a more nuanced refusal for particular purposes. For marketing data use, this right is more or less absolute and has to be honoured at any time. I am highlighting the objection to using profiling in this section because in marketing, lots of 'profiles' are used. Even though the automatic decisions are made using profiles, i.e. customer segments and attributes, that do not lead to serious harm, once there is an objection, the use of profiles must stop. That means no more tailoring messages to this person and instead communicating 'default ad', whatever that is, to this customer. However, if the data is used in the context of scientific research or for statistical purposes, such as for market research, it is less clear to what extent the right to object is valid.

Right to access (Article 15 GDPR)

Article 15 and the right to access data, or Subject Access Request (SAR) as privacy professionals refer to it, is the cornerstone of data protection, and an enabler of informational self-determination. The objective of this right, as stated in Recital 63 of GDPR, is to allow data subjects to be aware of and verify the lawfulness of the processing. For marketers and data protection officers, on the other hand, this right presents a challenge. It also represents a big chunk of work for the regulators. According to the 2023 annual report of the ICO, more than a third of all cases they received were about SAR (ICO, 2023a). Article 15 gives customers the right to receive, among other things, a copy of their personal data as well as specific information about it. However, the right to data access is, as many other rights are, not an absolute right, according to Recital 5 of GDPR (legislation.gov.uk, 2016). The EDPB's guidance document on the right of data access says that even this cornerstone right must be balanced against other fundamental rights, which include the freedom to conduct business which is strongly related to marketing (EDPB, 2020). Similarly, exemptions to the SAR must be considered when it can disadvantage the rights and freedoms of others. That is why, when providing a copy of the data, the documents may have to be redacted so that trade secrets and other sensitive information are not exposed.

PROVIDING A COPY OF ALL DATA

When GDPR speaks of *providing a copy of personal data undergoing processing*, it literally means all personal data; from email exchange to assigned RFM, structured as well as non-structured data. Yes, it means you not only need to check the CRM, campaign management systems, etc., but also your company's data lake.

To illustrate the extent of data you need to provide, in one ruling, the German Federal Court, the highest court in the country, judged that even personal notes written down about the data subject need to be provided under SAR (BGH, 2021). In another ruling, the European Court of Justice declared that answers to exams, and even comments of examiners, must be disclosed in full (ECJ, 2017). It needs to be noted that the access right is only extended to personal data, which means contracts or other supplementary documents usually do not have to be presented (ECJ, 2023).

In any case, the information that needs to be given to the requestor of SAR has dramatically broadened compared to the era of the 1995 Data Protection Directive. At the same time, GDPR waived the fee for data subjects under the 95 Directive, which organizations were allowed to charge for SARs. The UK Data Protection Act from 1998 allowed companies to charge a small fee of up to £10 for data subjects to get a SAR response (legislation.gov.uk, 1998; House of Commons, 2015). Fees charged for access requests in the Netherlands were also dropped with GDPR coming into effect (wetten.overheid.nl, 2018). Although these small sums for SARs did not make a big difference to organizations, financially, the change did make it easier for consumers to submit a SAR. As a result, the amount of work required in handling data access rights has increased in both quantity and breadth of information to be sent back to the requestor-customer. HR departments, rather than marketing, seem to have the broadest range of information to dig through for SAR; providing a copy of personal data for them means going through numerous emails and internal documents – and redacting them where necessary.

FIGURE 7.1   Hashed email with attributes

Hashed email	Degree of urbanisation	Car	Age	Nr. of website visit last week
3df39280a2eed1053681e 59c3ebc94ac8aea9dad 62986792e6cc09c471cd17d1	Suburban	Yes	45	10

DISCOVERING MORE INFORMATION RELATED TO A CUSTOMER

Sometimes, all that a marketer has are email addresses or other identifiers in a hashed format, with some values attributed to it (see Figure 7.1).

Under normal circumstances, you will not be able to find out to whom this record belongs, because the identifier, the email address, is hashed. Also, the attributes assigned to this email address are too generic, making it impossible for your marketing department or anyone else in your company to reveal the person behind this record. Then one day your customer, Samantha Satsuma from 25 Mozart Avenue, raises an SAR. In doing so, she provides you with her email address, ssatsuma@hello.com. You can now hash this email address the same way all other email addresses are hashed, and search in the hashed email database to see if there is a match with the hashed value of Samantha's email address (SHA256 hash: 3df39280a2eed1053681e59c3ebc94ac8aea9dad62986792e6cc09c-471cd17d1). If you find a matching record, you know that that hashed email and associated attributes are related to Samantha. You can now include all data associated with this record as well when providing a copy of all personal data relating to Ms Satsuma. Note that without Samantha giving you her email, this would not have been possible.

PROVIDING A COPY OF DATA IN THE BACKUP

As we discussed in the section on data erasure rights, going through backups is not a pleasant experience. For SAR, the EU regulators suggest personal data in the backup to be shared with the requestor when two conditions are met; (1) there is more information stored in the backup than in the live system and (2) it is technically feasible to provide access to the data in backup (EDPB, 2020). I noticed that in the EDPB guideline on SAR, the EU regulators are silent about the time, resources and effort required to retrieve the information. In any case, the suggestion here is to remain transparent about the data stored in the background, whether you provide a copy to them or not.

EXCEPTIONS TO THE RIGHT TO DATA ACCESS

Perhaps regulators have seen many organizations experiencing SARs that were problematic. One such situation is where a consumer sends the request to just anyone in the organization. It is usually quite easy to guess someone's business email address if you know the systematics of how they are generated. Say, Lucas Alberto from your marketing department spoke at the Marketing and AI Technology Conference. Your company, XYZ Ltd's website is www.xyz.co.uk. A frustrated and impatient customer can take a wild guess that sending an email to l.alberto@xyz.co.uk or lucas.alberto@xyz.co.uk might reach Lucas, and he can forward the SAR to the person in charge of responding to data protection queries. EU regulators take the position that a query sent to Lucas, who has nothing to do with SAR, does not have to be responded to, provided that the company provides clear information on where to send access requests. When, however, the SAR is sent to an info@ address, regulators expect your organization to respond to the request (EDPB, 2020).

Lastly, Recital 27 specifies that deceased persons do not have the right to data access because GDPR only applies to persons who are alive. EU member states can create exceptions to this rule. Italy, where the right to data protection of persons who have passed away has existed for a long time, continues this tradition. Persons such as heirs and executors or a representative, or someone who is safeguarding the deceased person or their family's interest, may request an SAR of the deceased unless this was explicitly refused by the deceased (Pinotti and Sforza, 2019).

Key takeaways

1 Data subjects, including your customers, have data protection rights they can exercise.

2 There are norms, including the verification of identity, which are helpful when data protection requests are made, and deadlines need to be observed.

3 Rights to rectification, portability, erasure, object and SAR are permanent in nature. The right to restrict processing is temporary.

4 When SAR is raised, copies of all personal data including emails and correspondences must be provided.

Conclusion

The right to data protection is a relative right that should be weighed against other rights. However, GDPR has stepped up the rights of data subjects so that customers can evaluate in much greater detail whether your company is using the data lawfully. There are practical challenges, such as data in backups, but there are also solutions like suppression files that marketers have been using for many decades. Responding to data protection requests from customers can be laborious and complicated. If you have this under control, then the risk of the issue escalating to the regulator will be minimized. Don't forget to document everything, be transparent with the enquiring customers and never forget to have a smile on your face. Being polite regardless of the situation will always help you in the long run!

Bibliography

BfDI (2019) BfDI verhängt Geldbußen gegen Telekommunikationsdienstleister, Pressemitteilung 30/2019, 9 December 2019, Bonn/Berlin, www.bfdi.bund.de/SharedDocs/Pressemitteilungen/DE/2019/30_BfDIverh%C3%A4ngtGeldbu%C3%9Fe1u1.html (archived at https://perma.cc/E2YX-L623)

BGH (2021) Bundesgerichtshof Urteil des VI. Zivilsenats vom 15.6.2021 – VI ZR 576/19, Verordnung (EU) 2016/679 Art. 15; BGB § 362 Abs. 1 Zur Reichweite des Auskunftsanspruchs nach Art. 15 Abs. 1 DS-GVO, https://juris.bundesgerichtshof.de/cgi-bin/rechtsprechung/document.py?Gericht=bgh&Art=en&Datum=Aktuell&Sort=8195&nr=119995&pos=27&anz=706 (archived at https://perma.cc/G4HB-CPC7)

curia.europa.eu (2017) European Court of Justice, Peter Nowak v Data Protection Commissioner, C-434/16, 22 June 2017, https://curia.europa.eu/juris/document/document.jsf?docid=198059&doclang=EN (archived at https://perma.cc/5JD4-TPLY)

curia.europa.eu (2023) European Court of Justice, CRIF GmbH v Österreichische Datenschutzbehörde, C-487/21, 4 May 2023, https://curia.europa.eu/juris/document/document.jsf?text=&docid=273286&pageIndex=0&doclang=EN&mode=req&dir=&occ=first&part=1&cid=4256058 (archived at https://perma.cc/DDE5-8J52)

EDPB (2020) European Data Protection Board Guidelines 01/2022 on data subject rights – Right of access, Version 2.0, adopted on 28 March 2023, https://edpb.europa.eu/our-work-tools/our-documents/guidelines/guidelines-012022-data-subject-rights-right-access_en (archived at https://perma.cc/R8BV-SP34)

Gola, P (2017) Datenschutz-Grundverordnung: VO (EU) 2016/679, Verlag C H Beck oHG, München, Germany

House of Commons (2015) The Department of Human Resources and Change and
Information Rights and Information Security (IRIS) Service, Data Protection Act
1998: Personal information about constituents and others, updated March
2015, www.parliament.uk/globalassets/documents/foi/Advice-for-Members-and-
Data-Protection-Feb15-WEB.pdf (archived at https://perma.cc/B6QG-WQDW)

ICO (2023) UK Information Commissioner's Office: A guide to individual rights,
19 May 2023, https://ico.org.uk/for-organisations/uk-gdpr-guidance-and-
resources/individual-rights/individual-rights/ (archived at https://perma.cc/
94BM-MAHN)

ICO (2023a) UK Information Commissioner's Office, Information Commissioner's
Annual Report and Financial Statements 2022/23, HC1440, 13 July 2023,
https://ico.org.uk/media/about-the-ico/documents/4025864/annual-report-
2022-23.pdf (archived at https://perma.cc/T6K9-Q3BD)

legislation.gov.uk (1998) Data Protection Act 1998, 16 July 1998, www.legislation.
gov.uk/ukpga/1998/29/section/7/1998-07-16 (archived at https://perma.
cc/9KNL-EAKY) (see section 7 Right of access to personal data)

legislation.gov.uk (2016) Regulation (EU) 2016/679 of the European Parliament
and of the Council, 27 April 2016, www.legislation.gov.uk/eur/2016/679/
contents (archived at https://perma.cc/3X7G-YPXR)

legislation.gov.uk (2018) Data Protection Act 2018, 23 May April, www.
legislation.gov.uk/ukpga/2018/12/contents/enacted (archived at https://perma.cc/
D7TB-P9S6)

OECD (2021) Data portability, interoperability and digital platform competition,
OECD Competition Committee Discussion Paper, http://oe.cd/dpic (archived at
https://perma.cc/8MBC-GDBG) www.oecd.org/daf/competition/data-portability-
interoperability-and-digital-platform-competition-2021.pdf

Open Knowledge Foundation (2023) Open Data Handbook, http://
opendatahandbook.org/glossary/en/ (archived at https://perma.cc/N4SV-5A4S)

Pinotti, V and Sforza, M (2019) GDPR Guide to National Implementation: Italy –
A practical guide to national GDPR compliance requirements across the EEA,
White & Case, 13 November 2019, www.whitecase.com/insight-our-thinking/
gdpr-guide-national-implementation-italy (archived at https://perma.cc/
H3XU-YEWJ)

UK Parliament (2023) Data Protection and Digital Information Bill, Government
Bill, Originated in the House of Commons, Sessions 2022–23, 2023–24, last
updated 12 February 2024 at 17:17, https://bills.parliament.uk/bills/3430
(archived at https://perma.cc/CJ4Z-YWYG)

wetten.overheid.nl (2018) Besluit kostenvergoeding rechten betrokkene Wbp,
Geldend van 01-07-2012 t/m 24-05-2018, Regeling vervallen per 25-05-2018,
https://wetten.overheid.nl/BWBR0012565/2012-07-01 (archived at https://
perma.cc/3QNX-QNCF)

8

Working with partners and suppliers

You may be able to guess it from my first name, I am Japanese. I have been living in Europe for many years, and incredibly, after all these years, I still get homesick. Over the years, I found out that the best way to recover from homesickness is through food. Food from home. One day, when I felt I missed 'home', I went to a speciality butcher selling Shimofuri Kobe beef, the kind my grandmother orders for her birthday. While I waited for my turn, I noticed a man sitting at a table, trying out one tiny piece of cooked meat after another. 'All right, next one', he would say after chewing through the pieces. It turned out that he was the big boss of the butcher, and he was checking the quality of the meat from his supplier. 'Many of our customers are famous restaurants. They buy our meat because the quality is consistently high. "Our supplier messed it up" is not an excuse.' That is exactly how it works with data protection, too. Your customers expect you to treat their data, even when you use external service providers to work on it, in a compliant manner. In this chapter, we look into the working relationships with partners and suppliers of marketing departments, and how the working relationships can be formalized to ensure your customer data is protected.

Partners and suppliers of marketing departments

Marketing departments have many partners they can potentially work with. Those who sell products and services to similar customers are all potential companies to do joint promotions with, like the automobile manufacturer and a classical music foundation I described in Chapter 4. It is also possible to team up with a company from your supply chain and present your customer with a packaged solution. For instance, a social media company can team up with an analytical software company and provide their customers with both audience selection and advanced measurement capabilities to differentiate themselves from other social media outlets.

Then there are suppliers. Your marketing department can be working with a wide variety of suppliers. Jobber and Ellis-Chadwick (2024) suggest that a marketing department can be functionally structured. Each such function, Search Engine Optimization, content, social media, paid media, (digital) marketing analytics and web development, can have suppliers assisting their activities.

In addition, marketing can make use of infrastructure suppliers, such as cloud hosting services, backup service providers and file transfer services, procured centrally on a corporate level.

Working with partners and suppliers that touch personal data requires formal agreements. Later on in this chapter, we will take a deep dive into contracts.

Working relationships from a data protection perspective

Let me do a quick recap of what we have covered in Chapter 3. There we discussed the concepts of controller, joint controller and processor. Controller determines the purposes and means of the processing of personal data. In other words, controllers are the first ones fingers will point to should anything go wrong with the processing. When more controllers together determine the purposes and means, then it means there is a joint controller arrangement. Processors do not determine the purposes and means. They work on the data on the controller's behalf, under their instructions. There are different constellations in which controllers and processors work together.

Controller-to-controller relationship

In a controller-to-controller relationship, two (or more) organizations work with a set of personal data independently from one another. Each company is accountable for its own processing activities. In examining whether an organization is a controller, EDPB suggests looking into who has determined 'why' the data has to be processed (purpose of processing) and 'how' the data shall be processed (means of processing) (EDPB, 2021, 14, No. 35).

When the organization determines the purposes and the means of processing, that organization is a controller.

For instance, when a marketing data supplier A Ltd licenses a list of dentists to a marketing department of a medical equipment company B Ltd, the personal data is transferred from A Ltd to B Ltd on a controller-to-controller basis. The marketer of the medical equipment company B Ltd can decide to use the data for contacting the dentists to promote the newly launched precision drill. B Ltd is hence a controller. The marketing data supplier A Ltd, on the other hand, continues to license the same file to other organizations so that they can generate revenue. Therefore, A Ltd is also a controller of the data, using the data independently from whatever B Ltd is doing with the list of dentists.

Joint controller

In addition to the short description provided in Chapter 3 regarding the joint controller, it should be pointed out that at times it requires careful analyses to differentiate a joint-controllership arrangement from that of a controller-to-processor arrangement. Regulators suggest starting by taking a closer look at the decision that is made, whether there is either a 'common decision' or a 'converging decision' between the organizations. When a common decision is made, there is a common intention between the companies, which leads to the decision. Converging decisions, on the other hand, do not need organizations to have a common intention. If they are in a situation where something cannot be achieved without the participation of the other company, there is a converging decision. The court cases in the box below will explain the two types of decisions within the legal context in greater detail. Interestingly, an organization can be a controller even without having access to data, as long as it is able to decide on the purposes and means of processing (curia.europa.eu, 2018).

JOINT-CONTROLLERSHIP RULINGS FROM THE COURT OF JUSTICE OF THE EUROPEAN UNION

There were so far three milestone rulings on the concept of controller and joint controller from the European Court of Justice. The first ruling relates to Wirtschaftsakademie Schleswig-Holstein GmbH, an institution that provides vocational education and training. The company created an online presence, called a 'fan page', on Facebook (curia.europa.eu, 2018). The second case that followed concerned a Finnish religious group, Jehovah's Witness Community and its members, regarding the data collected by members through door-to-door visits (curia.europa.eu, 2018). The third case again involves Facebook and relates to Fashion ID GmbH & Co. KG, an online fashion retail business. Fashion ID embedded a 'Like' button on Facebook, creating data traffic from their website to Facebook (curia.europa.eu, 2019).

Are these companies controllers?

Because the Wirtschaftsakademie ruling was there first, the other two rulings referenced this ruling, which in turn confirmed the first ruling multiple times. Before establishing whether organizations are joint controllers, the court examined in all cases whether the purpose and means of the processing were determined by the respective organizations. In terms of 'why' the data had to be processed, in the case of Wirtschaftsakademie it was most likely because the company wanted a social media presence for promotional and communication purposes. The court case, however, focused on the fact that they were able to access information about their visitors by using functions provided by Facebook. Wirtschaftsakademie achieved its goals by setting up a fan page on Facebook. The 'why' of the processing for the Jehovah's Witness Community was to spread their belief, and that of Fashion ID was to obtain more 'Likes'. In terms of deciding 'how' the data should be processed, Jehovah's Witness Community decided to have their members visit families door-to-door, and Fashion ID to embed the 'like' button on their website.

In assessing whether organizations were indeed determining the purposes and means of processing, the court focused on what was actually taking place rather than purely relying on contractual arrangements or the lack thereof. At first look, Wirtschaftsakademie appeared to be a mere user of the social media platform. They were nevertheless able to gain statistical insight into the visitors to their page, generated by using personal data, through the functions available to a fan page administrator. The Jehovah's Witness Community neither collected nor otherwise directly processed personal data collected by their members. Nevertheless, it was the Jehovah's Witness Community that orchestrated the door-to-door visits.

It is also noteworthy that none of the three organizations, Wirtschaftsakademie, Jehovah's Witness Community or Fashion ID, had access to the personal data concerned. For Wirtschaftsakademie and Fashion ID, only the social media platform had access to personal data, and as for Jehovah's Witness Community, they never received the data from the members. However, not having access to data did not deter these three organizations from determining the purposes and means for the processing, perhaps the most important criterion used for assessing whether an organization is a controller or not.

Joint participation in determining the purposes and means

When two organizations are joint controllers, they need to 'jointly determine the purposes and means of processing' (Article 26 GDPR) (legislation.gov.uk, 2016). For Jehovah's Witness Community, there is a common intention between the two parties, namely the Community and the members, so it is possible to see them as making a decision together; here, a 'common decision', a term coined by the EU regulators, was made. In the two other cases, Wirtschaftsakademie and Fashion ID, the two respective companies did not have common intentions with Facebook. Wirtschaftsakademie wanted fan page presence (and the statistical information of the visitors) and Fashion ID wanted more likes, neither of which can be considered interest for the social media platform. However, the court realized that without Wirtschaftsakademie participating in the processing, Facebook would have not been able to obtain new visitors from the educational institution's website to their platform. Without Fashion ID setting a like button, Facebook would not have received additional visitor traffic from Fashion ID's website. While the benefits sought by the companies differ, the purposes and means of processing in both cases complement each other. Or, to put it another way, without the participation of both companies, the processing would not have been possible. The EDPB calls such types of decisions 'converging decisions', and those making converging decisions of the purposes and means are joint controllers. That sounds as though the ruling has expanded the definition of joint controllers extensively.

Thankfully, the Advocate General of the European Court of Justice for the Fashion ID case recognized the existence of an 'overall chain of processing' that may exist in data use. He continued that, somewhere in that chain, a line must be drawn for organizations not to be party to the 'converging decision'. Here is the quote from the Advocate General's opinion on this topic (curia europa.eu, 2018a):

74. Furthermore, what about the other parties in a 'personal data chain'? When pushed to an extreme, if the only relevant criterion for joint control is to have made the data processing possible, thus in effect contributing to

that processing at any stage, would the internet service provider, which makes the data processing possible because it provides access to the internet, or even the electricity provider, then not also be joint controllers potentially jointly liable for the processing of personal data?

75. The intuitive answer is of course 'no'. The problem is that the delineation of responsibility so far does not follow from the broad definition of a controller. The danger of that definition being too broad is that it results in a number of persons being co-responsible for the processing of personal data.

Joint controllers can allocate different degrees of responsibilities

The Advocate General of the Wirtschaftsakademie case acknowledged that the existence of shared responsibility over the same data processing does not automatically mean the data protection obligations must be shared equally among the participating organizations. Rather, the level of responsibility related to data protection must be assessed for each circumstance and can be allocated as they are deemed acceptable (curia.europa.eu, 2017).

WHEN CAN AN ORGANIZATION CLEARLY BE A PROCESSOR AND NOT A JOINT CONTROLLER?

Unlike controller-to-controller and controller-to-processor arrangements, which we will discuss in the next section, the extent of responsibilities and hence the liability each company has over a single processing is unclear. Reflecting the unequal allocation of responsibility, drawing up fair liability clauses in a joint-controller agreement is not an easy task.

To marketers, I would like to make the following suggestions:

1 When you are using a service provider that is going to work with your customer data, make sure that this is contractually fixed, properly. Do not forget to check the actual workflow until you are satisfied that at no point the contractor will, for instance, create aggregated statistics for them to improve their production process (converging decision). This will make them a joint controller.

2 When working with partners, understand the overall data use and process flow. Identify which parts, if any, of the process can fall under joint controller. Make sure it is clear to all parties when the joint controllership starts and ends, or which exact part of the processing activities can fall under joint controllership.

Controller-to-processor

This arrangement is most commonly used by your marketing department when they use service providers. As discussed in Chapter 3, processors are bound by the instructions of the controller. This by default means that a processor is another company. Your marketing department instructing your engineering department does not constitute a controller-to-processor relationship between the two departments (EDPB, 2021, p 26, para 79). Where there is a controller-to-processor relationship, the processor must be acting on behalf of the controller. The regulators explain this as the processor serving someone else's (controller's) interest. When the marketing data files of your company are stored at an external backup service provider, your company is doing so mainly to have business continuity in case data is lost. The backup service provider does not benefit from your company's business continuity. They do the backup for your company, in exchange for a fee, which is their business model (EDPB, 2021).

Service providers to your marketing department must also strictly follow their instructions to be a processor. For instance, if the instruction to the service provider is 'calculate the possibility of churn, using file X', then that must be executed. To be realistic, there must also be a margin of manoeuvre for the processor. Your marketing department does not have to specify, for instance, which data analytics tool the service provider uses. They as a processor can choose if they use SAS or SPSS for analysing your marketing data. You can also let the service provider decide on detailed security measures. For instance, your marketers don't need to specify which password management program they use. Such practical measures taken by the processors are referred to as 'non-essential means of processing' about which processors can make their own decisions (EDPB, 2021).

On the other hand, your marketing department must decide and instruct the 'essential means' of processing, such as which records should be selected to be analysed by the service provider, or how long the service provider should keep the data.

Contractual arrangements

Contractual arrangements, alongside the factual working of processing, determine whether the working relationship your company has with a partner or a service provider is that of controller-to-controller, joint-controller or controller-to-processor. Becoming controllers or joint controllers will mean more data protection responsibilities for all companies involved, and hence more liability and work for both you and your partners and service providers. To begin with, your customers need to be informed that there is another company that is a joint controller. You would most probably need to update your data protection documents, such as the Records of Processing Activities and Legitimate Interest Assessments. We will discuss these documents in detail in Chapter 10.

Because GDPR does not specify a contractual arrangement for the controller-to-controller relationship, usually you will see a paragraph which covers data protection aspects, that data will be processed lawfully by both parties in a commercial agreement. Some indemnification wording is also common in such agreements. Some organizations, where they, for instance, perceive an elevated level of data protection risk, would insist on putting a controller-to-controller data protection agreement, which resembles the SCC and/or the IDTA for controller-to-controller construction.

For joint controller arrangements, the contracts must clearly state which party is responsible for what parts of the processing. For instance, it can be arranged so that your company will be responsible for responding to data protection requests, and the other controller will be responsible for informing the customers about the processing they are doing together.

Data protection agreement

In establishing a controller-to-processor relationship, there must be a data protection agreement. The first sentence of Article 28(3) of GDPR says so (legislation.gov.uk, 2016):

> Processing by a processor shall be governed by a contract or other legal act under Union or Member State law, that is binding on the processor with regard to the controller and that sets out the subject matter and duration of the processing, the nature and purpose of the processing, the type of personal data and categories of data subjects and the obligations and rights of the controller.

Data Protection Agreement, or DPA for short, must be specific. Having said that, risk-based approach can be applied to DPAs (EDPB, 2021). When the processing risk is low, the DPA does not have to be so detailed. I can only imagine how long and detailed DPAs for clinical trials must be, in comparison to DPAs we usually come across in the field of marketing.

GDPR lists information that needs to be contained in a DPA in Article 28(3) (legislation.gov.uk, 2016).

PROCESS DATA ONLY ON DOCUMENTED INSTRUCTION FROM THE CONTROLLER (ARTICLE 28(3)A GDPR)

The DPA with your service provider must clearly state that the service provider, be it a company analysing customer data of your marketing department or cloud hosting company, is handling your data on your company's behalf. With this clarification, the working relationship between your company and the service provider is clear that it is controller-to-processor.

This section of GDPR also specifies that the instruction must be documented. However, it does not mean that all the detailed instructions have to be in the contract. Rather, a DPA can set out an overall instruction of what your marketing department wants the supplier to do to the data. DPA is often an addendum to the main commercial agreement with the supplier. For that reason, the scope of services, durations of the contract, price etc. are usually in the main commercial contract.

GDPR's Article 28(3)a also states that the requirements for transferring data outside of the EU or the UK, depending on where you are based, must be specified in the DPA.

CONFIDENTIALITY OF PROCESSING (ARTICLE 28(3)B GDPR)

Your DPA must bind your service provider to confidentiality. Employees of your service provider who handle your marketing data must have signed a confidentiality agreement that prohibits them from disclosing your data or any other information related to it without authorization. Many service providers either have such a clause integrated into their employment contract or have a separate employment agreement addendum to this effect. Contractors must also commit to the same level of formal confidentiality.

SECURITY PRECAUTIONS (ARTICLE 28(3)C GDPR)

It may sound obvious, but there must be a section on security requirements in the DPA with your company's service provider. This is important because it is ultimately your company that is accountable for how the service provider protects your customer data. The EDPB expects a certain degree of detail to be included in the DPA (EDPB, 2021).

In Germany, many companies were using a similar structure in listing out security measures in detail in a special section of a DPA, even before GDPR came into force. The descriptions of the security measures were referred to as TOMs, short for Technical and Organizational Measures, or *Technische und organisatorische Maßnahmen* in German, and it seems like this term is spreading.

Today, TOMs are usually found as an appendix of the DPA and are expected to contain the following details (eur-lex.europa.eu, 2021):

- measures of pseudonymization and encryption of personal data
- measures for ensuring ongoing confidentiality, integrity, availability and resilience of processing systems and services
- measures for ensuring the ability to restore the availability and access to personal data in a timely manner in the event of a physical or technical incident
- processes for regularly testing, assessing and evaluating the effectiveness of technical and organizational measures in order to ensure the security of the processing
- measures for user identification and authorization
- measures for the protection of data during transmission
- measures for the protection of data during storage
- measures for ensuring physical security of locations at which personal data are processed
- measures for ensuring events logging
- measures for ensuring system configuration, including default configuration
- measures for internal IT and IT security governance and management
- measures for certification/assurance of processes and products
- measures for ensuring data minimization
- measures for ensuring data quality
- measures for ensuring limited data retention
- measures for ensuring accountability
- measures for allowing data portability and ensuring erasure

OUTSOURCING BY SERVICE PROVIDERS (ARTICLES 28(3)D AND 28(4) GDPR)

The DPA with your service provider must say that if the service provider intends to outsource any of the processing of your data to another company, or sub-processor, your company must be informed about it and approve the use of that sub-processor. The approval can be given to specific sub-processors or your company can give general approval. Either way, the contract should clearly state that intended changes to sub-processors have to be notified to your company. This way, your company will have the chance to decide if a particular sub-processor is acceptable or not.

Furthermore, the DPA with your service provider must also state that they put a DPA between them and the sub-processor, which contains the same protection obligations as specified in the DPA between your company and the service provider. In the DPA with your service provider, it must say that they, and not your company, are liable in case the sub-processor fails to comply with data protection obligations.

DUTY TO ASSIST WITH DATA SUBJECTS' REQUESTS (ARTICLE 28(3)E GDPR)

Because your company can receive a data protection request from your customers, which requires the help of your service provider, the DPA must state that your service-provider-processor must assist in responding to these requests when you need them. For instance, you might need the help of a measurement company, your processor, if they hold any information about a particular customer who is raising an SAR. Sometimes you might find out that data was processed in an unexpected manner, and you need help from your service provider to assist in finding out what went wrong with the processing. In any case, most of the time, when you need your service provider's assistance, it will be about asking for information or data from them. This needs to happen promptly so that you can respond to your customer's data protection queries within a month.

Since the responsibilities related to your customers' rights stay with your company, the controller, fixing appropriate assistance contractually is very important.

DETAILS ON HOW THE SERVICE PROVIDER MUST HELP WITH YOUR COMPANY'S EFFORT TO ENSURE COMPLIANCE (ARTICLE 28(3)F GDPR)

In your DPA, you also need a section that commits your service provider to support your organization in three other situations. Firstly, your service provider must be contractually bound to assist your company in adopting adequate TOMs to ensure data security. Secondly, in case of data breach notification, your service provider must assist your organization so that all the obligations are met. As an example, when your service provider falls victim to a cyber-attack, and your data is affected, the service provider must provide all necessary information so that you can report it in a compliant manner. Thirdly, your processor must help where you need to carry out a data protection impact assessment. Your marketer may be interested in new ways of measuring the effects of campaigns by using pedestrian traffic measurement tools in front of all of your company's retail outlets in the country. The service provider of the measurement tool must provide the necessary information for your organization to carry out a proper assessment. Similarly, the DPA with your service provider must state that in case your company decides to solicit the opinion of the competent data protection authority, the service provider must assist.

DELETE OR RETURN ALL DATA AT THE END OF SERVICE PROVISION (ARTICLE 28(3)G GDPR)

The DPA must state how the data will be handled once the engagement of the service provider comes to an end. Your company can decide if the entrusted personal data must be deleted or returned to you. In doing so, your company's processor must carry out the deletion or physically send back the data in a secure manner.

In my experience, deletion is more common nowadays, because the method of transfer has changed over the years. In bygone years, data was transported on CD-ROMs, DVDs and external hard drives. Nowadays, file transfers are usually carried out online.

RIGHT TO CHECK AND AUDIT (ARTICLE 28(3)H GDPR)

The DPA with your service provider must have a clause that allows you to obtain information so that your company can find out whether the processor is protecting your data as they have contractually agreed. The actual wording in GDPR is 'makes available to the controller all information necessary to demonstrate compliance with the obligations laid down in this Article and allow for and contribute to audits, including inspections, conducted by the controller or another auditor mandated by the controller' (legislation.gov.uk, 2016).

However, auditing is time-consuming, perhaps more so for your organization than the service provider. In case this has to be a physical audit, your company may even have to send someone to the service provider's offices and inspect activities in person. Even if travelling is not necessary, going through the information provided by your service provider's IT department, for instance, is time-consuming. Hence it is a relief that GDPR does not say controllers must carry out an audit! The form of how to control the adherence of the processor to an agreed level of data protection is not fixed.

Having said that, the DPA must provide the possibility for your company to conduct a full audit in case you wish to do so.

In practice, you may send a questionnaire at a regular interval, say once a year, to your service provider and request they fill it out. Your data protection department or compliance department can then go through the responses. As a side note, that is why it is always great if the service provider can provide a certificate issued by an auditing organization that can demonstrate their compliance that way. It saves your data protection and compliance departments a lot of time and work.

Large service providers nowadays have a clause in the DPA that says your company will appoint a specific auditor who will provide you with audit results. Theoretically, organizations can decide whether or not to use the auditor presented by the service provider. Practically, if you lack the bargaining power, you may have no choice but to accept the suggested auditor.

Lastly, your company's negotiation power will determine who will pay for the audit.

STANDARD CONTRACTUAL CLAUSES, INTERNATIONAL DATA TRANSFER AGREEMENT AND THE ADDENDUM (ARTICLE 46(2)D GDPR, S119A(1) DATA PROTECTION ACT 2018)

In Chapter 6 we discussed data transfer or restricted transfer to third countries, where I mentioned that official template contracts, International Data Transfer Agreement (IDTA) and the Addendum and the standard contractual clauses (SCCs), are widely used as legal instruments for this purpose (eur-lex.europa.eu, 2021; ICO, 2022).

The SCC of the EU contains several modules and users can choose the one that suits their particular situation:

Module 1: Controller-to-controller transfer (your organization is controller, company abroad is controller)

Module 2: Controller-to-processor transfer (your organization is controller, company abroad is processor)

Module 3: Processor-to-sub-processor transfer (your organization is processor, company abroad is sub-processor)

Module 4: Processor-to-controller transfer (your organization is processor, company abroad is controller)

IDTA requires the status of the exporter and importer, meaning controller, processor or sub-processor, to be clarified at the beginning of the agreement.

Nowadays, we see service provider companies that incorporate SCC and IDTA in the DPA. Such contracts will simply state that SCC or IDTA will apply to the DPA in case personal data is sent from the EU or the UK to a third country for processing.

It would then go on to explain how the blank text boxes in SCC or IDTA should be filled out, for instance, that your company is the data exporter and that the service provider is the data importer, or who the sub-processors are and so on.

When signing such a DPA, it is important to ensure that the contract says where there is a conflict between the DPA, the main commercial contract and the SCC or IDTA, that the clauses of the SCC or IDTA prevail.

Another trend is for service providers, mostly those based outside of the UK and EU, to make DPA, SCC and IDTA available on their website, sometimes even with the signature of an authorized signatory. If the service provider which your marketing department wants to use provides this service, download this, review it and, if there is nothing you feel has to be negotiated, countersign and archive this.

Key takeaways

1 Working relationships with partners and data suppliers can be categorized into controller-to-controller, joint-controller or controller-to-processor relationships.

2 Joint-controller arrangements are more difficult than controller-to-controller or controller-to-processor constructions.

3 When using a service provider, it is essential to have a robust DPA. The required content of such DPA is listed in Article 28(3) of GDPR.

4 When your partner or service provider is located in a third country, you must ensure that the data can be transferred in a compliant manner. SCC for the EU or IDTA for the UK are standard contracts that can be used as legal instruments for transferring your customer data to third countries.

Conclusion

Marketers might have many opportunities to work with partners and service providers. When working together with external organizations, the working relationship with those organizations must be clearly defined. In whichever constellation your organization is working, being controller or joint controller will allocate the bulk of data protection responsibilities. In a joint-controller arrangement, your company can decide with the other company who is responsible for what, and allocate the data protection responsibilities accordingly. Depending on the situation and negotiation power, this may be challenging. When appointing a service provider as a processor, a robust DPA must be in place, which allows your company as the controller to ensure that the data protection obligations are met at your processor's end. When data is transferred to a third country, your company can use SCC for the EU and IDTA for the UK, contractual templates for data transfer issued by the EU Commission and the ICO respectively.

Bibliography

curia.europa.eu (2017) In Case C-210/16, Request for a preliminary ruling under Article 267 TFEU from the Bundesverwaltungsgericht (Federal Administrative Court, Germany), made by decision of 25 February 2016, received at the Court on 14 April 2016, in the proceedings Unabhängiges Landeszentrum für Datenschutz Schleswig-Holstein v Wirtschaftsakademie Schleswig-Holstein GmbH, https://curia.europa.eu/juris/document/document.jsf?text=&docid=-202543&pageIndex=0&doclang=en&mode=lst&dir=&occ=first&part=1&cid=11565657 (archived at https://perma.cc/N5B9-9REM)

curia.europa.eu (2018) Tietosuojavaltuutettu v Jehovan todistajat — uskonnollinen yhdyskunta, Case C-25/17, ECLI:EU:C:2018:551, Judgment of the Court (Grand Chamber), 10 July 2018, https://curia.europa.eu/juris/document/document.jsf?pageIndex=0&docid=203822&doclang=EN&text=&cid=2758546 (archived at https://perma.cc/5BM9-PS3L)

curia.europa.eu (2018a) Fashion ID GmbH & Co. KG v Verbraucherzentrale NRW eV, Case C-40/17, ECLI:EU:C:2019:629, Opinion of advocate general Bobek, 19 December 2018, https://curia.europa.eu/juris/document/document.jsf?text=&docid=209357&pageIndex=0&doclang=en&mode=lst&dir=&occ=first&part=1&cid=2758217 (archived at https://perma.cc/CWF5-87ZT)

curia.europa.eu (2019) Fashion ID GmbH & Co. KG v Verbraucherzentrale NRW eV, Case C-40/17, ECLI:EU:C:2019:629, Judgment of the court (Second

Chamber), 29 July 2019, https://curia.europa.eu/juris/document/document.
jsf?text=&docid=216555&pageIndex=0&doclang=en&mode=lst&dir=&occ=fi
rst&part=1&cid=2758217 (archived at https://perma.cc/2285-QBH6)

EDPB (2021) European Data Protection Board Guidelines 07/2020 on the concepts
of controller and processor in the GDPR, Version 2.1, adopted on 7 July 2021,
https://edpb.europa.eu/our-work-tools/documents/public-consultations/2020/
guidelines-072020-concepts-controller-and_en (archived at https://perma.
cc/7EYJ-GLRF)

eur-lex.europa.eu (2021) Standard Contractual Clauses implemented by the
Commission Implementing Decision (EU) 2021/914 of 4 June 2021 on standard
contractual clauses for the transfer of personal data to third countries pursuant
to Regulation (EU) 2016/679 of the European Parliament and of the Council, 7
June 2021, https://eur-lex.europa.eu/eli/dec_impl/2021/914/oj (archived at
https://perma.cc/6LCX-6F99)

ICO (2022) Information Commissioner's Office: International data transfer
agreement and guidance, 2 February 2022, https://ico.org.uk/for-organisations/
uk-gdpr-guidance-and-resources/international-transfers/international-data-
transfer-agreement-and-guidance/ (archived at https://perma.cc/7V7S-WN2M).
IDTA and the Addendum is also available from this link as download files.

Jobber, D and Ellis-Chadwick, F (2024) *Principles and Practice of Marketing*,
McGraw Hill, Maidenhead, p 856

legislation.gov.uk (2016) Regulation (EU) 2016/679 of the European Parliament
and of the Council, 27 April 2016, www.legislation.gov.uk/eur/2016/679/
introduction (archived at https://perma.cc/FCA8-FS47)

9

Data security

I have an extremely confidential piece of information on a particular sheet of paper. This A4-sized paper contains a list of Christmas presents I plan to give to my family members. To make sure that no one gets access to this information, I have hidden it in my home office, in the cupboard next to my desk. There you find a chunky English dictionary. When you open the page where 'Christmas' is listed, you will find my precious list, carefully folded into two. But what if my children or my other half comes to look something up in an analogue dictionary? Arguably, the risk is small, but I am not taking any chances. I have a secret language called Japanese. My family might find that piece of paper, but all they will see will be タータンチェックの野球帽 and 腕時計, which are basically hieroglyphs to them. Thanks to this, my family enjoys wonderful moments exchanging gifts every Christmas. Just writing about this makes me grin, imagining the surprised faces and a burst of laughter, surrounded by the green scent of the Christmas tree and the obligatory mulled wine. This motivates me to conceal this highly sensitive information even more! In this chapter, we will discuss how companies and their marketing department can protect their secrets, and their data, so that they too can bring a smile to their customers' faces.

Understanding information security

In some games, you have this 'get out of jail card'. With these cards, you can avoid missing out on a round of games. What if I said GDPR has something similar? It is called data security. The GDPR provisions for data security are in line with the risk-based approach embedded in law, where risk is minimized, and more flexibility is given to controllers. For instance, when regulators decide on fines, they must take security measures companies have put in place to protect the data into consideration (see Article 83(2)c of GDPR) (legislation.gov.uk, 2016). Say your laptop is stolen. If it was encrypted, you do not need to inform your customers that there was a data breach. Not having to inform your customers saves the brand image your marketing department has been building for years. That is one reason why data security is such an important discipline. Many organizations have a separate security department and a Chief Information Security Officer who heads the functional areas. Those marketers who had security incidents published by news outlets must know how life-saving security colleagues can be in times of need.

Definition of information strategy

The word data security is not found in Article 4 of GDPR, the article where definitions are listed. Instead, the word 'security' appears in Article 5 where the basic premises of the data protection law are described. In other words, data security is one of the main principles of the GDPR, 'integrity and confidentiality'. GDPR expects organizations to ensure the prevention of unauthorized or unlawful processing, accidental loss, destruction or damage of data as one of the starting points for protecting personal data. TOMs must be implemented to this end so that the integrity and confidentiality of the data are protected (Article 5(f) GDPR) (legislation.gov.uk, 2016).

Outside of GDPR, information security is defined as follows:

Information security is the safeguarding of information and information systems against deliberate and unintentional unauthorized access, disruption, modification and destruction by external or internal actors. (Gartner, Inc., 2023)

Information security is the technologies, policies and practices you choose to help you keep data secure. (gov.uk, 2018)

Information security: The protection of information and information systems from unauthorized access, use, disclosure, disruption, modification, or destruction in order to provide confidentiality, integrity, and availability. (NIST, 2023)

Approach to information security

Just as marketing professionals created strategic frameworks – 4Ps, 7Ps, 4Cs and so on – so the school of information security strategy has come up with frameworks – the CIA triad and the Parkerian Hexad. CIA stands for

Confidentiality, Integrity and Availability. Donn Parker, a security consultant, later expanded this framework with three more elements, namely Utility, Authenticity and Possession. Below is a brief description of the six aspects of the Parkerian Hexad (Bosworth et al, 2009).

AVAILABILITY

Availability refers to the ability of the organization to access data. When, for instance, there is a loss of power and your marketers cannot access customer data, it is considered an availability problem. The file is there, so it is not stolen. However, the marketer is temporarily unable to access the particular data.

UTILITY

Utility of the Parkerian Hexad relates to the problem of losing the usefulness of the data. For instance, if a campaign manager loses the encryption key to the data, the data is still there, and it can be accessed. However, the data cannot be used because the emails needed for carrying out an email campaign are encrypted so they are useless.

INTEGRITY

Maintaining integrity refers to preventing unauthorized changes to the data. For instance, if an intern of the marketing department accidentally deletes the field 'purchased more than two items' within the dataset, this is an integrity-related security incident. If the manager of the intern can undo the deletion of the field, then the integrity of the data is intact. Typically, integrity is maintained by assigning different access rights, such as read-only access for interns and read-and-write access for the marketing manager.

AUTHENTICITY

Authenticity relates to the attribution of data or information to the rightful owner or the creator of that data or information. Imagine a situation where your advertising agency, acting as your data service provider, receives a fake email which instructs them to delete all your customer data. The agency might think that it is a genuine instruction from your company, and executes the command. This is then an authenticity problem.

CONFIDENTIALITY

When someone unauthorized gets access to a particular marketing analytic file, confidentiality is being breached.

POSSESSION

The Parkerian Hexad uses the term possession to describe situations where data or information is stolen. For instance, a malevolent employee of the marketing department downloads all the sales contact information to a mobile device and then deletes them from the network. This is a possession problem.

Risk management

In addition to understanding the problems you are facing, using the Parkerian Hexad, your organization must know the potential security risks for the business. Andress suggests a useful and generic five-step risk management process, for a variety of situations (Andress, 2019).

STEP 1: IDENTIFY ASSETS

Before your organization can start managing your marketing department's risks, you need to map out all data assets belonging to your marketing department. In doing so, all data, some distributed in different systems or entrusted to service providers, must be accounted for. Once this exercise is completed, your marketing department can determine which data files are the most critical. RoPA with all processes of personal data mapped out can be leveraged for this exercise.

STEP 2: IDENTIFY THREATS

For all data files and processes identified in the previous step, potential threats are determined. This may mean holding a brainstorming session with marketers and security and data protection departments to go through the data and processes one by one. The Parkerian Hexad from the previous section can be a great help in guiding through such sessions. It will also be helpful to identify the most critical data and processes during this exercise.

STEP 3: ASSESS VULNERABILITIES

In this step, for each data-use surfaced in Step 2, relevant threats are identified. In doing so, the context of your organization's operation, products and services sold, vendor relations as well as the physical location of the company premises are considered.

STEP 4: ASSESS RISKS

In this step, the threats and vulnerabilities for each data and process are compared and assigned risk levels. Vulnerabilities with no corresponding threats or threats with no associated vulnerabilities will be seen as not having any risk.

STEP 5: MITIGATE RISKS

For the risks that surfaced in Step 4, measures necessary to prevent them from occurring will be determined during this stage. Andress identifies three types of controls that can be used for this purpose. The first type of control, logical control, protects the IT environment for processing your customer data, such as password protection and the placing of firewalls. The second type of control is administrative control, which is usually deployed in the form of corporate security policy, which the organization can enforce. The last type of control is physical control. As the name suggests, this type of control protects the business premises and makes use of tools such as CCTV, keycard-operated doors, fire alarms and backup power generators.

With the time, risks may change. For instance, your marketing department may be physically relocated to a new building, changing the physical security needs, or your company might decide to migrate from a physical server to a cloud-based hosting service, which means your customer data will have to move too. Both such situations necessitate a new round of the risk management process to kick off. In general, it is advisable to revisit the risk management process on a regular interval, say annually, to keep your company on top of all risks your marketing department, and beyond, carry.

Approaching risk management with Three Lines of Defence

Institute of Internal Auditors (IIA) established a risk management model called Three Lines of Defence. The model requires three internal roles, (1) the governing body, with oversight of the organization, (2) senior management, which takes risk management actions and reports to the governing body, and (3) internal audit, which provides independent assurance, to work together and act as robust protections to the organization (IIA, 2020).

The elements of the Three Lines of Defence are (IIA, 2020):

First line of defence: Manage risks associated with day-to-day operational activities. Senior management has the primary responsibility, and emphasis is put on people and culture. Marketing managers' task here is to make sure that their department is aware of data protection risks, including security risks, and are following relevant corporate policies.

Second line of defence: Identify risks in the daily operation of the business. Security, data protection and risk management teams carry out monitoring activities. Senior management, including the CMO, is ultimately accountable for this line of defence. A well-functioning second line of defence requires good cooperation between marketing and security, data protection and risk management teams. Practically, it would mean understanding the importance of operational-level auditing and providing input to the security team, even when there are other pressing deadlines and business issues.

Third line of defence: Provide independent assurance on risk management by assessing the first and second lines of defence. Independent corporate internal audit teams usually have this role. Here, too, the marketing department will be asked to cooperate during audits. Assurance results reported to the governance body inform the strategic business actions for the senior management team.

GDPR's focus on security matters

Article 32 of GDPR is the main article that covers security. In this article, the topic of security is approached on the principle of accountability, which means that for everything you want to claim there must be documented evidence. For example, if your organization has implemented TOMs, this must be documented and ready for third-party audits. Similarly, GDPR approaches information security with a risk-based approach. For instance, organizations can be exempted from notifying of personal data breaches to regulators and consumers if the security measures in place decrease the risk to the rights and freedoms of the data subjects.

Security policy

The first piece of security-related documents regulators would inspect, if you are in that unfortunate situation, is your organization's security policy. Some companies use international information security standards, such as ISO 27001, to structure their security policies. Working with an accredited framework is a plus if your company intends to be certified by that standard. Regardless of the framework your organization decides to use, very helpful information to be included upfront in the policy is the information classification, where data classification is a sub-category. Typically, information is categorized according to sensitivity and gets labelled 'restricted', 'confidential', 'internal use only' and 'public' accordingly. On top of these classifications, the data taxonomy discussed in Chapter 4 can be added as additional layers to determine the precise level of data sensitivity relevant to data protection.

Protecting data

As part of the greater organization, your marketing department must be mindful of how to technically protect personal data, which would most likely be your customer and prospect data. Data can be at rest, in motion or in use. In all three situations, there are the best ways of protecting the data technically. For data at rest, this can be encryption, or, where files are stored on physical media, robust physical security. Data in motion refers to data that are being transmitted from one place to another, where encryption is the primary data protection method. Many organizations use a Virtual Private Network (VPN) tunnel when allowing employees remote access to files on an internal network, for instance, when they are working from a home office. VPNs encrypt the connection between the mobile device, say a laptop, and the server or the cloud storage. Data in use may be the most difficult to protect, particularly when legitimate users are accessing the files. Encrypting data while it is in use may either not be possible or significantly slows down the processing, making running analytical queries or converting files very time-consuming.

In any case, protecting data itself is a popular security measure, which both practitioners and regulators see as a promising way to provide data use flexibility while protecting the right to data protection of the data subjects. Currently, we are seeing a comeback of privacy enhancing technologies (PETs), digital privacy and confidentiality solutions that use pseudonymization and anonymization techniques (OECD, 2023).

PSEUDONYMIZATION AND ENCRYPTION
GDPR defines pseudonymization in Article 4(5) (legislation.gov.uk, 2016):

> 'pseudonymisation' means the processing of personal data in such a manner that the personal data can no longer be attributed to a specific data subject without the use of additional information, provided that such additional

information is kept separately and is subject to technical and organisational measures to ensure that the personal data are not attributed to an identified or identifiable natural person.

In other words, when you can replace the personal identifier with an ID, and if you maintain the lookup table separately, which allows the IDs to be decoded to the original personal identifiers, then the record in question may be considered pseudonymous. Table 9.1 below shows how plain text identifiers, name, address and email, can be replaced by a pseudonym, in this case, an ID. Since attributes are still available in clear text, marketing data scientists can still analyse this information, and create, for instance, customer segments with it.

ENISA explains pseudonymization as the protection of data by hiding the identities of persons in the dataset. There are four main pseudonymization techniques discussed in the ENISA document (ENISA, 2022).

Counter technique: This pseudonymization technique assigns a new incremental number, or monotonic counter, for each unique identifier. With this technique, the first customer on your CRM file, for instance, can be assigned '1' and the second customer '2' and so on. The counter can also start from a different value, for instance from 1001. In this case, the first customer will be assigned '1001' and the second '1002'.

Random number technique: Random number pseudonymization technique assigns a random value between a minimum and maximum value you set, whereby everyone in the dataset receives a unique number. If your marketing department decides that the value of the pseudonym should be between 10000 and 99999, the first customer can be assigned a randomly generated number '61946' and the second '16914'.

TABLE 9.1 Pseudonymizing customer records

Name	Address	Email address	Has a dog	Owns a SUV	Lives in a house with a garden
Henk de Vries	Perroen weg 4, Maastricht	henk@gmail.com	Yes	No	yes
Fleur Bakker	Van Moerkerkenlaan 1a, Groningen	Fbakker@outlook.com	No	Yes	no

ID (Pseudonym)			Has a dog	Owns a SUV	Lives in a house with a garden
d2f1995ad002f7			Yes	No	yes
3b7c2586dde68b			No	Yes	no

Hashing technique: Hashing basically scrambles the input identifier to a fixed-length hash value, or an output, using a mathematical function. Hashing is a cryptographic function that cannot be reversed. This is why they are also called 'one-way hash'.

Even when it is difficult to re-identify the person from hash values, when an identical record is put through the same hash algorithm, the hash value will be the same. That means it can be used to match records without ever using clear text data. Message-Digest algorithm 5, better known as MD5, is widely used for hashing email addresses for online advertising by large publishers. Publishers provide precise instructions on how the advertiser's input file should look. It would specify, for example, that the first letter of the first name must be capitalized, street names must be in all capital letters and delivered in a separate column from the house number and so on. This is because even when the records belong to the same consumer, the smallest differences in the format of data, such as capitalising the first letter, create a different hash value. When hash values are different, the records will not match, and your customers will not be selected as an audience. Once the audience file is in the specified format, organizations upload the MD5 hashed file to the designated account of the publisher. Where there is a match, the publisher can display the video or picture your creative team has prepared to their selected user audience.

While MD5 is still used commonly for matching purposes, the Bavarian data protection authority once raised a concern that MD5 can be decoded (BayLDA, 2015). Perhaps this is why the hashing method called Secure Hash Algorithm 256 (SHA256) is currently the technique most widely used. SHA256 is much more robust than MD5.

Key-coded hashing technique: Key-coded hashing techniques, including hash-based message authentication codes, are basically hashing techniques with additional protection through the use of a unique alpha-numeric key called salt. Without knowing the salt, you cannot have the same hash value created, even when the input identifier is identical. In GDPR language, salt is the *additional information*.

Encryption technique: Encryption is a 'two-way' technique. Encryption often uses advanced cryptographic algorithms, and, like key-coded hashing techniques, it uses keys for re-identifying files to provide extra protection to the data. PGP, which stands for Pretty Good Privacy, is one of the first strong encryption techniques, and it is still widely used today for pseudonymizing (and anonymizing) personal data.

ANONYMIZATION

Then there is the ultimate protection method of personal data, which is anonymization. Unlike pseudonymization, when anonymized, data cannot be related or associated with a natural person. The key difference to pseudonymization is that the 'additional data' required to re-identify persons either does not exist or is not available to the organization. Since GDPR only applies to personal data, the law and all the obligations that come with it do not apply when the data is anonymous.

The simplest way to anonymize data is to aggregate. When calculating the average spend of a certain customer segment, that data 'average spend' is information that cannot be associated to a specific person but rather to a group of persons. This means that while the process of calculating the average requires data on an individual level, the resulting value of the 'average spend' of a group is no longer on the same level. When creating a file that only has the name of the customer segment in column one and the value of 'average spend' in column two, this dataset is no longer personal data and hence GDPR does not apply.

Besides aggregation, there are four anonymization techniques marketers may have heard of or may already be using in their daily work.

Trusted Third Party (TTP): Putting TTP as intermediaries that de-identify records can create complete anonymization. Marketers may have used TTPs when, for instance, working on a joint industry study where all participating companies send over a selection of their customer data to a TTP. The TTP then matches the different datasets, strips off the identifiers and perhaps carries out other treatments to the data, before making it available to the participating organizations' marketing data scientists. The marketing scientists are then able to gain an industry-wide view of the consumers. ICO sees TTP as an effective anonymization arrangement that can facilitate collaborative research projects like the one I have just described. ICO, however, reminds organizations that an agreement for the collaboration using a TTP must cover security, anonymization and anti-re-identification measures (ICO, 2012, p 43).

There is also a variation of TTP where the anonymising entity is not a separate organization, but rather a computationally created environment, where participating organizations are not able to gain access to the data with identifiers, similar to a normal TTP (Goldwasser and Lindell, 2005).

Synthetic data: Synthetic data, as the name suggests, is fake data. The European Data Protection Supervisor's office explains synthetic data as follows (Riemann, 2023):

> Synthetic data is artificial data that is generated from original data and a model that is trained to reproduce the characteristics and structure of the original data.

Synthetic data are created in such a way that the structure as well as the relationships between variables are kept intact, so that marketing data scientists can run regression, CHAID, factor analyses and all the rest, to provide the marketing team with the most intriguing insights. The challenge is that creating synthetic data requires specialist knowledge, and can take a long time. This is one area AI can help marketers, as we will discuss in Chapter 12.

Differential privacy: Where synthetic data is built entirely by using fake data, differential privacy injects a small amount of fake data in real datasets so that users will not know if a particular record is real or faux. In other words, the approach creates anonymity by inserting noise into the dataset.

When differential privacy is applied, three rules must be followed. Firstly, the noise should not change the study outcome in the big picture. Secondly, the attributes of an individual should not reveal that person in the dataset, and lastly, leaving out any record from the analysis should yield a similar outcome (Kearns and Roth, 2019).

I first came across this concept in 2009 at the 31st International Conference of Data Protection and Privacy Commissioners in Madrid, presented by an Israeli scholar. Since then, differential privacy has been discussed in many conferences and seminars. This makes me think that the method will soon appear on one or the other regulator guidelines as one of the preferred anonymization methods.

Homomorphic encryption: The last type of anonymization technique I will introduce in this section is homomorphic encryption. Simply put, this is a special encryption method that allows marketing data scientists to analyse encrypted data and produce an encrypted outcome. When, however, the encrypted result is decrypted, they are identical to the results that are produced by performing the same analysis on a cleartext dataset (Yi et al, 2014).

There is one challenge in using homomorphic encryption. As with every encryption, homomorphic encryption requires large computational power. For most companies, and their marketing departments, this anonymization technique remains out of reach for this reason, for now.

ANONYMIZATION, REGULATORS AND THE EUROPEAN COURT OF JUSTICE

Since GDPR does not define anonymous data, EU regulators have been debating how to differentiate anonymous data from pseudonymous data (Art 29 WP, 2007; Art 29 WP, 2014). Pseudonymized data falls under the category of personal data, but anonymized data does not. In the 2014 guidance, the EU regulators evaluated different pseudonymization and anonymization techniques with the criteria 1) if records can be singled out, and 2) if records are linkable and 3) can be inferred to a particular person using inference. Using these three benchmarks, they determined if the pseudonymization or anonymization method in question indeed creates anonymous data. In their own words (Art 29 WP, 2014):

> The opinion elaborates on the robustness of each technique [to turn personal data anonymous] based on three criteria:
>
> (i) is it still possible to single out an individual,
>
> (ii) is it still possible to link records relating to an individual, and
>
> (iii) can information be inferred concerning an individual?

At current, the only form of anonymity which EU and UK regulators can agree upon is data in an aggregated form. The Article 29 Working Party stated:

> Only if the data controller would aggregate the data to a level where the individual events are no longer identifiable, the resulting dataset can be qualified as anonymous. (Art 29 WP, 2014, p 9)

Other institutions concur. The Geo Business Code of Conduct published by the Ministry of Economics of Germany states that data is considered anonymous when it is aggregated on at least four households (SRIW, 2015). Since the average number of persons per household in Germany is two, the position of the Ministry can be understood as considering data which aggregates information of at least eight persons are anonymous (Global Data, 2023).

As discussed in Chapter 3, the European Court of Justice's interpretation of anonymity needs to be closely followed. The ruling on IP address says whether the data is anonymous or not differs depending on whether the organization has access to ways to re-identify the person (curia.europa.eu, 2014). Another ruling on data anonymity at the General Court of Justice, involving the European data protection supervisor, confirms the relative approach (curia.europa.eu, 2023).

On the other side, ambiguities in the 2014 ruling on IP addresses open the ruling to another interpretation. While adopting a relative approach to anonymity, the ruling also mentioned that if there is a legal way to re-identify a person, no matter how unlikely the applicability of this law will be, information is not anonymous. Since there will always be one or the other law, perhaps those that deal with national security, crime or emergency situations, which could permit the re-identification of a person, it can be argued that an outcome similar to an absolutist approach to anonymity (if anyone can re-identify, data is not anonymous even if you cannot re-identify the person) has been taken by the IP-address case (curia.europa.eu, 2014).

If the relative approach becomes the definite approach, pseudonymous files where data is encrypted can be anonymous, if your company does not have access to the encryption key. Marketers are advised to follow the legal development of anonymity.

CASE STUDY
Anonymized insights in practice

Cartography and micro-geographic information have been around for many decades. This group of disciplines studies the characteristics of locations, including the traffic, building and resident types of the area. Billboard companies use geographic information to decide where best to place their billboard. The labels 'A+ location' and 'A location' are calculated based on micro-geographic information like the distance to a tube station, day-time and night-time population and socio-demographics of the residents of the immediate vicinity. Estate agents can then use this description to efficiently market the property in question to prospects from the gastronomic or retail industries. City planners and private property developers make decisions based on cartographic information to issue planning permits for nurseries and hospitals or choose a location for a new supermarket.

Micro-geographic information has also been deployed for marketing for many years. Door drops, which used to promote anything from the grand opening of a garden centre to 1990s-style dance parties, used to select only the most relevant neighbourhoods using geographic insights.

Advantages of using micro-geographic information

Micro-geographic information relates to a geographic location or property and does not relate to a person. In addition, to avoid accidentally capturing personal information, for instance, because a property or micro-geographic area only has a single resident, strict rules are applied to ensure that all records are available on an aggregated level. This makes micro-geographic information outside of the realm of GDPR.

In addition, micro-geographic information by default covers the entire population of the country. That means companies can append insight information to all the records; a stark comparison to online match rates of cookies. With micro-geographic intelligence, brands can make data-driven decisions on campaigns for all touchpoints, throughout the marketing eco-system.

Choosing a cohort framework that works for marketing use cases

The first step of developing micro-geographic or cohort data is to find a framework that allows the consumers to be grouped together into cohorts that are small enough so that the dataset can deliver intelligence for highly relevant personalization. At the same time, it should be aggregated to a level large enough to make sure that data does not lead to a single person.

The official government frameworks in the UK for geographic partitioning are usually based on boundaries set by the Office of National Statistics (ONS), like counties, electoral wards, parishes and Output Areas (OA) for census statistics. However, even the smallest geographic unit, the OA, contains 100 persons. ONS frameworks are helpful in understanding wider area traits that can deliver key insights, such as the urbanicity of the area. Nevertheless, using these frameworks is not ideal if you want to understand the subtle differences in consumer characteristics, such as demographics and lifestyle.

Another popular scheme is the national postcode framework, which divides the UK into approximately 1.7 million compartments, on average containing 30 people. Since it contains a much smaller number of persons, consumer characteristics aggregated on postcode levels have proven to create sufficient 'lift' for audience performance. 'Lift' in data jargon expresses the incremental added value of any given marketing activity. For instance, a lift can be the margin by which the number of click-throughs of the test group, created using the insight data, has improved, compared to the control group. However, postcodes are established to assist postal services in distributing letters and parcels, and not for grouping households and persons based on, for instance, their consumption patterns.

Hexagons and geo-tiles separate the country in geometric meshes, in six-sided polygons or squares. The uniform shape applied to all geography, as well as the scalability of the sizes of the mesh, make these frameworks attractive and are hence practical for use cases that deal with movement data like a pedestrian traffic heat-map. However, similar to the postcode framework, hexagons and geo-tiles do not create homogenous consumer groups. For instance, two neighbouring buildings with no street connection, one a council dwelling and the other a high-end development estate, can be grouped into a single cohort.

Acxiom has therefore created a unique framework, called micro-cell, which groups buildings in the immediate vicinity with similar characteristics, which introduces a strong factor of homogeneity of persons that are living in those buildings (Acxiom Ltd, 2024). In total, approximately 5 million micro-cells were created for the whole country, each containing a minimum of 5, and on average 10 residential addresses. Micro-cells consolidate household and individual level information to an anonymized level, yet at the same time provide the accuracy and predictability needed for delivering relevant messages.

Populating the framework

In the next stage, official statistics, points of interest and property information were gathered. Then individual-level survey data that contains attributes such as socio-demographics, hobbies and product preferences were aggregated into micro-cells, using iterative statistical techniques. The results were then tested on various datasets to ensure that micro-cell level information created stable insights, and more importantly, provided better lift.

In terms of accuracy, micro-cell data presented results that were very similar to the original individual-level record, in particular, insights generated on key marketing attributes such as income level band, home ownership status and marital status were practically identical. This in turn convinced the business to replace all individual-level attributes with those on the micro-cell level.

Performance of aggregated micro-cell data in real-life campaigns

Let us pick an unusual example, which comes from the business-to-business marketplace. Channel 4, a public service broadcaster, offers brands their streaming platform to display advertising to their approximately 30 million customers. The broadcaster wanted to improve advertising sales and hence decided to enrich its customer database with Acxiom's micro-cell data, consisting of more than 400 data attributes. Through a subsequent analysis phase, 150 audience segments were created that offer high-yielding granular audience packages called 'Approved' on

Channel 4. Channel 4's customers, mostly brands, can then select the audience segments that are best suited for their communication needs.

A study was then conducted by MTM, a research company commissioned by Channel 4, which measured the advertising campaigns of an estate agency, a security company and an insurance company. They found that there was a 60 per cent jump in spontaneous brand awareness and a 43 per cent increase in recognition of the advertisement among the exposed audience compared to the control audience. In addition, there was a 23 per cent increase in consideration of the advertised brand compared to the pre-stage audience (Acxiom Ltd, 2024a).

Identification and authentication

Let us get back to covering other aspects of information security, relevant to GDPR's Article 32. In protecting personal data, organizations must be able to check the identity of system users, persons accessing your company's CRM or even entering your office premises.

Identification starts with the presentation of usernames, account numbers or ID cards. In the next step, the presented identity document is checked through an authentication process. Two authentication factors marketers may be using today daily are 'something you know' such as passwords or PINs, and 'something you have' such as a security token generator or a badge. These factors and others can be combined to create a multifactor authentication, which gives you a stronger sense of certainty about who you are dealing with.

Managing authorization and access controls

Have you ever been frustrated because you were unable to access a marketing campaign file or a presentation deck because you are not authorized to access them? Organizations protect personal data by creating different levels of authorization. The example of an intern and the manager having different rights, discussed earlier in this chapter, describes the authorization and access control situation. Another example can be your IT department's system administrator having the right to change the settings of the cloud server's account. Your marketers are not authorized to do so.

Access controls are typically managed by a so-called Access Control List (ACL), maintained by the IT or security departments of your organization.

The list determines which files or directories a brand manager can read or write. Some other ACLs manage network access or directory access, limiting it to persons for whom it is necessary to access a particular section of your organization's network.

Physical security

Physical security also deals with access control, but in an off-line setup, such as managing who can enter which building or facility. These are often managed by cards and badges, which also authenticate persons. Physical security also covers personal data that needs to be physically protected. Possible threats include extreme temperatures and problems with the power supply, which can corrupt or lead to the loss of a file. Security experts also use deterrents such as a huge sign saying 'CCTV in operation', burglar alarms and mechanical locks (Andress, 2019).

Protecting network and operation systems

Protecting personal data requires a well-thought-through network design. Firewalls that control the data traffic between your company's internal network and anything external to it, on the internet, are a must if marketers want to protect customer, prospect and other personal data from being accessed without proper authorization. There are different types of firewalls, such as the proxy server that protects apps, deep packet inspection that can inspect the content of incoming data traffic, or packet filtering that allows control of the traffic based on IP addresses, port numbers and the protocol used. In addition to firewalls, your organization might deploy an intrusion detection system to prevent hacker attacks.

When data is accessed from outside of the organization, a VPN can be used, as we discussed earlier in this chapter. As a frequent business traveller, I often access the network through a VPN tunnel, using hotel WiFi access. This way, I can access my files on the company network more securely. Similarly, when files are transferred to and from external parties, like customers and service providers, security aspects need to be considered. Transferring audience files to platforms usually takes place over an API. For sending files elsewhere frequently, Secure File Transfer Protocol, or SFTP, is the preferred option for many organizations. SFTP prevents hackers from tapping into the file transfer traffic. A growing number of file transfer is supported by Software as a Service (SaaS) file transfer solutions, where organizations upload the file, and the recipient downloads it at their end. In most cases, these solutions are hosted on a server outside of your organization, which means SaaS file transfer companies are your processors.

Operating systems also need to be protected as they can be subject to a hacker attack, potentially granting unauthorized access to your customer and prospect data. Andress describes a technique, Operation System Hardening, which makes use of six principles (Andress, 2019):

- remove unnecessary software
- remove unneeded services: disable software that loads automatically when the system starts
- alter default accounts: change permissions and passwords from the default setting
- use principles of least privilege: only allow absolute minimum permissions
- perform updates
- implement logging and auditing

In addition, your company's system administrator must protect the operating system from malware that allows hackers to, among other things, steal or alter your precious personal data.

Mobile computing and Bring Your Own Device (BYOD)

Mobile computing made working from home and while being on the road easier. To protect against vulnerabilities, your company's security department can deploy software on mobile devices, which controls the configuration of your laptop or smartphone. The software can also block network access from mobile devices in case they are stolen.

Managing personal devices, because your company supports BYOD policy, may be more nuanced. This is because your company does not own the device in question. The minimum your company can do is to limit BYOD devices to email access only, with a prerequisite to have the same end-point protection as any corporate-owned device. All other access can be made only by using company-owned devices (Andress, 2019).

Security training

Your organization's personnel, be it from marketing, accounting or HR departments, are themselves security vulnerabilities. Employees can be tricked into giving intruders access to, for example, files containing customer data. By systematically training employees, the chances of attacks being recognized and reported to the security department increase. This leads to better prevention of serious incidences.

Social engineering attacks, manipulating people to access data and networks, can also take a physical form. Tricking an employee into letting an intruder access your company's premises is one example. You may have received messages from your security department, reminding you time after time not to open suspicious emails, and not to click on links that are embedded in a commercial email. That is because it can be a phishing attempt, a digital form of social engineering. Clicking through a malicious link can land you on a fake website that installs malware or collect information from you that can be used for future network attack.

A good training programme is therefore important for protecting your customer and prospect data. Security training can create awareness of suspicious activities, and how to report them to the security department. Employees can also be asked to familiarize themselves with the corporate security policies and procedures during security training.

As a small note, the marketing department is usually part of the incident management team. This is usually described in your organization's security policy and process documents. When incidents become public and journalists start contacting your organization for statements, marketers will be put on the spot. Determination of incident communication strategy, including the preparation of drawer statements, must be swiftly carried out, in coordinated action with senior leadership, data protection, legal and security teams. Some incidents may necessitate breach notification to both the data protection authority and your customers. We will discuss the topic of notification later on in this chapter.

Audit and accountability

Since GDPR is based on accountability principles, setting up a structure, also for security matters, is expected. Concretely, systematic logging and monitoring of data access, in combination with identification, authentication and authorization policies, can hold departments and specific persons accountable. Such measures can constitute non-repudiation, giving compelling evidence that there is no space to deny the validity of a particular claim (NIST, 2023). Non-repudiation can work as a deterrent against misbehaviour and ultimately prevent intrusion.

The best way to prevent security incidents is to map out the weak points and fix them before incidents happen. Through an audit, your company can systematically discover the vulnerabilities. There are also methods to test your company's preparedness by mimicking a hacker attack. This particular type of audit is called a penetration test or simply pen test.

In Chapter 8, we briefly mentioned how helpful it is to work with a processor with credentials. Getting your organization certified to an accredited certification standard using third-party auditors can also give assurances to your customers and partners, that your organization is buttoned up. There are general security standards, such as ISO 27001, but also industry-specific data protection standards such as QuLS for marketing and TISAX for automotive industries.

Breach notification

GDPR also governs situations where data breach happens. There are three types of actions companies need to take, depending on the severity of the impact of the breach on the rights and freedoms of the data subjects. When a data breach happens, your company needs to either just document the incident, document the incident and report to the regulator, or document the incident, report to the regulator and inform the affected customers.

Article 4(12) of GDPR defines personal data breach (legislation.gov.uk, 2016):

> 'personal data breach' means a breach of security leading to the accidental or unlawful destruction, loss, alteration, or unauthorised disclosure of, or access to, personal data transmitted, stored or otherwise processed.

In other words, the damage, in the form of destruction, loss, alteration, disclosure and access to personal data, has to be present for any incident to be classified as a personal data breach. Just the presence of a risk of such damage does not count as a breach. For instance, a virus software was accidentally turned off for an hour, presenting a risk that customer data in the CRM system could have been accessed during this period. Unless there is evidence to suspect unauthorized access, in this case, it is not considered a personal data breach.

If, however, a personal data breach has occurred, it must be documented (see Article 33(5)) (legislation.gov.uk, 2016). In addition, your organization must notify the regulator within 72 hours, after becoming aware of the personal data breach (Article 33(1)) (legislation.gov.uk, 2016). GDPR does not say 'Report within 72 hours from the moment the incident took place'. The regulators interpret the expression 'become aware' as meaning your organization has a reasonable degree of certainty that the incident has compromised personal data (Art 29 WP, 2018, pp 10–11). That moment usually arrives sometime after when the incident has happened.

Article 33(1) also implies that a well-functioning incident management policy is put in place, as otherwise reporting it to the regulator without undue delay is not possible. The report to the competent data protection authority must contain at least the following information (Article 33(3) GDPR) (legislation.gov.uk, 2016):

a. … the nature of the personal data breach including where possible, the categories and approximate number of data subjects concerned and the categories and approximate number of personal data records concerned;

b. … the name and contact details of the data protection officer or other contact point where more information can be obtained;

c. … the likely consequences of the personal data breach;

d. … the measures taken or proposed to be taken by the controller to address the personal data breach, including, where appropriate, measures to mitigate its possible adverse effects.

Notification can be made in phases, so that you don't have to wait until all information is available before notifying the regulator (Article 33(4) GDPR) (legislation.gov.uk, 2016).

Once your organization has established that a personal data breach has taken place, it must be assessed whether the incident is likely to have caused risks to the rights or freedom of your customers. When in doubt, you can consult the 'Recommendation for a methodology of the assessment of the severity of personal data breaches', a document prepared by the European Union Agency for Cybersecurity, ENISA (ENISA, 2013). They proposed a formula that can be used by marketers to assess how serious the breach is. For instance, if a loyalty care database of a supermarket chain containing names, email addresses and loyalty card numbers was compromised, the level of risk according to the formula would be 'low: individuals either will not be affected or may encounter a few inconveniences, which they will overcome without any problem (time spent re-entering information, annoyance, irritation etc.)' (see ENISA, 2013, p 6). Using the formula, I presume that the loss of audience files your marketing department uploads to a publisher for digital activation will carry an even lower risk than that of a supermarket loyalty programme example. Most audience files contain nothing more than MD5 hashed email addresses or IDs. Unless your organization stores sensitive data, such as information on health or religion, I expect the loss of data in the field of marketing to carry a generally lower risk than, say, personal data files used in the fields of criminal investigation, clinical research or insurance industries.

If your organization has assessed that there is indeed a high risk to the rights and freedoms of your customers, your marketing department must realize that customers – more precisely, customers impacted by the incident – must be notified. This is a catastrophe! As I mentioned earlier, the wonderful trusting relationship your marketers are working hard to build up can be destroyed by just one notification. Besides, customers might panic, fearing the worst, such as identity theft.

There are measures your company can put in place to avoid this disaster in case of a problematic personal data breach. Firstly, keep the data in a pseudonymized form wherever possible. If the data was pseudonymized, and there is no way for others to decipher the data, your customers do not need to be notified about the breach (Article 34(3)a GDPR) (legislation.gov. uk, 2016). Similarly, if your company was able to take immediate action to mitigate the risk, for instance through a well-functioning Incidence Response Plan or robust TOMs, customers do not need to be notified either (Article 34(3)b GDPR) (legislation.gov.uk, 2016). Lastly, if contacting the customers becomes a disproportional effort, for instance, because you cannot identify which of the customers were affected, notification is not required (Article 34(3)c GDPR) (legislation.gov.uk, 2016).

In any case, your DPO, if your organization has appointed one, will be able to advise you most appropriately. We will discuss the topic of DPO in Chapter 11.

Key takeaways

1 Data security, referred to as integrity and confidentiality, is one of the main principles of GDPR.

2 Parkerian Hexad gives a structure to analyse the nature of security problems.

3 Security departments make use of risk management steps to prioritize vulnerabilities. Three Lines of Defence is a well-known model for risk management.

4 Security policy, accompanied by implemented measures such as authentication, authorization, network security, training and regular audits, allow the company to implement robust security measures.

5 Data itself can be protected by pseudonymization or even anonymization. When data is anonymized, GDPR is not applicable. When aggregated, data is anonymous.

6 Personal data breaches must always be documented. Some breaches must be notified to the regulator and, in some cases, even the consumers must be notified.

7 Putting in appropriate data security safeguards can save organizations from notifying the customers of the breach.

Conclusion

The discipline of information security protects data and information systems. Approaches such as the Parkerian Hexad guide organizations to systematically approach security incidents. Security departments also go through risk management steps to identify relevant risks for the organization. GDPR takes a risk-based approach. When data is protected in such a way that it can be rendered anonymous, the data no longer requires legal protection under the GDPR. Apart from protecting the data itself, security measures must be extended to proper authentication and system access authorization, network and physical security, protection of mobile devices, and training. A regular audit will help organizations better prevent security incidents. Despite the preparation, when a personal data breach takes place, this might need to be reported to the regulator or even the customers. Whether or not notification is required also depends on how well the data in question has been protected.

Bibliography

Acxiom Ltd (2024) Acxiom InfoBase®, Unleash the full potential of customer insights: discover Acxiom's comprehensive and powerful data solutions with InfoBase, www.acxiom.co.uk/customer-data/infobase/ (archived at https://perma.cc/YD34-DZDA)

Acxiom Ltd (2024a) Case study: Channel 4 uses Acxiom's InfoBase® data to optimise advertising on their streaming platform, www.acxiom.co.uk/case-studies/channel-4s-use-of-acxioms-infobase-data-to-optimise-advertising-on-their-streaming-platform/ (archived at https://perma.cc/U3CC-ADEE)

Andress, J (2019) *Foundations of Information Security,* No Starch Press

Art 29 WP (2007) Article 29 Data Protection Working Party, 00323/07/EN WP 131 Working Document on the processing of personal data relating to health in electronic health records (EHR), adopted on 15 February 2007, https://ec.europa.eu/justice/article-29/documentation/opinion-recommendation/files/2007/wp131_en.pdf (archived at https://perma.cc/M57B-NGHN)

Art 29 WP (2014) Article 29 Data Protection Working Party, Opinion 05/2014 on Anonymisation Techniques, adopted on 10 April 2014, https://ec.europa.eu/justice/article-29/documentation/opinion-recommendation/files/2014/wp216_en.pdf (archived at https://perma.cc/ZQ73-3TEG)

Art 29 WP (2018) Article 29 Data Protection Working Party, WP250rev.01 Guidelines on Personal data breach notification under Regulation 2016/679, adopted on 3 October 2017, last revised and adopted on 6 February 2018, https://ec.europa.eu/newsroom/article29/items/612052 (archived at https://perma.cc/N63V-MU9H)

BayLDA (2015) Bayerisches Landesamt für Datenschutzaufsicht: 6. Tätigkeitsbericht 2013/14, www.lda.bayern.de/media/baylda_report_06.pdf (archived at https://perma.cc/QZX3-TS38)

Bosworth, S, Whyne, E and Kabay, M E (2009) *Computer Security Handbook*, 5th edn, Wiley, chapter 3: Toward a new framework for information security, Donn B Parker

curia.europa.eu (2014) Patrick Breyer v. Bundesrepublik Deutschland, European Court of Justice, Case C-582/14, https://curia.europa.eu/juris/document/document.jsf?text=&docid=184668&pageIndex=0&doclang=en&mode=req&dir=&occ=first&part=1&cid=1130557 (archived at https://perma.cc/6BNW-DC4L)

curia.europa.eu (2023) Single Resolution Board (SRB) v European Data Protection Supervisor (EDPS), General Court, Judgment of 26. 4. 2023 – CASE T-557/20, https://eur-lex.europa.eu/legal-content/EN/TXT/PDF/?uri=CELEX:62020TJ0557 (archived at https://perma.cc/F7E3-QCZN)

ENISA (2013) European Union Agency for Cyber Security: Recommendations for a methodology of the assessment of severity of personal data breaches, Working Document, v1.0, December, www.enisa.europa.eu/publications/dbn-severity (archived at https://perma.cc/Q4ZC-F5EX)

ENISA (2022) European Union Agency for Cyber Security: Deploying pseudonymisation techniques, www.enisa.europa.eu/publications/deploying-pseudonymisation-techniques (archived at https://perma.cc/9J2M-ZDP3)

Gartner, Inc. (2023) Information technology: Gartner glossary, www.gartner.com/en/information-technology/glossary/information-security (archived at https://perma.cc/JP27-6CAN)

Global Data (2023) Average size of households in Germany (2010–2021), www.globaldata.com/data-insights/macroeconomic/average-household-size-in-germany-2096124/ (archived at https://perma.cc/XK77-B2FU)

Goldwasser, S and Lindell, Y (2005) Secure multi-party computation without agreement, *J Cryptology* 18, 247–87, https://doi.org/10.1007/s00145-005-0319-z (archived at https://perma.cc/JBP4-HK8A)

gov.uk (2018) Gov.uk Service Manual, Technology: Securing your information, Technology community (technical architecture), updated 21 May 2018, www.gov.uk/service-manual/technology/securing-your-information (archived at https://perma.cc/3ZVQ-USU5)

ICO (2012) Information Commissioner's Office: Anonymisation – managing data protection risk code of practice, https://ico.org.uk/media/1061/anonymisation-code.pdf (archived at https://perma.cc/96BH-EL9K)

IIA (2020) The Institute of Internal Auditors (IIA), The IIA's Three Lines model, an update of the Three Lines of Defense, July 2020, www.theiia.org/globalassets/documents/resources/the-iias-three-lines-model-an-update-of-the-three-lines-of-defense-july-2020/three-lines-model-updated-english.pdf (archived at https://perma.cc/9HX7-AU4H)

Kearns, M and Roth, A (2019) *The Ethical Algorithm: The Science of Socially Aware Algorithm Design*, Oxford University Press, New York, USA

legislation.gov.uk (2016) Regulation (EU) 2016/679 of the European Parliament and of the Council, 27 April 2016, www.legislation.gov.uk/eur/2016/679/article/4 (archived at https://perma.cc/7AT2-RG2V)

NIST (2023) National Institute of Standards and Technology, US Department of Commerce, Computer Security Resource Centre, Information Technology Laboratory, Glossary, updated 28 May 2023, https://csrc.nist.gov/glossary/term/information_security (archived at https://perma.cc/TE3Z-LN94); https://csrc.nist.gov/glossary/term/non_repudiation (archived at https://perma.cc/DJ4A-44N2)

OECD (2023) Emerging privacy-enhancing technologies: Current regulatory and policy approaches, 8 March 2023, www.oecd.org/publications/emerging-privacy-enhancing-technologies-bf121be4-en.htm (archived at https://perma.cc/Y69S-GBTH)

Riemann, R (2023) European data protection supervisor: Synthetic data, https://edps.europa.eu/press-publications/publications/techsonar/synthetic-data_en (archived at https://perma.cc/D8WM-2GS3)

SRIW (2015) GeoBusiness Code of Conduct (CoC) GeoBusiness und Datenschutz, Verhaltensregeln gemäß § 38 a BDSG zur Geodaten-Nutzung durch Wirtschaftsunternehmen des Vereins Selbstregulierung Informationswirtschaft e. V. (SRIW) und der Kommission für Geoinformationswirtschaft des Bundesministeriums für Wirtschaft und Energie (GIW-Kommission) V1.3, Stand 13, January 2015, https://sriw.de/fileadmin/sriw/files/20150113_GeoBusiness-Code-of-Conduct-_CoC__GeoBusiness-und-Datenschutz_V1.3_SRIW.pdf (archived at https://perma.cc/6A6A-8XLN)

Yi, X, Paulet, R and Bertino, E (2014) Homomorphic encryption, in *Homomorphic Encryption and Applications*, SpringerBriefs in Computer Science, Springer International Publishing, pp 27–46, Cham, Switzerland

10

Templates for GDPR

At the beginning of my career, going on a business trip started with a sense of anxiety. Every time I left home, unnecessary thoughts would come to my mind. 'Did I pack my hairbrush?' 'I hope I brought the plug adapter.' Five minutes later, I would turn around and walk straight back through the entrance door to partially unpack the otherwise meticulously packed cabin-size trolley. This wasteful ritual had to stop. One day, I had an epiphany and created a checklist called 'Things to bring on a business trip'. There are 30 odd items, from umbrella to passport, and I tick them off as I pack them in my suitcase. Since then, I no longer return home five minutes after leaving. I am confident that I have absolutely everything with me the moment I shut my front door, thanks to that checklist.

In this chapter, we explore four checklists or template documents for data protection, which will hopefully give you peace of mind that you haven't forgotten something important, data protection-wise, before starting to use your data.

RoPA, LIA, DPIA and TIA

As discussed in Chapter 3, GDPR requires organizations to be accountable. Regulators expect organizations to present them with certain documents that prove that due attention is given, and actions are taken to safeguard personal data. This, needless to say, is also the case for using customer and prospect data.

There are four documents that you need to create for compliance reasons, except in situations in which your organization is exempted. The four documents are Record of Processing Activities (RoPA), Legitimate Interest Assessment (LIA), Data Protection Impact Assessment (DPIA) and Transfer

Impact Assessment (TIA). In the UK, TIAs are referred to as Transfer Risk Assessments (TRAs). There are privacy technology companies that provide solutions that automate the creation of these and other compliance documents, and your legal and data protection colleagues may ask you to type in your answers directly in the system. In other cases, your legal and privacy department may ask you to fill out a form they have created themselves. The law does not set a fixed format for maintaining these documents, so both approaches are fine.

A small caveat. The examples provided in the sample documents in this chapter are fictitious and serve as illustrations of how such documents can look. Every process and every organization are operating in different contexts, and are hence carrying different levels of inherent risks. To ensure that your data protection documents are compliant, please work with your legal advisor or your data protection officer, which we will discuss in the next chapter.

DPDI Bill, RoPA and DPIA

One of the aims of DPDI Bill is to reduce the amount of paperwork. Accordingly, the general requirements to maintain a RoPA has been removed. Instead, organizations carrying out high-risk processing are required to maintain a documentation of the processing. Similarly, the requirement of a DPIA is dropped in favour of a risk assessment where high risk processing takes place. The format of the assessment is not specified in the new law (UK Parliament, 2023).

Record of Processing Activities – RoPA

A RoPA is a mandatory document under Article 30 of the GDPR. By creating a RoPA, you are mapping out all data processing activities in the organization, including those of the marketing department. This document can also give an overview of data use to the marketers, or, in other words, what data and processing need to be protected from a compliance perspective.

A RoPA must be developed with utmost care because Article 30(4) of GDPR requires organizations to provide this document when requested by the regulators. A RoPA is a key piece of information for them to get an initial insight into the processing they are interested in, as well as get the feeling of the level of compliance of the organization. A RoPA must be in a written form, and the document can be kept digitally (Article 30(3) and (4)) (legislation.gov.uk, 2016). The ICO suggests hyperlinks should be used in a RoPA, encouraging additional information to be provided with this document (ICO, 2023). The Irish regulator, DPC, on the other hand, cautiously reminds us that the links should either work when clicked from outside your organization or provide the information separately to the regulator when they ask for a copy of your RoPA if the links do not work (DPC, 2023).

GDPR has exemptions for keeping a RoPA. If your organization has fewer than 250 persons employed, you can be exempt from maintaining a RoPA. This can be seen as an effort to alleviate SMEs from administrative burden. However, that is not all. Even if your organization is exempt due to the 250-person threshold, you will still have to do a RoPA if what your company does with personal data carries risks to the freedoms and rights of the data subject. For instance, if your company provides genealogy services using DNAs, which is genetic data, considered to be sensitive under GDPR, it will be difficult to argue that there is no risk to the use of personal data (Article 9) (legislation.gov.uk, 2016). That means even if the organization has 30 persons, a RoPA will nevertheless be required.

But this is not all. It is actually the criteria 'processing is not occasional' which will knock out most SMEs carrying out marketing activities using personal data from using the RoPA exemption. The Article 29 Working Party, the predecessor of the EDPB, defines the word 'occasional' in the following way (Art 29 WP, 2018):

> The WP29 considers that a processing activity can only be considered as 'occasional' if it is not carried out regularly, and occurs outside the regular course of business or activity of the controller or processor.

This can mean that even if, say, a charity organization carries out a campaign only once a year, before Christmas, this will be considered as a *processing activity carried out regularly*.

However, I consider the RoPA a helpful and fundamental tool for data protection. Even if marketing data, or for that matter any other data processing within your organization, makes your organization fall within the exemption, even if eventually DPDI Act does not require one, I would still find maintaining a RoPA to be helpful.

What is required in a RoPA

To find out what you need to have on your RoPA, look no further than Article 30. GDPR requires the following information in a RoPA from a data controller (Article 30(1)) (legislation.gov.uk, 2016):

a. the name and contact details of the controller and, where applicable, the joint controller, the controller's representative and the data protection officer;

b. the purposes of the processing;

c. a description of the categories of data subjects and of the categories of personal data;

d. the categories of recipients to whom the personal data have been or will be disclosed including recipients in third countries or international organizations;

e. where applicable, transfers of personal data to a third country or an international organization, including the identification of that third country or international organization and, in the case of transfers referred to in the second subparagraph of Article 49(1), the documentation of suitable safeguards;

f. where possible, the envisaged time limits for erasure of the different categories of data;

g. where possible, a general description of the technical and organizational security measures referred to in Article 32(1).

Your service provider, processing your customer or prospect data on your behalf, is expected to have the following information in their RoPA (Article 30(2)) (legislation.gov.uk, 2016):

a. the name and contact details of the processor or processors and of each controller on behalf of which the processor is acting, and, where applicable, of the controller's or the processor's representative, and the data protection officer;

b. the categories of processing carried out on behalf of each controller;

c. where applicable, transfers of personal data to a third country or an international organization, including the identification of that third country or international organization and, in the case of transfers referred to in the second subparagraph of Article 49(1), the documentation of suitable safeguards;

d. where possible, a general description of the technical and organizational security measures referred to in Article 32(1).

TABLE 10.1 An example of a RoPA

Vacuum Cleaner Ltd.
123 High Street, Dublin 16, D27 NR46
info@
company.ie
Managing Director: C. Murphy
DPO: S. Doyle
DPO E-Mail: dpo@company.ie

Record of Processing Activities

Processing	Business Function	Purpose of Processing	Description of Processing	Business Process Owner	Categories of Data Subjects	Type of Personal Data	Recipient of Data	Transfer to 3rd Countries	Transfer Instrument	Retention Period	TOM	Legal Base
Direct mail postal campaign	Marketing	maintain contact details for communication	link to description	J. Quinn	customer	name, address	Lettershop	Indonesia	SCC	5 years	Link to TOM	6(1)f Legitimate Interest
Email christmas promotion	Marketing	maintain email for communication	link to description	J. Quinn	customer	email address	n.a.	n.a.	n.a.	3 years	Link to TOM	6(1)a Consent
Web analytics	Marketing	measure effectiveness of website	link to description	J. Quinn	consumer	Customer ID, cookie, campaign ID	n.a.	n.a.	n.a.	3 months	Link to TOM	6(1)f Legitimate Interest

(continued)

TABLE 10.1 (Continued)

Processing	Description of Processing	Business Function	Purpose of Processing	Business Process Owner	Categories of Data Subjects	Type of Personal Data	Recipient of Data	Transfer to 3rd Countries	Transfer Instrument	Retention Period	TOM	Legal Base
File Referencing	link to description	Marketing	maintain customer and other consumer files correct and up to date	L. O'Brien	consumer	name, address, telephone number, email address	n.a.	n.a.	n.a.	see contract	Link to TOM	6(1)c Legal Obligation
Segmentation creation	link to description	Marketing	identify customer groups for differenciated messaging	J. Quinn	customer	customer ID, 3rd party lifestyle and demographics on geo level, purchase behaviour	n.a.	n.a.	n.a.	1 year	Link to TOM	6(1)f Legitimate Interest
Suppression	link to description	Marketing	respect customer and consumer choice	L. O'Brien	customer, ex-customer, consumer	name, address, email address	n.a.	n.a.	n.a.	n.a.	Link to TOM	6(1)c Legal Obligation

An example of a RoPA

The Irish DPC carried out a so-called sweep to understand the state of a RoPA kept by organizations. The following example of a RoPA is based on a table presented in DPC's guidelines (DPC, 2023).

Note that while information about business function and the business owner is not required in Article 30, I find it practical to have this information on a RoPA. This way, you can contact the person in charge of a particular processing, when you have questions. Also, a column dedicated to legal base, included in Table 10.1, is not necessary under Article 30 of GDPR. Nevertheless, I find it helpful to have this information in the overview.

Legitimate Interest Assessment – LIA

As discussed in Chapter 5, Legitimate Interest is my preferred legal ground for marketing use cases. The prerequisite to use this legal ground, however, is to check if there are no overriding interests, freedoms or rights of the data subjects that speak against your data use.

In contrast to the RoPA, GDPR neither explicitly states that an LIA document must be generated, nor specifies the content of LIA. However, indirectly, the LIA is indeed a requirement. Let me explain. In Article 5(2) of GDPR, it is made clear that the accountability principle must be abided by.

> The controller shall be responsible for, and be able to demonstrate compliance with, paragraph 1 ('accountability').

To demonstrate compliance, measures must be documented. The *paragraph 1* in the sentence above refers to this sentence in Article 5(1):

> **Personal data shall be:**
>
> (a) **processed lawfully,** fairly and in a transparent manner in relation to the data subject ('lawfulness, fairness and transparency').

This means, to process personal data lawfully, you need a legal ground. One of the legal grounds is Legitimate Interest, and GDPR sets out the conditions for using this legal ground as follows:

> Processing shall be lawful only if and to the extent that at least one of the following applies:...
>
> (f) processing is necessary for the purposes of the legitimate interests pursued by the controller or by a third party, except where such interests are overridden

by the interests or fundamental rights and freedoms of the data subject which require protection of personal data, in particular where the data subject is a child. (Article 6(1)f)

Putting these points together, this means that organizations must be able to demonstrate that personal data is processed lawfully, which can be based on Legitimate Interest. When using Legitimate Interest, companies need to demonstrate compliance that there are no overridden interests of the data subject that will prevent the use of the data. To demonstrate compliance, you need to have documented evidence. So, in a way, LIA is a legal requirement for organizations to use Legitimate Interest as a legal ground.

What is required in an LIA

As discussed in Chapter 5, to use Legitimate Interest as your legal ground, you need to go through the following six steps, namely:

Step 1: Is what I want to do legitimate, and why do I have an interest in doing this?

Step 2: Is the processing necessary to achieve the personal interest?

Step 3: Do either the interests or fundamental rights of the data subjects override my interest? (the first balancing test)

Step 4: What additional safeguard can I put in place? (the second balancing test)

Step 5: Documentation and transparency

Step 6: Be prepared to facilitate data subjects exercise their rights

The ICO cleverly summarizes the above steps into three tests, namely the 'purpose test' (step 1), 'necessity test' (step 2) and 'balancing test' (steps 3 and 4). Step 5, the documentation is the LIA itself, and step 6 are necessary in any case, as organizations must respect the rights to data protection of its customers and prospects. In the LIA document, we therefore focus on these three tests.

An example of an LIA

There are LIA templates available from privacy consultancy organizations and law firms, as well as regulators such as the ICO and the Bavarian Data Protection Authority of Germany. The example taken here is created by

Data Protection Network, in cooperation with several trade associations, law firms and companies in the UK (Data Protection Network, 2018) (See Table 10.2).

In the example the Data Protection Network provides, a vehicle telemetric processing, used for fleet management, is examined. Here, I have used a fictitious example of a vacuum cleaner manufacturer, relying on the processing of names and addresses to promote their products to their customer base, instead.

Data Protection Impact Assessment – DPIA

The law expects organizations to develop processes that take Data Protection by design and default into consideration. DPIAs are integral parts of Data Protection by Design and Default. In addition, GDPR takes a risk-based approach. Where there are risks, the law does not automatically prohibit the processing but rather encourages organizations to first examine the possibilities of minimizing the risk. For instance, marketers might identify a particular data use that may carry high risk. The flagged risk is then put through a DPIA. In the course of the DPIA, possible measures to reduce the risk, such as pseudonymization and data minimization, can be suggested. These measures may reduce the risk to an acceptable level. When, however, the level of risk is still too high, but the particular data use case is vital to the organization, then the management of your company can solicit the opinion of the competent data protection authority, as per Article 36 of GDPR (legislation.gov.uk, 2016; Art 29 WP, 2017).

There are situations in which carrying out a DPIA is mandatory. Article 35(3) lists the situations out as follows (legislation.gov.uk, 2016):

A data protection impact assessment referred to in paragraph 1 shall in particular be required in the case of:

(a) a systematic and extensive evaluation of personal aspects relating to natural persons which are based on automated processing, including profiling, and on which decisions are based that produce legal effects concerning the natural person or similarly significantly affect the natural person;

(b) processing on a large scale of special categories of data referred to in Article 9(1), or of personal data relating to criminal convictions and offences referred to in Article 10; or

(c) a systematic monitoring of a publicly accessible area on a large scale.

TABLE 10.2 An example of an LIA.

Reproduced with kind permission of Data Protection Network, 27 November 2023 (Data Protection Network, 2018).

Legitimate Interest Assessment

A) IDENTIFYING A LEGITIMATE INTEREST

	Question	Answer	Guidance
1	What is the purpose of the processing operation?	Send hard copy promotional information per post on our products, including accessories, to our customers.	The first stage is to identify to a Legitimate Interest – what is the purpose for processing the personal data?
2	Is the processing necessary to meet one or more specific organisational objectives?	Yes. The processing is necessary for the business to retain current customers by keeping customers' interest in our product, so that they will buy our products again instead of that from our competitors.	If the processing operation is required to achieve a lawful business objective, then it is likely to be legitimate for the purposes of this assessment. The focus when answering this question should be on your business objectives not the interests of your consumers.
3	Is the processing necessary to meet one or more specific objectives of any Third Party?	Yes. Our campaign will be supported by marketing service providers, such as lettershop that will be printing the envelopes and the collaterals.	For this question, a Third Party is any organisation or individual with whom you may share data with for their own purposes. While you may only need to identify one Legitimate Interest for the purposes of an LIA – the interest that you are seeking to rely on – it may be useful to list all apparent interests in the processing, those of you as the Controller, as well as those of any Third Party who are likely to have a Legitimate Interest.

#	Question	Answer	Guidance
4	Does the GDPR, ePrivacy Regulation or other national legislation specifically identify the processing activity as being a legitimate activity, subject to the completion of a balancing test and positive outcome?	Yes. Recital 47 of the GDPR says marketing may be Legitimate Interest.	For example: Legitimate Interests might be relied on where an individual's (including client or employee) information is processed by a group of companies for the purposes of administration (Recital 48).
5	Why is the processing activity important to the Controller?	By communicating relevant information to retain existing customers, we can have more or stable revenue flow, which will help us being in business, continue employments of our employees. It also is an integral part of the freedom of our company to conduct our business. In addition, this contributes to reaching goal 8 of the Sustainable Development Goal of the united nation which aims to guarantee decent jobs and economic growth.	A Legitimate Interest may be elective or business critical; however, even if the Controller's interest in processing personal data for a specific purpose is obvious and legitimate, based on the objectives of the Controller, it must be a clearly articulated and communicated to the individual.
6	If applicable, why is the processing activity important to Third Parties the data may be disclosed to?	By providing services and generating business from this, the third party data processor is able to exercise their freedom to conduct business.	A Legitimate Interest could be trivial or business critical, however, the organization needs to be able to clearly explain what it is. Some purposes will be compelling and lend greater weight to the positive side of the balance, while others may be ancillary and may have less weight in a balancing test. Consider whether your interests relate to a fundamental right, a public interest or another type of interest.

(continued)

TABLE 10.2 (Continued)

Just because the processing is central to what the organization does not make it legitimate. It is the reason for the processing balanced against the potential impact on an individual's rights that is key.

It is important to consider whose Legitimate Interests are being relied on. Understanding this will help inform the context of the processing. In combination with the reason the Personal Data is being processed, this information will determine the weight of the Legitimate Interest that needs to be balanced.

B) THE NECESSITY TEST

	Question	Answer	Guidance
1	Is there an alternative way to achieve the objective without conducting this processing activity?	We have considered many alternative solutions, which includes communication of the information via email. However this cannot substitute the feeling paper printed material gives, which gives the experience a special touch. In addition, the traditional (recycled paper-based) promotional material strengthens the positioning of our product being traditional and down to earth.	• If there isn't an alternative, then clearly the processing is necessary; or • If there is an alternative but it would require disproportionate effort, then the processing may still be necessary; or • If there are multiple ways of achieving the objective, then a Data Protection Impact Assessment should have identified the least intrusive means of processing the data which would be necessary.

C) THE BALANCING TEST

	Question	Answer	Guidance
1	Would the individual expect the processing activity to take place?	Yes they will, as we have informed them in our privacy policy (link to privacy policy). In addition, there is a general awareness that data is used for marketing activities among consumers (link to consumer research 2022). In other words, our customers can expect to receive promotional materials from us.	If the individual would not expect the processing to take place, this could in particular override the Controller's interests. Consider the expectations of the individual, would this processing activity be within their reasonable expectations? Have they been informed? Consider including here any evidence you may have of their expectations that this processing would occur.
2	Does the processing add value to a product or service that the individual uses?	In the brochure, there is information about add-on products they can purchase to improve the user experience of our product, making the product they have purchased more valuable for them. Our customers can benefit by acquiring these.	If the individual would not expect the processing to take place, this could in particular override the Controller's interests. Consider the expectations of the individual, would this processing activity be within their reasonable expectations? Have they been informed? Consider including here any evidence you may have of their expectations that this processing would occur. If the processing adds value for the individual this may strengthen the case for Legitimate Interest.
3	Is the processing likely to negatively impact the individual's interests and/ or rights?	They might consider the use of paper to be leaving a carbon footprint, which is something they are trying to avoid.	Consider here whether the processing could lead to discrimination, financial loss, reputational damage, loss of confidentiality or professional secrecy. Or any other economic or social disadvantage. (Please note this is not an exhaustive list.) Does the processing prevent data subjects exercising control over their personal data? (See GDPR Recital 75.)

(continued)

TABLE 10.2 (Continued)

4	Would the processing limit or undermine the rights of individuals?	No. We do not believe it does.	If processing would undermine or frustrate the ability to exercise those rights in future this might well affect the balance.
5	Is the processing likely to result in unwarranted harm or distress to the individual?	No. We do not believe that it will as they were already interested enough in our product to purchase it.	
6	Would unwarranted harm or distress to the individual occur if the processing did not take place?	Maybe. If they have not received the promotional material, and they found out that others who have also purchased a similar product from our competitor have, they might feel slightly irritated.	
7	Would there be a prejudice to the Data Controller if processing does not happen?	Yes. We will be less able to retain the customers, as well as miss out on additional sales opportunity.	Would there be a negative organizational or commercial impact on the Data Controller if this processing were not to take place?
8	If applicable, would there be a prejudice to the Third Party if processing does not happen?	Yes. Our lettershop will have missed out from their revenue opportunity.	Would there be a negative organizational or commercial impact on a Third Party if this processing were not to take place?
9	Is the processing in the interests of the individual whose personal data it relates to?	Yes. They may be interested in other products and accessories of the product they have purchased, which will help them with cleaning their house.	Focus your response on the customer and any potential benefits of this processing. What are the benefits to the individual or to society?

#	Question	Answer	Guidance
10	Are the interests of the individual aligned with the party Looking to rely on their Legitimate Interests for the processing?	We believe so.	If the processing is to the benefit of the individual, then it is more likely that Legitimate Interests can be relied on, as the individual's interests will be aligned with those of the Controller. Where the processing is more closely aligned with the interests of the Controller or a Third Party than with those of the individual, it is less likely that the interests will be balanced, and greater emphasis needs to be placed on the context of the processing and relationship with the individual.
11	What is the connection between the individual and the organization?	Customer.	Identify the connection: • Existing customer • Lapsed/cancelled customer • Employee or contractor • Business client • Prospect (never purchased goods or services) • Supplier • None of above
12	What is the nature of the data to be processed? Does data of this nature have any special protections under GDPR?	Name and address. No special protection is given to these data under GDPR.	What types of personal data are being processed, e.g. contact data, financial details, etc.? Is it data relating to a child? If processing Special Categories of Personal Data, an Article 9 condition must be identified in addition to a lawful basis under Article 6.

(continued)

TABLE 10.2 (Continued)

| 13 | Is there a two-way relationship in place between the organization and the individual whose personal information is going to be processed? If so how close is that relationship? | No. | Where there is an ongoing relationship, or indeed a more formal relationship, there may well be a greater expectation on the part of the individual that their information will be processed by the organization. The opposite is also possible, but it does depend on the purpose of processing. Consider the nature of the relationship, is it:

• Ongoing
• Periodic
• One-off
• No relationship, or relationship has effectively ceased? |
| 14 | Has the personal information been obtained directly from the individual, or obtained indirectly? | Directly, when the individual ordered the product from us. | Consider whether personal information has been collected:

• Directly
• Indirectly
• A mix of both

If the information was obtained directly from the individual then you should take due consideration of the Fair Processing Notice, the relationship with the individual and their expectations of use. If the data was collected directly and these factors are positive, then it may tip the balance in favour of the processing operation. Where Personal Data is not collected directly, there may need to be a more compelling Legitimate Interest to overcome this. It will also depend on the context of the processing and if the organization has a two-way relationship with the individual. |

15	Is there any imbalance in who holds the power between the organization and the individual?	No.	If the organization has a dominant position, this places more responsibility on the Controller to ensure that the interests and rights of the individual are protected. The Controller will need to consider how it addresses any imbalance of power to ensure individuals' rights are not impacted.
16	Is it likely that the individual may expect their information to be used for this purpose?	Yes. See answer to question 1 under 'Balancing Test' above.	<ul><li>Yes</li><li>No</li><li>Not sure</li></ul> Given the relationship between the parties, services/products being provided, including the information notices available, would the individual reasonably expect or anticipate that their information would be used for those or connected purposes? The stronger the expectation, the greater the chances that Legitimate Interests can be relied on.
17	Could the processing be considered intrusive or inappropriate? In particular, could it be perceived as such by the individual or in the context of the relationship?	We do not believe so. The promotional printed material, if it is not interesting to the customer, will be thrown away into the paper waste.	Processing should not be unduly intrusive–intrusion into the private life of an individual may be justified based on the nature of the relationship or special circumstances. However, the greater the intrusion, perceived or otherwise, the more overwhelming the Legitimate Interest should be and the more the rights of the individual must be considered within the balance. Consider here the way the data is processed (e.g. large scale, data mining, profiling, disclosure to a large number of people or publication).

(continued)

TABLE 10.2 (Continued)

18	Is a Fair Processing Notice provided to the individual, if so, how? Are they sufficiently clear and up front regarding the purposes of the processing?	Our customers are provided with a notice through our privacy policy. The privacy policy is available on our website.	Remember that the more unusual, unexpected or intrusive the processing, the greater the importance of making the individual aware of the processing. Particularly where Legitimate Interests are to be relied on.
19	Can the individual, whose data is being processed, control the processing activity or object to it easily?	Yes. They can exercise their rights through sending us a letter, filling out an online form or by sending us an email.	• Yes (cover how you do this in the next section on 'Mitigation and Compensating Controls'). • No • Partly Giving the individual increased control or elements of control may help a Controller rely on Legitimate Interests where otherwise they could not. If individual control is not possible or not appropriate, explain why.
20	Can the scope of the processing be modified to reduce/mitigate any underlying privacy risks or harms?	No. Names and addresses are the minimum we need to send out promotional materials.	If yes (cover how you intend to do this in the next section 'Mitigation and Compensating Controls'). This is a similar concept to a Data Protection Impact Assessment. Where a DPIA might identify potential privacy harms it also allows the organisation to mitigate the risk of non-compliance by adapting or altering the scope of the activity. The same is true for an LIA. If you conclude that the processing presents a privacy risk to the individual, the processing can be limited or adapted to reduce the potential impact.

D) SAFEGUARDS AND COMPENSATING CONTROLS

	Question	Answer	Guidance
			Safeguards include a range of compensating controls or measures which may be put in place to protect the individual, or to reduce any risks or potentially negative impacts of processing. These are likely to have been identified via a Privacy Impact Assessment conducted in relation to the proposed activity. For example: data minimization, de-identification, technical and organizational measures, privacy by design, adding extra transparency, additional layers of encryption, multi-factor authentication, retention, restricted access, opt-out options, hashing, salting, and other technical security methods used to protect data. Please include a description of any compensating controls that are already in place, or will be put in place, to preserve the rights of the individual.
1	What existing safeguards are in place?	Our data processing is carried out according to our policies and procedures, and are carried out according to the applicable laws. We keep personal data no longer than is necessary and store personal data securely.	
2	Will any further safeguards be put in place?	Data is encrypted in transit and in rest. In addition, the data is protected under our TOM (link to TOM) as all other personal data.	

(continued)

TABLE 10.2 (Continued)

E) REACHING A DECISION AND DOCUMENTING THE OUTCOME

Outcome of Assessment	Guidance
Having carried out the above balancing test and LIA we believe that the policies and procedures, as well as data security measures, we have put in place will ensure that our legitimate interests are not overreached by the rights of individuals whose personal data will be processed for sending promotional information on our new products and accessories to our customers	Using the responses above now document if you believe you are able to rely on Legitimate Interests for the processing operation. Please explain, perhaps using bullet points, why you are, or are not, able to rely on this legal basis. You should draw on the answers you have provided in this questionnaire.

Signed by: Role:

Date:

Reviewed by:

Date:

Furthermore, regulators suggest additional factors to be considered. Here are two factors that may be relevant to marketing data use (Art 29 WP, 2017):

1. Evaluation or scoring, including profiling and predicting, especially from 'aspects concerning the data subject's performance at work, economic situation, health, personal preferences or interests, reliability or behaviour, location or movements' (Recitals 71 and 91). Examples of this could include… a company building behavioural or marketing profiles based on usage or navigation on its website.

…

5. Data processed on a large scale: the GDPR does not define what constitutes large-scale, though Recital 91 provides some guidance. In any event, the WP29 recommends that the following factors, in particular, be considered when determining whether the processing is carried out on a large scale:

a. the number of data subjects concerned, either as a specific number or as a proportion of the relevant population;

b. the volume of data and/or the range of different data items being processed;

c. the duration, or permanence, of the data processing activity;

d. the geographical extent of the processing activity.

There are, however, situations in which, even when the above conditions apply, marketers will not have to carry out a DPIA – for instance, when the data use is unlikely to result in a high risk to the rights and freedoms of the customers or prospects (Article 35(1)). Also, if a similar data use case was put through a DPIA, your organization does not have to repeat the DPIA but just apply the results of the similar data use case (Art 29 WP, 2017). Some regulators, such as the Spanish regulator, la Agencia Española de Protección de Datos (AEPD), have come up with a supplementary list of situations. The Spanish regulator acknowledges that carrying out a DPIA can be costly, and specifies the general list of exceptions to DPIA requirements created by the EDPB/Article 29 Working Party further. The list of AEPD includes situations, such as when the processing is carried out according to an approved code of conduct, on this list (AEPD, 2022).

It is the responsibility of the organization or, more specifically, the managing director's responsibility, to ensure that the DPIA is carried out when it is required. In doing so, the DPO of your company should be consulted. Where it is appropriate, the persons or the representatives of persons whose data is used for the processing that should undergo a DPIA should be solicited. This in turn is a gentle nudge built into GDPR, that forces us to be open to other points of view when evaluating the data use (Article 35(9)) (legislation.gov.uk, 2016). In an HR context, this is quite easy. Management can ask some of their employees, or in case your organization has a works council, if they can be contacted as the representatives of that internal organization to provide feedback. In the marketing context, getting insights from customers and prospects may require a bit more work. Some companies, particularly in the business-to-business field, have customer advisory groups, where customers are regularly invited to exchange their views. During such meetings, their opinion of a particular data use can be put on the agenda. Another way is to conduct market research. If you are planning on carrying out a consumer survey or a focus group anyway, and if it is appropriate to ask questions that can be used for a DPIA, it would be a perfect opportunity to do so.

Lastly, there is no legal obligation to publish the DPIA; however, regulators believe that publishing at least a summary of the DPIA may foster trust between individuals. Marketers may consider this when discussing ways to better position the organization in the minds of the customers and prospects.

What is required in a DPIA?

Article 35(7) of GDPR lists out what DPIA needs to contain (legislation.gov.uk, 2016).

The [data protection impact] assessment shall contain at least:

1 a systematic description of the envisaged processing operations and the purposes of the processing, including, where applicable, the legitimate interest pursued by the controller;

2 an assessment of the necessity and proportionality of the processing operations in relation to the purposes;

3 an assessment of the risks to the rights and freedoms of data subjects referred to in paragraph 1; and

4 the measures envisaged to address the risks, including safeguards, security measures and mechanisms to ensure the protection of personal data and to demonstrate compliance with this Regulation taking into account the rights and legitimate interests of data subjects and other persons concerned.

A DPIA form

As with the RoPA and LIA, there are numerous templates available from commercial organizations, trade associations and regulators. CNIL, the French regulator, has a comprehensive template, supplemented by a document that explains the DPIA methodology, and a separate extensive reference guide titled 'Knowledge Bases'. You can find, for instance, best practices for online behavioural advertising in the Knowledge Bases (CNIL, 2018; CNIL, 2018a; CNIL, 2018b). In terms of the format, the DPIA template from the ICO has an easy-to-follow step-by-step approach to the assessment (ICO, 2023b).

In the DPIA guide, ICO reminds us that 'A DPIA should begin early in the life of a project, before you start your processing, and run alongside the planning and development process' (ICO, 2023a).

The steps to follow are (ICO, 2023a):

Step 1: identify the need for a DPIA

Step 2: describe the processing

Step 3: consider consultation

Step 4: assess necessity and proportionality

Step 5: identify and assess risks

Step 6: identify measures to mitigate the risks

Step 7: sign off and record outcomes

Note that the DPIA process, recommended by the ICO, concludes with a sign-off so that the decisions that are made are binding and documented.

The following DPIA template is based on the ICO template (ICO, 2023b) (See Table 10.3).

Transfer Impact Assessment and Transfer Risk Assessment – TIA and TRA

In July 2020, a landmark case at the Grand Chamber of the Court of Justice of the European Union brought down the validity of a US–EU data transfer instrument called the EU–US Privacy Shield. Among other things, the court ruled that the US authorities' use of EU personal data was neither restricted nor proportional. In particular, Section 708 of the Foreign Intelligence Surveillance Act (FISA), which applies to electronic communication service

TABLE 10.3 Template for a DPIA

Data Protection Impact Assessment

Step 1: Why is DPIA necessary?	**response in text unless otherwise indicated**

Provide the project goals and a descriptions of a processing. Link other documents as required.

Explain why a need for DPIA was identified.

Step 2: Processing Purposes

Description of the Processing

method of data collection

data use

data storage

data deletion

data source

data recipient

processing with high risk

Scope of the processing

nature of data

include special category of data?

volume of data in processing

frequency of processing

data retention

number of persons affected

geographic area

Context of processing

relationship with the individuals

amount of control by the individuals over the processing

do the individuals expect the processing to take place

are there children or other vulnerable groups of persons in the data?

concerns of security flaws

is the processing novel?

what is the current state of the art technology of this area?

(continued)

TABLE 10.3 (Continued)

Data Protection Impact Assessment

current issues of public concern over this processing

Purpose of processing

what do you want to achieve?

what is the intended effect on individuals?

benefits of the processing

Step 3: Consultation process

How to consult relevant stakeholders

when and how individuals' views are sought

if not, why is seeking individual's views not appropriate?

other organizations to involve in the consultation

required assistance from processor

will you consult experts (ex. Information security expert)?

Step 4: Assess necessity and proportionality

Describe compliance and proportionality measures

will the processing actually achieve the purpose?

is there another way to achieve the same outcome?

how to prevent function creep?

how will data minimization be ensured?

what information will be given to individuals?

how will the rights of data subjects be supported?

measures to ensure data processory comply

safeguard for international data transer

Step 5: Identify and assess risks

Describe source of risk and nature of potential impact on individuals

likelihood of occurance

harm

resulting risk   low, medium, high

Step 6: Identify measures to reduce risk

Identify additional measures you coule take to reduce or eliminate risks identified as medium or high risk in Step 5

(per risk) measures to reduce or eliminate risk

(continued)

TABLE 10.3 (Continued)

Data Protection Impact Assessment	
(per risk) effect on risk	eliminated, reduced, accepted
(per risk) residual risk	low, medium, high
(per risk) measure approved	yes/no
Step 7: Sign off and record outcomes	
Measures approved by:	name/position/date
actions integrated to project plan with date and person responsible for completion	yes/no
residual risks approved by:	name/position/date
if high resitual risk, consult the regulator	
DPO advice provided:	name/position/date
advice on compliance, if step 6 measures, and if the processing can proceed	
DPO advice accepted or overruled by:	name/position/date
explain why	
Consultation responses reviewed by:	name/position/date
explain why if not in line with the view of the consulted	
This DPIA will be kept under review by:	name/position/date

providers, and Executive Order 12333 which forms the basis of electronic surveillance, were considered problematic (curia.europa.eu, 2020).

At the same time, the court ruling confirmed the validity of SCCs as a data transfer instrument; however, it added that prior to the transfer, organizations must check whether EU personal data can be protected from foreign public authorities. Where necessary, organizations must put in place supplementary measures to protect the data to be transferred (curia.europa.eu, 2020). Hence this ruling triggered an additional data protection requirement, TIA in the EU and TRA in the UK.

A week after this ruling, the EDPB published a FAQ which digested the ruling and communicated, among other things, that there is no grace period for complying with the court decision. Companies were basically told to carry out the impact assessment of the data transfer, particularly to the US, with immediate effect (EDPB, 2020). After a round of consultation, the EDPB then published its recommendations for supplementary measures for transferring data to non-adequate third countries. Suggested supplementary measures include strong encryption, transfer of pseudonymous data, data encryption in transit, use of split or multi-party processing so that one party alone cannot reveal the identity of the data subject, and contractual measures (EDPB, 2021).

In the meantime, the UK ICO took a slightly different approach, focusing more on whether the transfer increases the risk to the protection of personal data, compared to whether the data remained in the UK. ICO says that it also accepts TRA based on the EU approach, which examines the inherent risks due to the laws that are in place in third countries (ICO, 2021). Helpfully, the ICO then created a TRA tool to help guide organizations in carrying out a TRA. The tool guides organizations through the assessment by using six key questions (ICO, 2021a):

Question 1: What are the specific circumstances of the restricted transfer?

Question 2: What is the level of risk to people in the personal information you are transferring?

Question 3: What is a reasonable and proportionate level of investigation, given the overall risk level in the personal information and the nature of your organization?

Question 4: Is the transfer significantly increasing the risk for people of a human rights breach in the destination country?

Question 5: Are you satisfied that both you and the people the information is about will be able to enforce the Article 46 transfer mechanism against the importer in the UK?

If enforcement action outside the UK may be needed: Are you satisfied that you and the people the information is about will be able to enforce the Article 46 transfer mechanism in the destination country (or elsewhere)?

Question 6: Do any of the exceptions to the restricted transfer rules apply to the 'significant risk data'?

The 'significant risk data' is the data you identify in Questions 4 and 5 as data which your Article 46 transfer mechanism does not provide all the appropriate safeguards for.

An example of TIA/TRA

One year after the Schrems II ruling, some of the data protection authorities of Germany, namely that of Baden-Württemberg, Bavaria, Berlin, Bremen, Brandenburg, Lower Saxony, Rhineland-Palatinate and Saarland, embarked on a random check to see whether organizations were properly carrying out

TABLE 10.4 An example of a TIA

	Transfer Impact Assessment	
1	Processing	Customer Contact–Postal
2	General description	link to description
3	Our role (Controller, Joint Controller or Processor)	Controller
4	Categories of Data Subjects	link to RoPA
4a	sensitive data	no
4b	childrens data	no
5	Type of Personal Data	link to RoPA
6	Data recipient in 3rd country	Address Processing Pro AG
6a	contact details (address, email address, telephone number)	Jl. M.H. Thamrin No.1, Menteng, Jakarta 10350, Indonesia, info@app.id, +62 490 558 75 21
6b	role of the data recipient (Controller, Joint Controller, Processor or Sub-Processor)	Processor
6c	existance of further Processor or Sub-Processor	no
7	Country to which data will be transferred	Indonesia
8	Start date of transfer	03-03-2024
9	Duration of transfer	3 months
10	Frequency of transfer	once
11	Processing purpose	link to RoPA
12	Legal basis	Legitimate Interest GDPR Article 6(1)f
13	Transfer mechanism (adequacy, SCC, BCR, exemptions under Article 49, other)	SCC
13a	if SCC, which version is to be signed with the data recipient (Ctrl-Ctrl, Ctrl-Proc, Proc-SubProc)	Ctrl-Proc
14	Have you carried out a legal assessment of the 3rd country?	yes

(continued)

TABLE 10.4 (Continued)

	Transfer Impact Assessment	
14a	if transfer is to the US, is the recipient subject to section 702 (FISA)?	n.a.
15	If you have concluded that the recipient can guarantee the fulfilment of the contractual obligations under the transfer mechanism, please describe in detail your reasons for this conclusion and provide appropriate evidence	Please see the assessment of the country published only by law firm ABC & Associates (link)
16	If you have concluded that the recipient cannot guarantee the fulfillment of the contractual obligations under the transfer mechanism, what additional measures are you taking?	n.a.
17	Legal situation in the 3rd country can change. How do you ensure a quick response to ensure compliance in the new situation? In particular, describe the notification and response process between your company and the recipient in the 3rd country	We have a subscription to data protection newsletters with alert service for Indonesia. The contractual agreement with the 3rd country data processor stipulates that any legal change that affects the protection to be reported to us immediately
18	Is the data encrypted?	yes
18a	if data is encrypted, which type of encryption is used?	TLS 1.3 and TDE encryption
18b	if data is encrypted, when is the encryption applied?	in transit and at rest
18c	if data is encrypted, when will the data be decrypted and by whom?	by data recipient in 3rd country
19	Provide the entry of RoPA for this processing	link to RoPA

TIAs (LfD Niedersachsen, 2021). As part of this exercise, the regulators generated questionnaires which can be used as a TIA template. I took this as the basis and translated it into English. Table 10.4 is an example of a fictitious TIA that uses a marketing example.

In assessing the legal situation of a third country, it is very helpful to tap into online resources, some provided free of charge, by law firms and privacy service providers. Subscribing to newsletters that provides regular updates on law changes in third countries that are relevant to data protection will help keep your TIA or TRA up-to-date.

Key takeaways

1 Four data protection documentations are often required, when you use personal data, namely RoPA, LIA, DPIA and TIA/TRA. This also applies when processing personal data in the marketing context. Under DPDI Bill, RoPA and DPIA will no longer be necessary unless the processing of personal data carries high risk.

2 RoPA provides an overview of all data processing and is a document that needs to be presented to the regulator upon request.

3 LIA is necessary for using the legal ground, Legitimate Interest.

4 The need for a DPIA is triggered by high-risk processing. A successful DPIA must take place prior to starting the processing which is considered risky.

5 TIA and TRA are used to assess the legal risk, or, in the case of TRA, the increase in the level of data protection risk when processing the data in third countries. Supplementary measures can reduce the risk of data processing in that third country.

6 Useful templates and guidelines are available online from regulators, law firms and privacy services organizations.

Conclusion

In this chapter, we reviewed four key data protection documents, namely RoPA, LIA, DPIA and TIA/TRA. Under the DPDI Bill, RoPA and DPIA will not be necessary in most cases. The RoPA provides an overview of the data processing marketers are engaged in. Even when an exemption would apply, which would be quite rare, it is recommended to carry out a RoPA to understand which data and which processing need to be protected. When Legitimate Interest is used as the legal base for a marketing data use case, LIA must be conducted and there must be a positive outcome. There may be marketing data processing that is considered as carrying higher risk. Those must be examined using a DPIA, especially when the data use case fulfils at least one criterion of the situations listed in Article 35(3) of GDPR. The

DPIA is considered an integral component of Data Protection by Design and Default. Lastly, the TIA and TRA, which assess the legal environment or the increased risk in processing the data in a third country, need to be drawn up if your customer or prospect data is to be processed in a third country.

Bibliography

AEPD (2022) Agencia Española de Protección de Datod – Indicative list of the types of data processing that do not require a data protection impact assessment under Article 35(5) GDPR, www.aepd.es/documento/listadpia-35-5-ingles.pdf (archived at https://perma.cc/52QP-9JBY)

Art 29 WP (2017) Article 29 Data Protection Working Party – Guidelines on Data Protection Impact Assessment (DPIA) and determining whether processing is 'likely to result in a high risk' for the purposes of Regulation 2016/679, as last revised and adopted on 4 October 2017, https://ec.europa.eu/newsroom/article29/items/611236/en (archived at https://perma.cc/4S3P-AEXM)

Art 29 WP (2018) Article 29 Data Protection Working Party – Position Paper on the derogations from the obligation to maintain records of processing activities pursuant to Article 30(5) GDPR, adopted on 3 October 2017, as last revised and adopted on 19 April 2018, https://ec.europa.eu/newsroom/article29/items/624045/en (archived at https://perma.cc/TBX9-E9CR)

CNIL (2018) Commission Nationale de l'Informatique et des Libertés, Privacy Impact Assessment (PIA) Methodology, February 2012 edition, www.cnil.fr/sites/cnil/files/typo/document/CNIL-PIA-1-Methodology.pdf (archived at https://perma.cc/J7CC-T3AG)

CNIL (2018a) Commission Nationale de l'Informatique et des Libertés, Privacy Impact Assessment (PIA) Templates, February 2018 edition, www.cnil.fr/sites/cnil/files/atoms/files/cnil-pia-2-en-templates.pdf (archived at https://perma.cc/VR4C-XJF5)

CNIL (2018b) Commission Nationale de l'Informatique et des Libertés, Privacy Impact Assessment (PIA) Knowledge Bases, February 2018 edition, www.cnil.fr/sites/cnil/files/atoms/files/cnil-pia-3-en-knowledgebases.pdf (archived at https://perma.cc/3NLK-UHZA)

curia.europa.eu (2020) Data Protection Commissioner v Facebook Ireland, Maximillian Schrems, Judgment of 16 July 2020 – CASE C-311/18, https://curia.europa.eu/juris/document/document.jsf?text=&docid=228677&pageIndex=0&doclang=en&mode=lst&dir=&occ=first&part=1&cid=9791227 (archived at https://perma.cc/HT5T-NTXB)

Data Protection Network (2018) Guidance on the use of Legitimate Interests under the EU General Data Protection Regulation, https://dpnetwork.org.uk/dpn-legitimate-interests-guidance/ (archived at https://perma.cc/6YJH-XF39)

DPC (2023) Irish Data Protection Commissioner: Guidance Note: Records of Processing Activities (RoPA) under Article 30 GDPR, April 2023, www.dataprotection.ie/sites/default/files/uploads/2023-04/Records%20of%20Processing%20Activities%20%28RoPA%29%20under%20Article%2030%20GDPR.pdf (archived at https://perma.cc/PZF6-BWEP)

EDPB (2020) European Data Protection Board: Frequently asked questions on the judgement of the Court of Justice of the European Union in Case C-311/18 – Data Protection Commissioner v Facebook Ireland Ltd and Maximillian Schrems, adopted on 23 July 2020, https://edpb.europa.eu/sites/default/files/files/file1/20200724_edpb_faqoncjeuc31118_en.pdf (archived at https://perma.cc/RA9H-YFUL)

EDPB (2021) European Data Protection Board: Recommendations 01/2020 on measures that supplement transfer tools to ensure compliance with the EU level of protection of personal data, Version 2.0, adopted on 18 June 2021, https://edpb.europa.eu/system/files/2021-06/edpb_recommendations_202001vo.2.0_supplementarymeasurestransferstools_en.pdf (archived at https://perma.cc/Q3C5-UHAD)

ICO (2021) Information Commissioner's Office: Transfer Risk Assessments, https://ico.org.uk/for-organisations/uk-gdpr-guidance-and-resources/international-transfers/international-data-transfer-agreement-and-guidance/international-data-transfer-agreement-and-guidance/transfer-risk-assessments/#TRA-tool (archived at https://perma.cc/CM53-5VJG)

ICO (2021a) Information Commissioner's Office: ICO TRA tool, https://ico.org.uk/media/for-organisations/documents/4022649/transfer-risk-assessments-tool-20221117.doc (archived at https://perma.cc/95SZ-6YCQ)

ICO (2023) Information Commissioner's Office: How do we document our processing activities? https://ico.org.uk/for-organisations/uk-gdpr-guidance-and-resources/accountability-and-governance/documentation/how-do-we-document-our-processing-activities/ (archived at https://perma.cc/D9ET-BPHJ)

ICO (2023a) Information Commissioner's Office: Data Protection Impact Assessments (DPIAs), https://ico.org.uk/for-organisations/uk-gdpr-guidance-and-resources/accountability-and-governance/data-protection-impact-assessments-dpias/ (archived at https://perma.cc/J5Z2-85C6)

ICO (2023b) Information Commissioner's Office: Sample DPIA template, https://ico.org.uk/media/for-organisations/documents/2553993/dpia-template.docx (archived at https://perma.cc/2RZC-4XZG)

legislation.gov.uk (2016) Regulation (EU) 2016/679 of the European Parliament and of the Council, 27 April 2016, www.legislation.gov.uk/eur/2016/679/article/4 (archived at https://perma.cc/5NGD-7HTT)

LfD Niedersachsen (2021) Die Landesbeauftragte für den Datenschutz Niedersachsen: Pressemitteilung – Prüfung zum internationalen Datenverkehr Landesdatenschutzbehörden kontrollieren Umset-zung des EuGH-Urteils Schrems II in Unternehmen, 1 June, https://lfd.niedersachsen.de/download/169280 (archived at https://perma.cc/6XXT-Z5JP)

UK Parliament (2023) Data Protection and Digital Information Bill, Government Bill, Originated in the House of Commons, Sessions 2022–23, 2023–24, last updated 20 December 2023 at 09:33, https://bills.parliament.uk/bills/3430 (archived at https://perma.cc/PD2P-AUWV)

11

Data protection officer

'… and she said they are going to create a privacy department in Europe!' Shortly after my employer was acquired by a US marketing services company, the delegation of its C-suite arrived in a CEO-flown private jet at our office in the Netherlands. Among the visitors was my boss-to-be, who eloquently explained that sustainable marketing intelligence business is only possible through responsible data use. Their visit also coincided with the period when I started to look for the next step in my career. 'That sounds cool. I think you'd love that', replied my husband when I asked what he thought about me becoming a DPO. The next day, I went straight to the managing director's office and told him that I wanted to become the privacy officer of our Dutch operation. He more or less immediately sent me off to a DPO training course, and the next thing I realized I had a DPO certificate and a new job title as a DPO. This is how I became probably the first DPO or the FG (*functionaris gegevensbescherming*) in the marketing and advertising industry of the Netherlands. After almost 20 years of being a DPO, I am still very thankful to everyone who helped me land my first privacy job, which has put me on an unexpected and fulfilling career path. This chapter will give you a glimpse of my daily work that I enjoy so much. You will also get to know why marketers are the best friends of a DPO.

What is a DPO?

A data protection officer or DPO can be described as an internal regulator for data protection compliance. When I started as a DPO, GDPR did not exist. European Data Protection Directive had a provision to appoint a DPO, so countries like the Netherlands and Germany adopted this possibility in their respective data protection laws (eur-lex.europa.eu, 1995). In the

Netherlands, the appointment of a DPO was voluntary, which prompted the Dutch association of DPOs to develop a handbook for organizations with a checklist to determine whether appointing a DPO would be beneficial (overheid.nl, 2001). The handbook also listed the advantages of having a DPO (translated from Dutch with emphasis and explanations in square brackets added) (NGFG, 2009):

What is the added value of a DPO?

- The data protection officer (DPO) is a legally recognized supervisor but is also part of the organization of the controller who appointed him. As a result, the DPO is well placed to assess issues concerning its controller and help think of appropriate solutions. [**DPO as a supervisor with an understanding of the specific business context**]

- The Cbp (data protection authority) will hold back in approaching organizations where a DPO oversees personal data protection compliance. DPOs will be included in the public register of data protection officers. [**Regulators stay away if an organization has a DPO**]

- The DPO is a permanent point of contact with a strong advisory role to the controller – which is usually the director or board of directors – in matters concerning (the improvement of) the use of personal data. The DPO can also act as an independent mediator and/or complaints handler. This does not then have to be carried out outside of the organization, which can benefit both parties. [**DPO as an advisor and a mediator**]

- Appointing a DPO is an appropriate measure when serious safeguards are required when registering and using personal data. The DPO has the capabilities to effectively assist the organization in striving to use personal data lawfully and carefully. The DPO can promote and maintain the privacy awareness necessary for this within the organization. By exercising its tasks and powers, the DPO contributes to guaranteeing the quality of data processing. [**DPO increases data protection awareness**]

With GDPR in force, the nuances of the advantages of appointing a DPO have changed. However, the core merit of having a DPO remains the same: overall, it improves the organizational accountability for protecting personal data.

As a side note, not every privacy officer, data protection counsel or director of privacy is automatically a DPO. Persons in these functions perhaps work in the area of data protection but do not necessarily satisfy the requirements listed in chapter 4, section 4 of GDPR (legislation.gov.uk, 2016). We will discuss the role of a DPO in detail, but before that let us take a look at when appointing a DPO becomes a legal obligation for your organization under GDPR.

When is appointing a DPO mandatory?

If your organization fulfils one of the following criteria, a DPO must be appointed (emphasis in bold added) (Article 37(1)). (legislation.gov.uk, 2016):

a. the processing is carried out by a public authority or body, except for courts acting in their judicial capacity;

b. the **core activities** of the controller or the processor consist of processing operations which, by their nature, their scope and/or their purposes, require **regular and systematic** monitoring of data subjects on a **large scale**; or

c. the **core activities** of the controller or the processor consist of processing on a **large scale** of special categories of data pursuant to Article 9 or personal data relating to criminal convictions and offences referred to in Article 10.

In case your organization concludes that it is not necessary to appoint a DPO, regulators recommend the analysis conducted to arrive at that decision be documented (Art 29 WP, 2017).

In many cases, organizations conducting marketing activities can be subject to (b) above. Let us take a closer look at the words 'core activities', 'large scale' and 'regular and systematic monitoring'.

Referring to Recital 97 of GDPR, regulators interpret the notion of 'core activities', appearing in (b) and (c) above, as key operations of your organization (legislation.gov.uk, 2016) (Art 29 WP, 2017). I think marketing for many organizations is an essential activity necessary to survive and thrive.

The EU data protection supervisors go on to use the following factors to decide whether processing is to be considered 'large scale' or not (Art 29 WP, 2017):

- The number of data subjects concerned – either as a specific number or as a proportion of the relevant population
- The volume of data and/or the range of different data items being processed
- The duration, or permanence, of the data processing activity
- The geographical extent of the processing activity

As examples of large-scale processing, EDPB mentions processing real-time geo-location data for statistical purposes, processing customer data by an insurance company or a bank, and processing data for behavioural marketing and search engines (Art 29 WP, 2017).

In addition, regulators include online behavioural advertising as an example of 'regular and systematic monitoring'. Email retargeting, location tracking and even data-driven marketing activities and loyalty programmes are considered 'regular and systematic monitoring' (Art 29 WP, 2017).

In other words, if your organization uses data-driven marketing to personalize communication with clients and prospects using behavioural advertising, the regulator most likely expects you to have a DPO.

OTHER SPECIFICITIES OF A DPO

GDPR explicitly mentions that companies can appoint a DPO voluntarily, even when none of the criteria under Article 37 is applicable. In that case, all requirements laid out in Articles 37 to 39 of GDPR must be fulfilled.

A DPO can be appointed for both controller and processor (legislation. gov.uk, 2016). Article 37 of GDPR also provides the possibility to appoint a single DPO for a group of companies (legislation.gov.uk, 2016). The EU-level regulators, however, raise a concern that in that case a DPO must be able to communicate with local data subjects and regulators effectively. In other words, regulators do not see problems in appointing one DPO for a group of companies based in one country; let's say one DPO for a group of companies with legal entities registered in Milan, Rome and Venice. If companies are thinking of appointing a single DPO for offices located in different jurisdictions, smooth communication with consumers as well as the regulators must be possible. One such way to overcome the mainly linguistic gap is to equip the DPO with local supporting teams (Art 29 WP, 2017).

A DPO can also be located outside of the EU, although EDPB believes that it is more beneficial if the DPO is located within the EU because contacting the DPO in many cases is easier that way (Art 29 WP, 2017). It must, however, be noted that this opinion is from 2017. With today's widespread use of video conferencing facilities and numerous communication apps, making time zones the only communication hurdle, regulators might change their opinion in this respect.

Lastly, once appointed, the contact details of your organization's DPO must be made public, according to Article 37(7) of GDPR (legislation.gov. uk, 2016). This does not mean that the name of the DPO must be published.

Rather, your organization should provide a way to contact the DPO to customers and prospects, as well as to employees and external business contacts. An example is to put a data protection hotline in place, or to create an online contact formula on your website that gets forwarded directly to the inbox of your DPO (Art 29 WP, 2017). On the other side, the name of the DPO must be disclosed to the data protection authority. After all, the DPO is the contact person at your organization for your data protection authority.

Qualification of a DPO

Your DPO must have expert knowledge of data protection laws and practices. DPO candidates can prove this with, among other things, academic degrees and certifications. This does not mean that legal knowledge is the only qualification the DPO must have. In my experience, persons with a law degree with a keen interest in data protection can very quickly acquire theoretical knowledge of this field. Much more challenging is to find a person who has both the expertise of data protection, as well as the knowledge of the specific business field. The regulators say that it is 'useful' to have business sector and organizational knowledge in their opinion paper (Art 29 WP, 2017). Depending on the complexity of your organization's marketing data use, I feel that meaningful data protection advice can only come from DPOs with a solid understanding of how marketers use personal data, in specific contexts such as Digital Out-Of-Home advertising. From my experience, many DPOs are versed in data protection topics related to HR, such as employee monitoring and whistleblowing. However, when it comes to marketing and advertising data use, there are not many DPOs that have in-depth knowledge. Organizations recruiting for a suitable DPO may have had similar experiences. In case your marketing operation is complex, it can take up to a year until a DPO without marketing or advertising knowledge can provide meaningful advice to your organization.

One option is to offer legal and data protection training and then appoint someone who is already employed by your company as a DPO. Here the challenge is to bring up this person's knowledge of data protection, though this is not impossible. I know DPOs who have come from the field of engineering and IT that are very effectively carrying out their duties.

When hiring a DPO with specific knowledge of marketing becomes a challenge, your company can also opt for hiring an external DPO, typically a law firm or a consultancy company, that has a wealth of knowledge and experience in both data protection and marketing. GDPR's Article 37(6) provides this possibility (legislation.gov.uk, 2016).

Apart from academic and vocational background, a DPO must have integrity and high professional ethics. EU regulators believe these personal qualities to be essential for a DPO to fulfil its tasks faithfully (Art 29 WP, 2017). Since the key role of a DPO is to foster a data-protecting culture, making it easier for your organization to implement policies and procedures required by GDPR, I strongly believe that to be a highly effective DPO you need to have excellent interpersonal skills. I will cover the topic of DPO and communication skills later on in this chapter.

The special status of a DPO

As an internal data protection supervisor, a DPO needs to have a degree of independence, as well as report to the most senior management. A DPO can have another job role; however, in that case it must be assured that there is no conflict of interest. Court cases have shown that persons holding a position as director of audit, risk management or compliance are usually considered not suitable for being a DPO at the same time (CNPD, 2021; GBA/APD, 2020).

Before GDPR was known in its final shape, I had several discussions with fellow DPOs about the problem of 'token DPOs'. Token DPOs are DPOs who are appointed more or less as an alibi, for the organization to pay a lip-service to data protection. They are characterized by having neither real independence from data processing decision making nor the chance to advise the stakeholders before deploying a particular data processing solution. We were concerned that one day companies would start appointing the secretary of an IT director or an admin person in the HR office as their DPO, whose decision can be overruled on a whim by their bosses.

The policymakers seem to have heard of this concern, and hard-wired the requirement that companies 'shall ensure that the data protection officer is involved, properly and in a timely manner, in all issues which relate to the protection of personal data' (Article 38(1) (legislation.gov.uk, 2016). Article 29 Data Protection Working Party expected a close working relationship between the DPO and the middle management, and for the advice of the DPO to be heard. In case management makes a decision not to follow the recommendation of the DPO, this must be documented in line with the accountability principle underlining GDPR (Art 29 WP, 2017).

So that DPOs can function properly, GDPR requires organizations to properly equip the DPO, including the provision of supporting staff, continuous training and time necessary to fulfil the work (Art 29 WP, 2017).

GDPR also protects DPOs from being laid off as a direct result of carrying out its tasks, like providing a negative assessment of a particular marketing data use (Article 38(3)) (legislation.gov.uk, 2016).

Tasks of a DPO

ADPO must not be in charge of implementing data protection measures like maintaining RoPA or deploying encryptions. These are on the shoulders of the business, or, more precisely, the management of your organization. Rather, your DPO is your organization's own data protection supervisor.

GDPR expects your DPO to help you, at a minimum in the following ways.

ADVISE THE ORGANIZATION

The first task GDPR assigns to a DPO is to inform and advise the organization. In particular, a DPO can tell you what you have to do, or what your obligations are, when processing personal data. What does that mean? If you have questions, for instance, what information should be given in the consent language when collecting email contact information in exchange for downloading an industry survey report on your website, your DPO should be able to give you practical advice.

MONITOR COMPLIANCE

The DPO is an internal supervisor of all things data protection who can assist your organization to monitor its compliance. It should be noted that the DPO is not the one to ensure that your organization is compliant; rather, the DPO supports the management of the organization to achieve compliance. It is up to the CMO or director of marketing to ensure that data is used for marketing, in line with GDPR and other data protection laws, as well as corporate policy.

DPO can flag non-compliance by gathering information to find out how data is being used by your company's marketers, in the form of an audit. DPO is also expected to take a deep dive into data uses, analyse them and check whether they are compliant. That way, the DPO can guide the management, which includes assigning responsibilities to the marketing department in improving compliance (Art 29 WP, 2017).

Your DPO is also expected to provide training to your company's staff, including the marketers. Your DPO should also undertake data protection awareness-raising activities. Data Protection Day is on 28 January, and it is a good moment for DPOs to hold privacy events or send out corporate-wide messages to remind everyone of the importance of protecting personal data.

ADVICE DURING DPIA

Article 35(2) explicitly requires your organization, and its management, to seek advice from the DPO during a DPIA. Article 39(1)c of GDPR in turn requires the DPO to provide advice, when requested, when your company is going through a DPIA (legislation.gov.uk, 2016).

If a particular data use, such as for location-based data capture, is identified as a DPIA candidate, marketers can ask the DPO (Art 29 WP, 2017):

- whether or not to carry out a DPIA
- what methodology to follow when carrying out a DPIA
- whether to carry out the DPIA in-house or whether to outsource it
- what safeguards (including technical and organizational measures) to apply to mitigate any risks to the rights and interests of the data subjects
- whether or not the data protection impact assessment has been correctly carried out and whether its conclusions (whether to go ahead with the processing and what safeguards to apply) are in compliance with the GDPR

This is not to say that the DPO's advice must always be followed. While your DPO can advise on aspects related to the processing of the persona data in question, and assess if what the marketer is proposing is compliant, marketers and other stakeholders may have other insights that need to be weighed when making a decision. For instance, they are able to take into consideration what the competitors are doing, or that the alternative more data-protection-friendly method will be frowned upon by existing customers. These additional aspects can give a very different perspective which might lead management to go against the advice given by the DPO. In such cases, EU regulators recommend organizations implement appropriate TOMs and include a statement in the DPIA documentation why not following the DPO's advice can be justified (Art 29 WP, 2017).

An important task of a DPO is to act as a contact person for the Data Protection Authority (DPA) and be a facilitator between your organization and the DPA. Most marketers might not know what exactly the regulators are looking for during an investigation. Armed with data protection expertise, DPOs in such instances can help marketers to put together an information package that is requested by the regulator. DPOs also have the right to approach the DPA with their own questions (Article 39) (legislation.gov.uk, 2016).

Article 39(2) is cryptic (legislation.gov.uk, 2016):

> The data protection officer shall in the performance of his or her tasks have due regard to the risk associated with processing operations, taking into account the nature, scope, context and purposes of processing.

According to this sentence, DPOs can approach their tasks with a risk-based approach. EDPB interprets this text such that DPOs should be paying more attention to processing activities with high risk, and deprioritizing those with low risk. This may explain why marketers will be questioned with intense rigour by the DPO, for instance, when applying facial-geometry-based mood-detection techniques for displaying advertising, while the collection of business cards at a trade show barely gets the attention of the DPO (Art 29 WP, 2017).

The DPDI Bill and the DPO

The DPDI Bill replaces the DPO with the Senior Responsible Individual, SRI for short. Unlike a DPO, the SRI must be a member of senior management, which means SRI is able to either make business decisions or is at least able to significantly influence business decisions. An SRI must be appointed if your organization is a public body, or carries out high-risk processing.

Marketers and DPO

What we have gone through so far in this chapter are the minimum requirements of a DPO. Your DPO can do much more, particularly with the help of your marketing department.

DATA PROTECTION OFFICER   229

Creating a data-protective culture

A motivated DPO with the firm backing of the C-suite or the senior management can achieve the goal of transforming the organizational culture to one that pays due respect to data protection. Adding the marketers to the mix, under the guidance of HR, will almost guarantee the success of such a transformation.

As discussed in the previous section, DPOs are expected to give training to increase data protection awareness in your organization. However, when it is the whole culture that needs to pivot, much more than just giving PowerPoint presentations and online training must be done. Let us review two approaches to managing organizational change, in this case, from a culture that is indifferent to data protection to one that embraces data protection.

Cameron and Quinn (2011), the authors of a classic textbook in the field of organizational behaviour, suggest a nine-step approach to initiating a cultural change:

1 reach consensus regarding the current organizational culture
2 reach consensus on the preferred future organizational culture
3 determine what the changes will and will not mean
4 identify stories illustrating the desired future culture
5 identify a strategic action agenda
6 identify immediate small wins
7 identify leadership implications
8 identify metrics, measures, and milestones to maintain accountability
9 identify a communication strategy

Navigating through organizational culture change looks a lot like developing a strategic marketing plan. Comparing this to the four elements of the marketing strategy we discussed in Chapter 2, a striking resemblance can be observed. Point 1 corresponds to 'where are we now?', points 2, 3 and 4 to 'where would we like to be?', points 5, 6, 7 and 9 'how do we get there?' and finally, point 8 triggers the same activities as the last element of developing a marketing strategy, 'are we on course?' (Jobber and Ellis-Chadwick, 2024).

It is assumed that the C-suite or the senior management will guide through the nine-step process, either by moderating the discussions themselves or by asking an external moderator. While the DPO can make meaningful contributions during all nine discussion phases, its input will be particularly valuable in determining what a data-protection-embracing organization will look like during point 2, and perhaps also point 3. My take is that marketing representatives will excel in discussions during point 4 above, because of the numerous storyboard sessions they may have had with the creative teams. Point 9 will be the place where the DPO and marketing representatives can play a leading role, jointly.

Another corporate culture change management approach focuses on major tasks that need to be carried out. Once a decision is made to turn the organization's culture to one that is more data protection conscious, the following four tasks need to be carried out (Bellingham, 2001):

Task 1: maximize commitment

- mobilize people behind the shared values, strategy and structure
- empower people
- recognize individual and team contributions

Task 2: build capacity

- develop people
- create a learning organization

Task 3: align the culture

- articulate the cultural requirements for success
- create a cultural revolution

Task 4: manage change

- promote understanding
- facilitate acceptance
- enable change

To accomplish the four tasks, to achieve a privacy-friendly company, will require a strong partnership between marketing and the DPO, under the guidance of HR. A DPO that can empower and mobilize employees in accomplishing Task 1 will give the organization a great head start.

HOW THE COLLABORATION BETWEEN MARKETING AND DPO KICKED OFF A CULTURE OF PRIVACY FRIENDLINESS

With a hefty sanction and associated negative publicity behind it in the recent past, one consumer-facing company decided to use the opportunity to change its culture to one that embraces data protection. The newly appointed DPO, in its effort to engage and motivate employees to become more data-protection-oriented, started a walk-in office hour. People were told that they could just stop by her office and ask any question related to data protection.

In the beginning, no one popped by. She then consulted the marketing department and she was advised to focus on one operational department at a time, just as marketers do in segmenting the consumer market to engage with each of them, separately, with more relevant messages. The marketing department also suggested sending different messages tailored to each department, using their internal social media platform. For departments with many employees who can access customer data, digital signage was placed at strategic locations, such as the reception area and the entrance to the kitchen, to attract employee attention. The marketing department also suggested the walk-in office hours be held in a room in the building of that department.

The support from marketing had an immediate effect. On the first day after these changes were made, one employee stopped by her office. She was asked if the particular data the team was analysing could be considered personal data and whether data protection laws would apply. In the following days, more and more employees started to visit her during the walk-in office hours as word-of-mouth spread.

This is a small success achieved on a grassroots level through the marketing department teaming up with the DPO. But there is more to the story. The DPO in question is a skilled communicator, and generally a fun person to hang out with. I am assuming that this helped increase the traffic to her walk-in office hours as well!

Internal marketing communication strategy

Devising a marketing communication strategy to promote data protection awareness is a good thing. Let me list out a few advantages of having one:

- **Improves compliance:** Employees that are aware and embrace the importance of data protection generally lead to better overall compliance of the company. Employees notice potential privacy problems and report them, and also take corrective actions themselves where necessary.

- **Boosts morale and supports privacy-conscious culture**: When a communication strategy on data protection awareness is deployed, it can foster a sense of pride in the minds of the employees, that the company they work for cares about their and everyone else's personal data.

- **Better collaboration**: Employees are empowered to share their thoughts, news and articles on the topic of data protection on internal social media and chat groups. This leads to an improved sense of being in a data protection community.

- **Better alignment to company's data protection goals**: With employees embracing the importance of protecting data, it is easier to ensure the focus in every project, every meeting or chat discussion is aligned with the company goal of becoming privacy-centric.

- **Smooth change management**: Well-executed communication strategy on data protection makes it easier to implement changes. For instance, a required change can be putting in a more cumbersome approval process for uploading customer data onto a SaaS platform. Employees will be more accepting of additional documentation requirements necessary for data protection compliance.

- **Become brand ambassadors**: Employees who are embracing data protection culture may become engaged on the topic of data protection, even outside your organization. Empowered employees might show interest in joining a data protection committee at a trade association. They may enthusiastically share what their employer does to better protect personal data, supporting the data-protecting culture wholeheartedly while having conversations with customers and partners as well as with friends and family.

There may be many other good reasons why your DPO might want to help develop an internal communication strategy, but they most likely will not have the skill set to develop one. Here, support from the marketing department will make a big difference.

How DPOs can help marketers

Now that we have discussed how DPOs can significantly benefit from working together with your marketing department, let's explore how your marketing department can benefit from working closely with your DPO.

The investor relations team, within the marketing team, need to inform the board of the company's views on a particular privacy issue in the news, or about the preparedness of the company for an upcoming law change. The DPO is usually able to give insightful advice that can be used to craft a convincing message to the board, which in turn may be communicated publicly.

In another situation, where data protection incidents such as security breaches or negative press coverage related to data protection take place, your company must prepare itself to act and, where necessary, draw up crisis communication. Crisis communication is all about managing the perception of reality, which in turn shapes public opinion (Fink, 2013). Your organization most probably has a security policy, which has a section on how a crisis should be managed: who should be involved, the process of escalation, who is the spokesperson and how to develop internal FAQs and drawer statements for the press (Bernstein, 2011).

The PR specialists, tasked with crafting the message, need to be supported by advice based on sound data protection knowledge. This is what your DPO is there for! The crisis management team, which counts your DPO as a member, will assess the situation to understand what has happened. Next, the impact on the marketplace and customers is predicted. Companies will also try to guess the reaction of the regulator. In doing so, your DPO's contribution will be essential, as it is the DPO who maintains direct contact with the data protection authority. When the crisis is in the public domain, the likely reaction of the general public must also be taken into consideration. Several alternative scenarios can then be developed so that the crisis management team, and ultimately the CEO, can make decisions on how to deal with the situation, and then execute a suitable communication plan. Fink (2013) suggests managers use a three-step process for breaking the bad news with the least damage.

> First, provide a positive statement about the progress being made.
> Second, deliver the bad news.
>
> Third, provide a positive statement and assessment about solutions going forward.

Assuming that this is how your organization will develop its communication materials, the DPO can conduct an analysis and report back to the team on what could have gone worse. From this, finding a positive statement can be made by the PR specialist. After delivering the bad news, solutions going forward can be developed, once again, with your DPO.

Your DPO can also be helpful to your marketing department to promote your products and services. For instance, there are numerous ways in which your DPO can also help position the company as a data-protection-compliant organization. In a business-to-business context, organizations can have their DPO as a speaker at their client event, allowing them to possibly boost their image as privacy leaders in the marketplace. The same can be achieved by featuring an article by your DPO in the company newsletter. If your DPO is active in privacy associations or is a frequent speaker at data protection conferences, your organization can indirectly position itself as a privacy leader in the field.

Communication skills are crucial to a DPO

We have discussed that your DPO must work closely with the marketing department to excel in nurturing a data protection culture. Let me shed more light on how important communication skills are to fulfil the role and tasks of a DPO.

GDPR lists, among other things, the following expectations from a DPO (legislation.gov.uk, 2016):

> Article 38(1)
>
> The controller and the processor shall ensure that the data protection officer is involved, properly and in a timely manner, in all issues which relate to the protection of personal data.
>
> Article 38(4)
>
> Data subjects may contact the data protection officer with regard to all issues related to processing of their personal data and to the exercise of their rights under this Regulation.
>
> Article 39(1)a
>
> [DPO] to inform and advise the controller or the processor and the employees who carry out processing of their obligations pursuant to this Regulation and to other Union or Member State data protection provisions.
>
> Article 39(1)b
>
> [DPO] to monitor compliance with this Regulation, with other Union or Member State data protection provisions and with the policies of the controller or processor in relation to the protection of personal data, including the assignment of responsibilities, awareness-raising and training of staff involved in processing operations, and the related audits;

Article 39(1)c

[DPO] to provide advice where requested as regards the data protection impact assessment and monitor its performance pursuant to Article 35;

Article 39(1)d

[DPO] to cooperate with the supervisory authority;

Article 39(1)e

[DPO] to act as the contact point for the supervisory authority on issues relating to processing, including the prior consultation referred to in Article 36, and to consult, where appropriate, with regard to any other matter.

All the tasks and roles associated with the DPO mentioned above require the DPO to be an advisor, trainer, contact person and someone who can work together with others. These imply that DPO has a job that requires intensive personal contact. To perform well, the DPO must have great interpersonal skills.

THE DPO AS A TRUSTED ADVISOR

Whether the senior management or the C-suite accept the suggestion from the DPO in its advisory role is largely dependent on how the DPO presents the recommendations, and how much trust the DPO has in the management or the C-suite.

Based on their experience, Doorley and Garcia (2020) conclude that trusted advisors of business leaders exhibit the following 10 personal attributes. Here I have replaced the original notion of 'communicator' which the authors use with 'DPO' to emphasize the point.

1 **Professional credibility**: Quality of strategic thinking and counsel

2 **Reliability**: Execution of strategy and provision of tactical support

3 **Integrity**: Trustworthiness, whether the DPO 'says what he or she means and means what he or she says'

4 **Motives**: Commitment to the advancement of the leader's agenda (even at a cost or inconvenience to the DPO)

5 **Likability/chemistry**: Whether it's easy and enjoyable to work with the DPO

6 **Business acumen**: The degree to which the DPO understands the business context

7 **Organizational credibility and relationships**: The degree to which the leader can benefit from the DPO's knowledge of the organization and participation in its informal networks

8 **Problem-solving:** The DPO's ability to assess obstacles and develop solutions

9 **Time management:** The DPO's ability to prioritize and get things done

10 **Energy management:** The DPO's energy, perspective and resilience (e.g. resistance to burnout)

In other words, to become an effective and trusted advisor to senior management, a DPO must exhibit the traits listed above. Similarly, when choosing a DPO for your organization, interviewers of candidates should look at all 10 aspects of the person, in addition to the skill sets and experience of the person.

ACTIVE LISTENING SKILLS CAN HELP YOUR DPO

Apart from being an advisor, a DPO has to communicate with your marketers and others in the organization in a variety of ways, from training and conflict resolution to negotiation. It may be surprising to hear that general communication skills can be acquired by consciously learning certain techniques. One such technique is active listening. Unlike just listening, active listening requires the participants of the communication to fully concentrate on what is being said, as opposed to passively *hearing* the conversation, which is perhaps the reason why the technique is the foundation of successful communication. When marketers sense that they are being listened to, and have all the focus of the DPO, it can lead to a feeling of being valued and heard. Active listening can hence create a sense of trust and strengthen working relationships. It also helps people retain more of the conversation (Guffey and Loewy, 2014).

Active listening requires actively engaging in listening, reflecting on and summarizing what has been said, asking appropriately timed questions, and displaying verbal and non-verbal messages reflective of being engaged – all while being non-judgemental (Clarke, 2023).

To begin with, it is important to have the right set-up for the conversation. The DPO should be mindful of choosing the right time, place and opportunity. This will help to get into the mindset necessary to start a good conversation. In doing so, the DPO must constantly remind themselves that the goal is to understand the marketing manager's or marketing data scientist's motivation and the real issue that is behind what is being said. Add to this mix the four-step active listening framework, and your DPO can improve their communication skills. Here are the steps that I have adapted from Koffman (2020) and Rosenberg and Chopra (2015):

Step 1: Listen and understand. Let the person talk.

Step 2: Offer encouragement so the person is motivated to tell more.

Step 3: Summarize what you have understood.

Step 4: Acknowledge the other person's perspective.

Steps 1 and 2 help your DPO embrace their curiosity as a listener, and the last two steps may help your DPO come across as an empathetic and responsive listener. When following these steps, conversations are bound to conclude on a positive note!

DPO ACHIEVING THE DESIRED OUTCOME WITH ACTIVE LISTENING

This is how the conversation could go if the DPO does not use the active listening technique:

(on a video conference)

Lilly the DPO: (typing along something on the computer) Hey, I haven't seen your DPIA pre-screening form for the audience measurement tool yet. I thought it was urgent.

Jamie the marketing manager: Sort of. We are planning to sign the licence agreement next week.

Lilly: (immediately snaps back) Next week? So, why didn't you put in the request? You know it needs to go through the entire procedure on our end. I thought that you were fully aware that the security team needs to have all the documents before they can even start reviewing. Do you think you are the only person wanting to put a new system in place? Our lives do not revolve around you!

Jamie: Sorry.

Jamie and Lilly: (both in a bad mood, no solution)

Notice how Lilly the DPO was not giving her full attention to Jamie from the very beginning. She is also not giving much space for Jamie to talk and just states her interpretation of the situation. I am not sure whether Jamie will fill out the DPIA pre-screening form after this conversation.

And here is how the conversation can develop when Lilly the DPO adopts active listening:

Lilly: (after sharing a funny anecdote from a party last week) Hey, Jamie, before I forget, I thought I'd ask you about something. What happened to the audience measurement tool? I thought you wanted to request a DPIA pre-screening?

Jamie: (slightly embarrassed) I honestly don't know where to start with the DPIA pre-screening form. My boss sent me a link where I can access the form. But it is just overwhelming. And we want to sign the licence next week!

Lilly: What do you mean, 'overwhelming'?

Jamie: I don't know what the ask is. (He clicks on something and shares his screen.) Like this one, what do you mean by 'Are you a Controller or a Processor?' Or this other one 'Who are the recipients of the data?' How would I know? The person assigned to whatever the project is from the marketing analytics team gets the results.

Lilly: Oh, I see. The questions are not clear enough. Did you click on the question mark buttons in the legend to the right of each question?

Jamie: I could have, yes. But let me tell you, I didn't want to click on every single question mark button on the form. I got fed up looking at it and decided to ask Tony from IT to fill it out for me. And forgot to do that too.

Jamie and Lilly: (both burst into laughter)

Lilly: Yeah, that happens. Glad you forgot to ask him because Tony has nothing to do with audience measurement tools. He would not be able to answer the questions, even if he knew what controller and processor were or what is meant by the recipient of data.

Jamie: True.

Lilly: Besides, you could have contacted me or anyone else in my team. We even have a link to a training video for using the DPIA pre-screening form.

Jamie: I didn't know that. It is so kind of you to offer help. But you know, your team spent so much time with us on the product launch campaign last week, so I didn't want to come to you yet again and ask for more help. I didn't want to be so demanding.

Lilly: Ah, so you thought you would be giving me more work by asking me for help?

Jamie: Yes, and also, perhaps, I felt a bit embarrassed. I bet I am the only person from the marketing team who was confused by the form.

Lilly: Not to worry. The UX of the form is not particularly great. But the form has to be filled out so that we can kick off and complete the evaluation in time. Our security specialists, for instance, always need to have all the relevant documents from the vendors and that typically takes time. And yes, needing to click all of the information buttons can put people off. Do try the training video and see how you get on.

Jamie: I will do that this afternoon.

Lilly: (after a short pause) You know what? Since we work so closely with your department, what about this? I see that we both have a free slot at 3 pm today. Why don't we set up a video conference call and I can walk you through the form, and we can fill it out together. Deal?

Jamie: You are an angel! Thanks so much. (Sends a calendar invitation for 3 pm to Lilly.)

Lilly first of all makes sure that the conversation starts in an upbeat mood. Her concentration is fully on Jamie. Notice how she started off the conversation to allow Jamie to tell her his side of the story. She then asks an open-ended question 'What do you mean by "overwhelming"?' which encourages Jamie to open up and tell more about these thoughts. Lilly also summarizes what she heard Jamie say and shows that she understands what Jamie's real issue is. He did not feel comfortable giving more work to Lilly and was also embarrassed that he lacked the knowledge to fill out the form. How nice of Lilly to offer him help, personally.

Active listening is a skill that can be learned. DPOs and marketers can have constructive conversations that can lead to positive long-term relationship building.

Key takeaways

1 A DPO is an internal data protection supervisor. The role and the tasks of a DPO are specified in GDPR.

2 Appointing a DPO is not mandatory unless your organization fulfils certain criteria. Organizations involved in personalized marketing will likely need a DPO.

3 DPOs' tasks are advisory, which makes it important for them to be able to work independently.

4 Teamwork between marketers and DPOs can help organizations become more data protection aware.

5 DPOs' tasks and functions require sound interpersonal skills. The ability to communicate effectively greatly improves the effectiveness of the DPO in making the company privacy-friendly.

Conclusion

Your DPO helps your organization to become more compliant with data protection laws through a variety of support measures, such as providing advice to the senior management and training. It is, however, the responsibility of the C-suite or the senior management to implement measures necessary to operate the business in a lawful manner. Beyond the tasks specified in GDPR, the DPO can assist senior management in bringing about cultural change to the organization, as it relates to attitudes towards data protection. Your marketing department can be of great assistance in such situations, particularly in shaping internal communication. A DPO can also contribute to the marketing effort, particularly where the organization wishes to position itself as a privacy-friendly company, or when crafting crisis communication materials. Interpersonal and communication skills of a DPO, not explicitly mentioned in GDPR, can make a significant impact on the effective functioning of the DPO. Such skills can be learned, just like knowledge of data protection laws or the specific operational context of a company or an industry.

Bibliography

Art 29 WP (2017) Article 29 Data Protection Working Party, Guidelines on Data Protection Officers ('DPOs'), adopted on 13 December 2016, last revised and adopted on 5 April 2017, https://ec.europa.eu/newsroom/article29/items/612048 (archived at https://perma.cc/A6JR-E2AF)

Bellingham, R ed. (2001) *The Manager's Pocket Guide to Corporate Culture Change*, HRD Press, Amherst, MA, USA

Bernstein, J (2011) *Manager's Guide to Crisis Management*, McGraw-Hill, New York, USA

Cameron, K S and Quinn, R E (2011) *Diagnosing and Changing Organizational Culture: Based on the competing values framework*, 3rd edn, Jossey-Bass, Hoboken , NJ, USA

Clarke, D (2023) Improving your listening skills (online video), www.linkedin.com/learning/improving-your-listening-skills-19238090/improving-your-listening-skills?u=2103289 (archived at https://perma.cc/TF72-7DDX)

CNPD (2021) La Commission nationale pour la protection des données – Grand-Douché de Luxembourg: Décision de la Commission nationale siégeant en formation restreinte sur l'issue de l'enquête n° ... menée auprès de la Société A Délibération n° 37FR/2021 du 13 octobre 2021, https://cnpd.public.lu/content/dam/cnpd/fr/decisions-fr/2021/Decision-37FR-2021-sous-forme-anomyisee.pdf (archived at https://perma.cc/KS54-QZWY)

Doorley, J and Garcia, F (2020) *Reputation Management*, 4th edn, Routledge, Abingdon

eur-lex.europa.eu (1995) Directive 95/46/EC of the European Parliament and of the Council of 24 October 1995 on the protection of individuals with regard to the processing of personal data and on the free movement of such data, https://eur-lex.europa.eu/LexUriServ/LexUriServ.do?uri=CELEX:31995L0046:en:HTML (archived at https://perma.cc/5VHL-DVFT)

Fink, S (2013) *Crisis Communications: The definitive guide to managing the message*, McGraw-Hill, New York, USA

GBA/APD (2020) Gegevensbeschermingsautoriteit/ Autorité de protection des données, Belgie/Belgique, Geschillenkamer, Beslissing ten gronde 18/2020 van 28 april 2020, Dossiernummer : AH-2019-0013, Betreft: Inspectieverslag over verantwoordelijkheid bij gegevenslekken en positie functionaris gegevensbescherming, www.gegevensbeschermingsautoriteit.be/publications/beslissing-ten-gronde-nr.-18-2020.pdf (archived at https://perma.cc/99CN-M8L2

Guffey, M E and Loewy, D (2014) *Business Communication: Process and product*, Cengage Learning, Andover

Jobber, D and Ellis-Chadwick, F (2024) *Principles and Practice of Marketing*, McGraw Hill, Maidenhead

Koffman, F (2020) Difficult conversations with Fred Kofman (online video), www.youtube.com/watch?v=_TNrSo1brdY (archived at https://perma.cc/ZP5F-V3DC)

legislation.gov.uk (2016) Regulation (EU) 2016/679 of the European Parliament and of the Council, 27 April 2016, www.legislation.gov.uk/eur/2016/679/article/4 (archived at https://perma.cc/TEZ5-5MU4)

NGFG (2009) Nederlands genootschap van functionarissen voor de gegevensbescherming, Privacywet en privacyfunctionaris: Val ik in de prijzen?

overheid.nl (2001) Wet bescherming persoonsgegevens, 1 September 2001, https://wetten.overheid.nl/BWBR0011468/2018-05-01 (archived at https://perma.cc/5RYS-3T6F)

Rosenberg, M B and Chopra, D (2015) *Nonviolent Communication: A language of life: Life-changing tools for healthy relationships*, Puddle Dancer Press, Encinitas, CA, USA

12

AI and marketing

My mother decided to create a new profile picture, using an AI-powered drawing app, for her social media account. She wanted to have the same motif she had been using for decades for her personalized stationery. On her notepads and envelopes, she had a picture of her playing the piano with the family dog curled up near the pedals. So, she typed in 'A woman in her 70s playing the grand piano with a fluffy white dog with black spots lying down next to her' in the tool. She was astonished to find out that her app only draws a young woman playing the piano, regardless of how she tweaks the command. After several attempts, she managed to have a silver-haired woman in the picture, but not playing the piano. Instead, the elderly lady was watching a young lady playing the piano. 'Is AI telling me that only youngsters are allowed to play the piano?' She was insulted. After all, she puts in two to three hours every day practising the piano. This is just one example that portrays one of the challenges of AI, namely that of bias by data. In this final chapter, we will take a look at AI used for marketing and the evolving legal environment, and how to leverage the knowledge of data protection governance to use AI tools responsively.

What is AI?

The expression Artificial Intelligence was first defined by John McCarthy in 1955 as: 'the science and engineering of making intelligent machines' (Manning, 2020). The sense of what AI is still remains in the most widely adopted definition today, the definition of the OECD:

> AI system: An AI system is a machine-based system that, for explicit or implicit objectives, infers, from the input it receives, how to generate outputs such as

predictions, content, recommendations, or decisions that can influence physical or virtual environments. Different AI systems vary in their levels of autonomy and adaptiveness after deployment. (OECD, 2023)

First and foremost, it is a machine. Secondly, AI or an AI system has objectives. Thirdly, there is an input, and lastly, it generates an output that influences the physical or the virtual world. Let me use this definition to assess whether my mother's drawing app fits the definition of an AI system. My mom's app is a machine, or to put it another way, the smartphone, within which it is embedded, is a machine. Its objective is to draw pictures and use graphic images, presumably from online sources, as input. It also uses my mother's instruction as an input to create its output, a digital drawing. The result can be shared virtually on my mother's social media with her friends, who might drop a comment or two on her new profile picture. I can therefore conclude that my mother's drawing app is an AI system.

Use of AI in marketing

When used correctly, AI is very useful. McKinsey's report on AI shows that most marketing and sales departments they surveyed made use of AI tools (QuantumBlack AI by McKinsey, 2023). There are five ways AI can augment or carry out marketing tasks, particularly those that do not require expert knowledge, namely, Text-based AI, Visual-based AI, Interactive AI, Analytical AI and Functional AI (Bekker, 2019).

Text-based AI

Text-based AI, like ChatGPT 3.5, can generate text content for marketing communication. The result can be blogs, email messages, web content or subtitles for video materials. What creative writers took hours to generate can be generated in a few seconds using text-based AIs. In the field of business-to-business, tailor-made digital catalogues can be generated on the fly, depending on which industry the buyer is from. For instance, for buyers of office products, stationery and consumable items will be featured prominently in the first couple of pages, while for buyers from the construction industries, information on different seals and screws can be placed in the first few pages instead. Email messages can also be personalized in real-time, giving marketers the possibility to weave in a sentence that refers to the last interaction with the customer, giving the email message a very personal touch.

Visual-based AI

AI can create logos, videos and pictures that can be embedded in websites, presentation slides and even on products. Without searching through photo stock libraries, marketers can also create the same picture of a family in several variations: a family sitting on a bench, relaxing at a beach or with a baby in a pram, within seconds.

Interactive AI

Interactive AI is the engine of chatbots. Chatbots need to be fed specific data and trained for your customers before they can be deployed. The advantage of chatbots is that they can interact with many customers simultaneously. This means shorter waiting times for the customers and fewer ticketed items internally for the call centre.

Analytic AI

The use of Analytic AI is perhaps most established in the field of marketing and advertising. Analytic AI taps into marketing data, kept in CRM, campaign management system, CDP or in a corporate data lake and generates recommendations and creates insights for the user. This type of AI democratizes analytics, as it makes insights from data accessible to all marketers, even those without the skill to mine raw data. While marketers today still need the assistance of an experienced marketing data scientist for complex analyses, simple queries can be made available to them without waiting for a junior analyst to work on them and return them.

Chaffey (2023) summarizes the main use of Analytic AI as follows (I added points 6 and 7 to this list):

1 **Customer segmentation:** Predictive analytics is used to segment customers based on various attributes, such as demographics, behaviour, lifetime value and purchase history.

2 **Lead scoring:** By analysing historical data and identifying patterns, predictive analytics can assign scores to leads, indicating their likelihood to convert into customers. This helps marketing and sales teams prioritize their efforts on high-potential leads, leading to more efficient lead management.

3 **Churn prediction**: Predictive models forecast which customers are at risk of churning (leaving) based on their behaviour and interactions. Marketers can implement retention strategies to reduce customer churn.

4 **Personalization and recommendation engines**: E-commerce and content platforms use predictive algorithms to suggest products, services or content to users based on their past behaviours and preferences. This enhances the user experience and drives sales or engagement.

5 **Marketing campaign optimization**: Predictive analytics can help optimize marketing campaigns by predicting which channels, messages and timing are most likely to yield the highest conversion rates. This maximizes the return on investment (ROI) of marketing efforts.

6 **Data anonymization**: Privacy enhancement technology (PET) is used to create calculation intensive synthetic datasets. AI-based PETs can also carry out homomorphic encryption of data, as well as analyse the encrypted records.

7 **Data preparation**: Many data preparation modules available through CDPs identify relevant customer data kept in different locations, put identified data first through standard hygiene (standardization, normalization, parsing, etc.), then through a PET, and match the resulting records to create marketing insight file.

Functional AI

Functional AI goes a step further compared to Analytic AI. Instead of just making recommendations or providing insights, functional AI uses the data and acts without the interference of a human. For instance, dynamic pricing AI will search e-commerce outlets and price comparison websites, and compare them with historical price movement data. Based on these inputs, it would adjust the price of your product in your online shop to attract more customers, or change the pricing so that it hits the right balance between profit margin and revenue (Marketing Evolution, 2022). It must also be noted that because functional AI makes automatic decisions, when personal data is used as input, GDPR's articles related to automated decision making may become applicable (legislation.gov.uk, 2016).

Concerns about using AI

AI, just like the personal data it often makes use of, is a double-edged sword. AI can bring a quantum leap in boosting marketing efficiencies, but it can also bring some challenges. Weizenbaum (1978), who programmed the first chatbot called ELIZA, pleaded the development of an ethical framework to protect mankind from AI harm as early as 1976. Extreme AI risks can be broadly categorized into four types (Hendrycks et al, 2023):

- **Malicious use**: Actors could intentionally harness powerful AIs to cause widespread harm. Specific risks include bioterrorism enabled by AIs that can help humans create deadly pathogens; the deliberate dissemination of uncontrolled AI agents; and the use of AI capabilities for propaganda, censorship, and surveillance. [...]

- **AI race**: Competition could pressure nations and corporations to rush the development of AIs and cede control to AI systems. Militaries might face pressure to develop autonomous weapons and use AIs for cyberwarfare, enabling a new kind of automated warfare where accidents can spiral out of control before humans have the chance to intervene. Corporations will face similar incentives to automate human labour and prioritize profits over safety, potentially leading to mass unemployment and dependence on AI systems... evolutionary pressures might shape AIs in the long run. Natural selection among AIs may lead to selfish traits, and the advantages AIs have over humans could eventually lead to the displacement of humanity. [...]

- **Organizational risks**: Organizational accidents have caused disasters including Chernobyl, Three Mile Island, and the Challenger Space Shuttle disaster. Similarly, the organizations developing and deploying advanced AIs could suffer catastrophic accidents, particularly if they do not have a strong safety culture. AIs could be accidentally leaked to the public or stolen by malicious actors. Organizations could fail to invest in safety research, lack understanding of how to reliably improve AI safety faster than general AI capabilities, or suppress internal concerns about AI risks...

- **Rogue AIs**: A common and serious concern is that we might lose control over AIs as they become more intelligent than we are. AIs could optimize flawed objectives to an extreme degree in a process called proxy gaming.

AIs could experience goal drift as they adapt to a changing environment, similar to how people acquire and lose goals throughout their lives. In some cases, it might be instrumentally rational for AIs to become power-seeking. [...] AIs might engage in deception, appearing to be under control when they are not. These problems are more technical than the first three sources of risk. [...]

Let's now bring it down to the discussion of risks to those that are not necessarily existentially threatening to mankind, which your marketers may already be confronted by today. OECD (2019) categorizes these harms into five categories, namely:

1 **Purposeful 'harm by design'**: Deepfake video designed to harm an individual's reputation and right to privacy.
2 **Harm caused by inherent 'side effects'**: Biased training data leading to discrimination. Social media algorithm promoting hate speech or false information.
3 **Harm caused by failure rates**: False positives by facial recognition in law enforcement.
4 **Harm caused by intentional misuse**: Political disinformation using data/AI systems.
5 **Harm caused by security breach**: Hackers taking control of autonomous vehicles.

By translating these harms into the context of marketing, the following picture emerges:

1 **Purposeful 'harm by design'**: Deepfake video designed to harm competitor's product, service or general reputation.
2 **Harm caused by inherent 'side effects'**: Biased training data leads to assigning customers to the wrong segments, leading to communicating irrelevant commercial messages.
3 **Harm caused by failure rates**: Matching wrong IDs will identify customers incorrectly. Falsely identified customers may be displayed advertisements that are not relevant to them or can be wrongfully told that they are not eligible for a particular discount.
4 **Harm caused by intentional misuse**: An AI-generated exaggerated claim of a laundry detergent advertising that makes white shirts stainless, which when used does not get rid of brownish-yellow coffee stains reliably.

5 **Harm caused by security breach**: Hackers messed up the audience assignment delivered to a DMP, resulting in students getting ads on investment strategies for early retirement and the elderly group getting ads for student loans.

Undoubtedly, these are unacceptable marketing disasters. However, it must be noted that the harm of using AI tools in a marketing context is not as dramatic as those in some other cases, such as law enforcement and medical use.

The EU AI Act

Noting both the advantages and the risks of AI, the draft of a comprehensive AI law, the Artificial Intelligence Act, was proposed by the European Commission in 2021 (eur-lex.europa.eu, 2021). The AI Act aims to nurture innovation with AI while ensuring that deployed AI systems, which affect EU-based persons, are safe and respect fundamental rights. In December 2023, during the trialogue phase of this dossier, the three EU institutions, the European Parliament representing the different EU parties, the European Council representing the member states and the European Commission, arrived at a political agreement on the key terms of the AI Act. The text as a result of the negotiation will be made final after technical details are fine-tuned, and the final editing and translations are completed. The AI Act is a regulation so it will be implemented in all EU member states, directly (eur-lex.europa.eu, 2021).

The final text of the AI Act will inform how your organization, and your marketing department, can prepare for the compliance obligations to come. I speculate that this law will become a blueprint for other comprehensive AI legislations around the globe, just as GDPR has influenced legislative activities on data protection laws worldwide.

Premises of the AI Act

The AI Act is expected to be adopted and published on the official journal of the EU in 2024. Twenty-four months after its publication, the Act will be fully enforceable. The final definition of AI, or more precisely AI systems, is not yet in the public domain (as of 4 January 2024). However, the Council of the EU has announced that the definition adopted is aligned with that of the OECD, discussed earlier in this chapter (Council of the European Union, 2023). This is expected to increase the interoperability of the EU AI Act with other laws around the world.

Furthermore, the AI Act applies to all systems impacting persons in the EU, which means that even if your organization is not located in the EU, the law can be applicable (Council of the European Union, 2023).

Just as GDPR recognizes the different capacities of organizations, controller or processor, the AI Act recognizes three distinct roles. The rough descriptions of these three roles are (Council of the European Union, 2022; European Parliament, 2023; eur-lex.europa.eu, 2021):

Provider: Organization that develops AI systems

Deployer: Organization using an AI system

Distributor: Organization that puts the AI system on the market.

In this chapter, I will focus on the applicability of the AI Act on deployer because, as far as marketing departments are concerned, they are usually acting in this capacity.

Classification of AI

Following the risk-based approach, the compliance obligations under the AI Act vary depending on the inherent risk of the AI system in question.

PROHIBITED AI SYSTEM

Legislators ban certain categories of AI systems outright. In her speech, von der Leyen, the president of the EU Commission explained (EU Commission, 2023a):

Unacceptable risk: AI systems considered a clear threat to the fundamental rights of people **will be banned**. This includes AI systems or applications that manipulate human behaviour to circumvent users' free will, such as toys using voice assistance to encourage dangerous behaviour of minors or systems that allow 'social scoring' by governments or companies and certain applications of predictive policing. In addition, some uses of biometric systems will be prohibited, for example, emotion recognition systems used at the workplace and some systems for categorizing people or real-time remote biometric identification for law enforcement purposes in publicly accessible spaces (with narrow exceptions).

For marketing AI use, it is very unlikely that current or envisaged AI use will fall under this prohibited AI category, provided that organizations adhere to the industry code of conduct and data protection laws.

HIGH-RISK AI

When an AI system is considered critical, regardless of whether the system is already commercialized or not, the AI Act requires that it fulfils numerous requirements. High-risk AI systems are listed in the annexes of the AI Act. Apart from AI systems used as safety components of a product, such as safety systems of motor vehicles, civil aviation, toys and medical devices, AI systems in the following categories will be considered high risk (Council of the European Union, 2022; European Parliament, 2023; eur-lex.europa.eu, 2021):

1 biometrics
2 critical infrastructure
3 education and vocational training
4 employment, workers management and access to self-employment
5 access to and enjoyment of essential private services and essential public services and benefits
6 law enforcement
7 migration, asylum and border control management
8 administration of justice and democratic processes

It is hence highly unlikely for marketing AI systems to be classified as high-risk AI. In case a marketing AI used by your marketers falls under the high-risk AI category, the following obligations need to be fulfilled (Council of the European Union, 2022; European Parliament, 2023; eur-lex.europa. eu, 2021):

1 carry out a Fundamental Rights Impact Assessment
2 there must be human oversight by trained, competent persons
3 input data must be relevant for the AI system use
4 when the system becomes a national threat, suspend the use of the AI system
5 inform the AI system Provider of serious incidents
6 retain automatically generated system logs

7 comply with registration requirements (applies to public authorities only)

8 perform, if required under GDPR, a Data Protection Impact Assessment

9 ensure compliance with the AI Act and support this with documented evidence (Accountability requirement)

10 inform people that they may be subject to the use of high-risk AI

MINIMAL-RISK AI

The AI Act further lists several AI uses that do not fall under prohibited or high-risk AI, but nevertheless require more precautions due to its sensitivity. These include AI systems which (Council of the European Union, 2022; European Parliament, 2023; eur-lex.europa.eu, 2021):

1 interact with people

2 use biometric categorization system

3 recognize emotion

4 generate or manipulate image, audio or video that can falsely appear authentic

When your marketing department uses an AI system falling under any of the four categories listed above, your customers and prospects need to be informed that AI systems are in use. For instance, when a chatbot is deployed on your website, web visitors need to be informed that they are interacting with a machine. When the creative wing of your marketing team is generating videos or images, using AI, which look very authentic, they must ensure that these artworks are clearly labelled as AI-generated images or videos.

For all other AI uses that are not prohibited, not high-risk and cannot be categorized under the four categories we just covered, no obligations are due under the AI Act. However, the applicability of the Act should be examined and documented. In other words, it is well worth the investment to prove that your organization did its homework and surveyed all the AI systems in use. Once mapped, AI systems can be once again systematically evaluated if they are prohibited, high-risk, sensitive or minimal-risk AI and appropriate measures have to be taken to fulfil the relevant obligations.

OVERSIGHT AND PENALTIES

A new oversight structure will be put in place once the AI Act is enacted. The Commission announced that an AI Office will be established within the

European Commission. The AI Office will be tasked to oversee advanced AI models, help foster standards and testing practices and ensure harmonization of the rules under the AI Act across the EU. There will also be a group of experts, referred to as a 'scientific panel of independent experts', who can advise the AI Office on technical issues (EU Commission, 2023a).

Governance on the member state level will be carried out by what the spokespersons of the EU institutions refer to as 'national competent market surveillance authorities'. The market surveillance authorities will supervise the implementation of the new rules (Council of the European Union, 2023).

Separately, the AI Board, comprising of EU member states' representatives, will be set up as an advisory board to the Commission. The AI Board will receive advice from an 'advisory forum' with stakeholders from the industry, academia and civil societies (Council of the European Union, 2023).

PENALTIES

What makes the AI Act a law with teeth is the size of its maximum fines. Using a prohibited AI system can cost an organization as much as €35 million or 7 per cent of the global annual turnover of the previous year, whichever is higher (Council of the European Union, 2023). In comparison, GDPR has a maximum penalty of 4 per cent of the global turnover. The maximum sanction is €15 million or 3 per cent of the global annual turnover for failing to fulfil the obligations in relation to high-risk AI and €7.5 million or 1.5 per cent of the global annual revenue for giving incorrect information to the market surveillance authority (Council of the European Union, 2023).

EU COMMISSION LOOKING FOR EARLY ADOPTERS

While the AI Act is still being worked upon, the Commission has started a so-called AI Pact, which will allow both organizations and the EU institutions to learn from each other on the workings of the AI Act before the law becomes enforceable. To join the AI Pact, the Commission asks the organizations to pledge, or to sign a declaration of engagement, to adhere to the AI Act voluntarily before it becomes enforceable. Invitation to the AI Pact is also extended to organizations that are not headquartered in the EU (EU Commission, 2023).

Towards responsible AI use in marketing

Because the AI Act's focus is on prohibited and high-risk AI, your marketing department will most likely not experience the level of stress they would have had in the run-up of GDPR coming into force. Nevertheless, in future-proofing your marketing team, it is advisable to make a head-start. The good news is, as I compare the two disciplines, data protection and AI governance, it is quite striking how principles and tools for data protection can be recycled for AI governance.

A quick and easy way to prepare for AI compliance is to map out AI systems in your company. Your marketers can make a start by taking an inventory of all AI solutions used by the team. A RoPA used for mapping out personal data processing for GDPR, which we discussed in Chapter 10, can be used as a starting point for this exercise. Once AI systems are mapped, your marketers can find out whether, for instance, AI is used in a way that triggers transparency obligations, and take actions accordingly. If high-risk AI is discovered, a Fundamental Rights Impact Assessment can be developed and implemented by copying the forms and processes that are already in place for a DPIA.

To do the work thoroughly, an effective and comprehensive AI governance strategy should be established. Since the AI Act's obligations for high-risk AI are evidence-based, mirroring the data protection governance model, built on the accountability principle, they can be a useful shortcut to developing an AI governance framework. To illustrate the point, I have taken the accountability wheel for data protection, introduced in Chapter 3, and adjusted the texts to suit AI governance.

1 **Establishing leadership and oversight for systems and the responsible use of systems,** including governance, reporting, buy-in from all levels of management and appointing appropriate personnel to oversee the organization's accountability programme and report to management and the board.

2 **Assessing and mitigating the risks** that the use of AI systems may raise to individuals, including weighing the risk of the information used against its benefits. Risk assessment also means conducting periodic reviews of the organization's overall AI governance programme and information uses in light of changes in business models, law, technology and other factors and adapting the programme to changing levels of risk.

3 **Establishing internal written policies and procedures** that operationalize legal requirements, create concrete processes and controls to be followed by the organization, and reflect applicable law, regulations, industry standards as well as the organization's values and goals.

4 **Providing transparency to all stakeholders internally and externally** about the organization's AI governance programme, procedures and protections, AI systems use the rights of individuals in relation to outputs that have an effect on them and the benefits and/or potential risks of AI systems. This may also include communicating with relevant regulators, business partners and third parties about the organization's AI governance programme.

5 **Providing training for employees and raising awareness** of the internal AI awareness programme, its objectives and requirements, and implementation of its requirements in line with the employees' roles and job responsibilities, as well as of the importance of AI governance in general. This ensures that AI use awareness is embedded in the culture of the organization so that it becomes a shared responsibility.

6 **Monitoring and verifying the implementation and effectiveness of the programme and internal compliance** with the overall AI governance programme, policies, procedures and controls through regular internal or external audits, other monitoring mechanisms and redress plans.

7 **Implementing response and enforcement procedures** to address enquiries, complaints, AI Act non-compliance and to enforce against acts of non-compliance.

The outcome seems perfectly applicable to AI governance. In other words, if your organization already has a mature accountability programme for data protection, this can be adjusted to be applied for AI governance, without re-inventing the wheel.

AI harms in marketing and codes of conduct

To begin with, the area of marketing and advertising is heavily regulated. Just in the UK, the UK Data and Marketing Association lists 57 laws and two codes of conducts that are applicable to marketing activities. The code itself sits atop these rules, which are aimed at enforcing higher industry standards with general principles 'respect privacy', 'be honest and fair', 'be diligent with data' and 'take responsibility', all of which can be applied to AI use (UK DMA, 2017).

The long-established ICC Advertising and Marketing Communication Code covers marketing and advertising, and is designed to combat a variety of issues, ranging from problematic guerrilla or ambush advertising to falsifying scientific claims. The wide coverage, including ethical topics of this code, makes it a suitable instrument for AI because it can be applied in a variety of marketing contexts (ICC, 2018).

Looking at the list of harms mentioned earlier, adherence to the ICC code would already address most of them. Here I list them out again, with the relevant articles of the ICC code that cover the issue, directly underneath each harm.

1 **Purposeful 'harm by design'**: Deepfake video designed to harm competitor's product, service or general reputation.

Relevant mitigation in the ICC code:

> Article 12 – Marketing communications should not denigrate any person or group of persons, firm, organization, industrial or commercial activity, profession or product, or seek to bring it or them into public contempt or ridicule.

2 **Harm caused by inherent 'side effects'**: Biased training data leads to assigning customers to the wrong segments, leading to communicating irrelevant commercial messages.

Relevant mitigation in the ICC code:

> Article 3 Decency – Marketing communications should not contain statements or audio or visual treatments which offend the standards of decency currently prevailing in the country and culture concerned.

> Article 4 Honesty – Marketing communications should be so framed as not to abuse the trust of consumers or exploit their lack of experience or knowledge. Relevant factors likely to affect consumers' decisions should be communicated in such as way and at such a time that consumers can take them into account.

> Article 5 Truthfulness – Marketing communications should be truthful and not misleading. Marketing communications should not contain any statement, claim or audio or visual treatment which, directly or by implication, omission, ambiguity or exaggeration, is likely to mislead the consumer, in particular, but not exclusively, with regard to:

> • characteristics of the product which are material, i.e. likely to influence the consumer's choice, such as: nature, composition, method and date of

manufacture, range of use, efficiency and performance, quantity, commercial or geographical origin or environmental impact

- the value of the product and the total price to be paid by the consumer
- terms for the delivery, provision, exchange, return, repair and maintenance
- terms of guarantee copyright and industrial property rights such as patents, trade-marks, designs and models and trade names
- compliance with standards
- official recognition or approval, awards such as medals, prizes and diplomas
- the extent of benefits for charitable causes

3 **Harm caused by failure rates**: Matching the wrong ID means not being able to identify customers correctly. Falsely identified customers may be displayed advertisements that are not relevant to them, or can be wrongfully told that they are not eligible for a particular discount.

Relevant mitigation in the ICC code:

Article 19(2) Data Protection and Privacy – Use of Data

Personal data should be:... accurate and kept up to date

4 **Harm caused by intentional misuse**: An AI-generated exaggerated claim of a laundry detergent advertising that makes white shirts stainless, which when used did not get rid of brownish-yellow coffee stains reliably.

Relevant mitigation in the ICC code:

Article 4 Honesty – see above point 2

Article 5 Truthfulness – see above point 2

5 **Harm caused by security breach**: Hackers messed up the audience assignment delivered to a DMP, resulting in students getting ads on investment strategies for early retirement and the elderly group getting ads for student loans.

Relevant mitigation in the ICC code:

Article 19(3) Data Protection and Privacy – Security of processing

Adequate security measures should be in place, having regard to the sensitivity of the data, in order to prevent unauthorized access to, or disclosure of, the personal data. If the data is transferred to third parties, it should be established that they employ at least an equivalent level of security measures.

In terms of the last harm, which relates to security breaches, information security policies and governance models, for instance, based on Three Lines of Defence discussed in Chapter 9, might already be functioning as an effective prevention, also for AI-related security breaches.

DPO and AI governance

With so many overlaps in compliance requirements between AI and data protection governance activities, knocking on the (virtual) door of your DPO for help with AI governance preparation sounds like the most logical thing to do. Your organization may decide to appoint a dedicated AI officer or opt for assigning internal AI oversight to your DPO. However your organization has decided to prepare for AI compliance, my suggestion is to work on the organizational culture at the same time. Just as it is important to have a data protection centric organizational culture for effective data protection compliance, for meaningful AI governance, the whole company must advocate safe AI use. The AI officer, or the DPO with additional AI governance responsibility, must have outstanding interpersonal skills to assist your organization in shifting the culture.

Key takeaways

1 AI is already used by many marketers. The use of Analytic AI, in particular, is well established in the field.

2 Outside the marketing context, AI has the potential to cause catastrophes to mankind. The level of harm that a marketing AI can cause, in comparison, is minimal.

3 The EU AI Act is the first comprehensive law that will govern AI systems. The focus of the law is on prohibited AI and high-risk AI. For low-risk AI, there are no obligations under the AI Act.

4 AI governance will not require your organization to reinvent the wheel. GDPR compliance, as well as adherence to the industry code of conduct, can be used as starting points for setting up an AI governance system.

Conclusion

AI is a double-edged sword, bringing with it tremendous opportunities as well as serious risks. In the context of marketing and advertising, AI use is unlikely to carry high risks. Marketers today use chatbots to interact with clients and prospects, data mining tools to predict trends, and text and image-generating AI tools to improve their operational efficiency. Recognizing the importance of nurturing responsible innovation with AI, legislators around the world are working on legal frameworks that allow AI innovation to flourish, while assuring the protection of fundamental rights. In the EU, the drafting started in 2021 and reached a political agreement in December 2023 on key areas of the law. The EU AI Act will focus on prohibited and high-risk AI. The AI Act takes a risk-based approach; the higher the risk, the more the obligations. Most marketing AI use will fall under the category of a minimal-risk AI system, which means there will be no or limited compliance requirements.

In preparing for the AI Act, and for general AI compliance, knowledge and experience gained through GDPR compliance can be used as there are many similarities between the two areas of governance.

Bibliography

Bekker, A (2019) 5 types of AI to propel your business, *ScienceSoft*, 13 May 2019, www.scnsoft.com/blog/artificial-intelligence-types (archived at https://perma.cc/6PC9-SSMQ)

Chaffey, D (2023) Trends in using AI for marketing: 2023–2024, *Smart Insights*, 29 September 2023, www.smartinsights.com/digital-marketing-strategy/trends-in-using-ai-for-marketing-2023-2024/ (archived at https://perma.cc/FQ4B-7QRR)

Council of the European Union (2022) Permanent Representatives Committee: Proposal for a Regulation of the European Parliament and of the Council laying down harmonised rules on artificial intelligence (Artificial Intelligence Act) and amending certain Union legislative acts – General approach, 14954/22, November 2022, https://data.consilium.europa.eu/doc/document/ST-14954-2022-INIT/en/pdf (archived at https://perma.cc/TBY5-9NYN)

Council of the European Union (2023) Press release: Artificial intelligence act: Council and Parliament strike a deal on the first rules for AI in the world, 9 December 2023, www.consilium.europa.eu/en/press/press-releases/2023/12/09/artificial-intelligence-act-council-and-parliament-strike-a-deal-on-the-first-worldwide-rules-for-ai/ (archived at https://perma.cc/D2PK-LMYM)

eur-lex.europa.eu (2021) A proposal for a Regulation of the European Parliament and of the council laying down harmonised rules on Artificial Intelligence (Artificial Intelligence Act) and amending certain Union legislative acts, COM/2021/206 final, Brussels, 21 April 2021, https://eur-lex.europa.eu/legal-content/EN/TXT/?uri=CELEX:52021PC0206 (archived at https://perma.cc/ZF8D-4LHR)

EU Commission (2023) Shaping Europe's digital future: AI Pact, November 2023, https://digital-strategy.ec.europa.eu/en/policies/ai-pact (archived at https://perma.cc/G5KR-DSR9)

EU Commission (2023a) Press release: Commission welcomes political agreement on Artificial Intelligence Act, 9 December 2023, Brussels, https://ec.europa.eu/commission/presscorner/detail/en/ip_23_6473 (archived at https://perma.cc/8KT7-D8YH)

European Parliament (2023) Amendments adopted by the European Parliament on 14 June 2023 on the proposal for a regulation of the European Parliament and of the Council on laying down harmonised rules on artificial intelligence (Artificial Intelligence Act) and amending certain Union legislative acts, COM(2021)0206–C9-0146/2021–2021/0106(COD)), 14 June 2023, Strasbourg, www.europarl.europa.eu/doceo/document/TA-9-2023-0236_EN.html (archived at https://perma.cc/67V2-8WN2)

Hendrycks, D, Mazeika, M and Woodside, T (2023) An overview of catastrophic AI risks, Center for AI Safety, 9 October 2023, www.safe.ai/ai-risk (archived at https://perma.cc/TK7G-MYH8)

ICC (2018) International Chamber of Commerce: ICC Advertising and Marketing Communications Code – Building consumer trust through responsible marketing, 892E, Paris, 25 September 2018, https://iccwbo.org/news-publications/policies-reports/icc-advertising-and-marketing-communications-code/ (archived at https://perma.cc/CDC4-CCUT)

legislation.gov.uk (2016) Regulation (EU) 2016/679 of the European Parliament and of the Council, 27 April 2016, www.legislation.gov.uk/eur/2016/679/article/4 (archived at https://perma.cc/5EEZ-6PLP)

Manning, C (2020) Artificial Intelligence definitions, Stanford University Human Centred Artificial Intelligence, September 2020, https://hai.stanford.edu/sites/default/files/2020-09/AI-Definitions-HAI.pdf (archived at https://perma.cc/PB4Q-XGK4)

Marketing Evolution (2022) What is AI marketing? A complete guide, 20 July 2022, www.marketingevolution.com/marketing-essentials/ai-markeitng (archived at https://perma.cc/9DAN-8R36)

OECD (2019) Artificial Intelligence and Responsible Business Conduct, OECD Centre for Responsible Business Conduct, Directorate for Financial and Enterprise Affairs, OECD workshop on Responsible Business Conduct and Digitalisation, 4 November 2019, https://mneguidelines.oecd.org/RBC-and-artificial-intelligence.pdf (archived at https://perma.cc/2RLP-BL7U)

OECD (2023) Recommendation of the Council on Artificial Intelligence, OECD/LEGAL/0449, adopted on 22 May 2019, amended on 8 November 2023, https://legalinstruments.oecd.org/en/instruments/OECD-LEGAL-0449 (archived at https://perma.cc/5VXC-7SWJ)

QuantumBlack AI by McKinsey (2023) The state of AI in 2023: Generative AI's breakout year expect significant effects on their industries and workforces, August 2023, www.mckinsey.com/capabilities/quantumblack/our-insights/the-state-of-ai-in-2023-generative-ais-breakout-year (archived at https://perma.cc/7LYL-DRST)

UK DMA (2017) Data and Marketing Association – The Code, https://dma.org.uk/the-dma-code (archived at https://perma.cc/CA92-TNA2)

Weizenbaum, J (1978) *Die Macht der Computer und die Ohnmacht der Vernunft*, suhrkamp taschenbuch wissenschaft, translated by U Rennert, Suhrkamp Verlag, Frankfurt am Main, Germany

INDEX

NB: page numbers in *italic* indicate figures or tables

Looking for another book?

Explore our award-winning
books from global business
experts in Marketing and Sales

Scan the code to browse

www.koganpage.com/marketing

Also from Kogan Page

SBN: 9781398610279

ISBN: 9781398606449

www.koganpage.com